Dear Younger Me
victim to victor

A Memoir

VICTORIA KING

© 2017 Victoria King. All Rights Reserved.

No part of this publication may be reproduced, stored in a retrieval system, or transmitted in any form or by any means—electronic, mechanical, photocopy, recording, or any other—except for brief quotations in printed reviews, without the prior permission of the publisher.

Scripture quotations are from the ESV® Bible (The Holy Bible, English Standard Version®), copyright © 2001 by Crossway, a publishing ministry of Good News Publishers. Used by permission. All rights reserved.

Scripture quotations also from THE HOLY BIBLE, NEW INTERNATIONAL VERSION®, NIV® Copyright © 1973, 1978, 1984, 2011 by Biblica, Inc.® Used by permission. All rights reserved worldwide.

CONTENTS

Introduction vii
Preface ix

Chapter 1	My Side of the Story 1
Chapter 2	The Umbrella 5
Chapter 3	The Book That Helped Saved My Life 22
Chapter 4	Journals Tell a Story 25
Chapter 5	How Did I Get Here? 32
Chapter 6	Meeting the Abuser 41
Chapter 7	Not Happily Ever After 46
Chapter 8	Moving Day Times 2 74
Chapter 9	Secrets Revealed 88
Chapter 10	Bring in the Cavalry: Counselors That Get It – Finally 94
Chapter 11	One Big Dysfunctional Family – Meet His Family ... 99
Chapter 12	The Narcissist's Sense of Entitlement, Lack of Empathy, and Art of Pretend 110
Chapter 13	Preparing for the Move South 115
Chapter 14	Medicine, Misery, and a Move 124
Chapter 15	The Sunshine of the South Awaits 137
Chapter 16	The Abuser Moves Out 149
Chapter 17	Destruction of my Youngest Daughter 172
Chapter 18	Unsuspecting Participants 216
Chapter 19	A Sociopath as a Husband and a Father 234

Chapter 20   Can a Narcissist Thrive in the Church?...................245
Chapter 21   Zebras Don't Change Their Stripes: The
               Narcissist Will Never Change................................259
Chapter 22   Help is Available..263

Acknowledgments 267
Epilogue..269
Legal Disclaimer 271

INTRODUCTION

For over three decades Victoria King lived life in her husband's Narcissist amusement park. She rode her Carnie's roller coaster of abuse, endured his daily choice of torment that produced the same heart racing startle as the pop of a Wack a Mole at the state fair. Like cotton candy, living with an abuser is sticky and messy. Every abusive Narcissistic driven encounter made her feel like she needed a shower to wipe away his slimy control residue. Her husband offered up his array of mental, emotional, physical, sexual and spiritual abuse like they were mouthwatering midway specials but none of them tasted good. Denials of his behavior saw him deceiving counselors, and the idea that the problem was her and not him was too often swallowed. In the church they attended, he parlayed precepts such as apology, repentance and forgiveness to con naïve leadership and worshippers. It took her too long to discover that her brokenness was not the same as his sickness and she could jump off her Carnie's Merry-Go-Round. As punishment for bravely ending her time in the Narcissist Circus the Carnie instituted calculated parental alienation tactics as he tried to destroy her mother-child relationships.

In this book Victoria intermingles sage advice, called Dear Younger Me, in case you too are riding a Narcissist's roller coaster.

PREFACE

I thank the many before me who have documented their domestic violence stories to create awareness. Every time this happens we collectively help other women realize these dysfunctions, and that they are not to blame as the perpetrators want them to believe. This subject is receiving widespread attention in today's media. It's needed. Each story bravely shared reveals the levels and depths of cruelty, violence, and control an abuser wields. Sharing brings a belief that we are not alone. Truth has the power to set us free and to heal the afflicted, but it inherently threatens the abuser since his lies can be shattered and dismantled in the face of it.

For some this book will bring healing, for some understanding, and for others a jump to defense and denial. The abuser and those he has conned may feel the need to discount, deny, or abuse me for now publicly revealing the abuse. This is a hard truth that will sometimes be emotionally difficult to read, but push on anyway. My book has a distinct Christian view because I am a Bible-believing, Jesus-loving Christian. If your beliefs are different, you will still find help and paths to healing in my true and heart-rendering story.

Along the way someone challenged me about using the words "Victim to Victor" in my title because the person felt there are no victors in domestic violence or in my story.

While I agree there are still hurdles, I no longer rise to a new day with any probability of a hand making impact with any part of my anatomy; no one whose primary goal is to control and suppress me in word or deed is sharing my space. My chest no longer feels anxiety; my mind is no longer overwhelmed with guilt from lack of escape plans or the feat of implementing them. His hits and throws did not bring a death blow and leave my children motherless. I now have a lovely home that is a serene, safe haven, and a superb career. My children graduated both high school and college with honors, though admittedly they too suffer internal scars. Perfection has not and will never be attained, but having lived under a cruel, violent, controlling man for over 20 years, I will celebrate that I was able to make that two-letter change: Victim to Victor.

I thank my adult son and one of my counselors for encouraging me to write this book. It was something I resisted, and has been one of the most gut-wrenching yet freeing things I have ever undertaken. In writing this I hope to bring truth into the light, explore the methods abusive people use to keep their victims captive, and help shed light on how perpetrators also loop in unsuspecting family members and by-standers.

You will find sections called "Dear Younger Me" in which I give the younger me advice and comfort that was so lacking during this scary path. I offer my pain as a platform to assist others, and hope many learn from my mistakes.

Chapter 1

My Side of the Story

Open the door and breathe in the fresh air called truth. My son recently said, "You should write a book so we can know your side." What a strange thing to say to your mother. "Your side"? To me that was a very telling statement. Yet, those I shared this statement with who walked with me through this trial failed to see what I believed to be so obvious. When pointed out, expressions changed, eyes opened wide, and jaws dropped. It was there in plain sight, so perfectly clear. If my son is saying I should tell my side, that means someone is telling him his side, or more accurately, telling his lies to my children … again. His process was and still is, "If I repeat my lies over and over, they will miraculously become truth."

Who is he? My ex-husband. The man who beat me with his fists. The man who physically, mentally, verbally, emotionally, and sexually abused me. His obsessive-compulsive behavior, sexual addiction, and need for control and power were a recipe for marital disaster. Health professionals later applied the labels Explosive Anger Disorder and Sociopath Narcissist.

When my son said I should write my story, it held a million meanings. I wanted to cry, to laugh, to surrender to

> His process was and still is, "If I repeat my lies over and over, they will miraculously become truth."

my knees. Had the answer to my long-awaited prayer come? Was the agony over? Was someone finally going to speak the truth? My son was telling me he had matured enough and was healthy enough to see his father's sickness, craziness, abuse, and lies. He now recognized the often-recounted stories his father spun were false. He had grown enough to see me not just as his mom, but as a woman whose character did not match the crazy one his father's words painted.

He could recall childhood memories and see his father's painful abusive actions toward him. Some of the abuse I record later are things done to this particular son, though I don't use names. The agony I endured was not just the abuse aimed at me. Following those words that flowed so innocently from my son's mouth insisting I tell my side, in my mind the words of the counselor who helped rescue me came flowing back: "Perhaps you should write a book." She added, "Just something to think about."

I discounted the thought. It was not something I believed I was capable of, nor something I wanted to do. Who wants to confess such horrendous things? We choose to tell people good things, nice things. We like to pretend to the world that all is fine, all is perfect. I felt embarrassed about what I endured, what I did not stand up to and escape. I know I am not alone in wanting to remain silent. Victims of abuse fear they will be judged. It's a lot to admit to yourself, much less another human being.

> Victims of abuse fear they will be judged. It's a lot to admit to yourself, much less another human being.

I personally have watched expressions change as I have dabbled in the waters of being transparent. I see the look that says maybe I did something to deserve it. That hurts. And that is exactly what my abuser insisted over and again: I deserved it. Please, do not greet a victim's confession with that attitude. It only confirms our fears.

One person flippantly called the abuse I endured "drama." My heart sank at this labeling. It trivialized the seriousness and criminal status of what I endured. Battered women, like me, are not the cause of violence, but the result of the crime of violence. Some said they would have been out of there the second it happened. For most abused women, leaving is a process. It took me 20 years.

When I finally found the strength to announce I was leaving, I was told, "Go ahead; you're not as pretty as you used to be and you will never find anyone else."

> You are not as pretty as you used to be, you will never find anyone else.

One of the most confusing aspects of being abused was how successfully my ex-husband could victimize himself, even though I was the one receiving the abuse. He convinced countless people of his willingness to make things work, and that I was unwilling and unforgiving; therefore, that made me the problem.

Crazy-making, gaslighting, withholding, countering, discounting, joking, teasing, blocking, diverting, accusing, blaming, trivializing, undermining, ordering, demanding, forgetting, denying, threatening, and delivering abusive anger, verbal abuse, mental abuse, sexual abuse, and emotional and spiritual abuse. These are the well-documented techniques of abusers and Sociopath Narcissists; these are the techniques my abusive ex-husband used on me. He also suffered from Obsessive Compulsive Disorder or OCD. The cycle of abuse is like the discomfort you feel when watching the murky habitat of a sleek river rat. He rises up with his high-set eyes and small ears that skim along the surface of the water and then abruptly disappears, only to resurface ten feet down river to make you jump when his beady eyes meet yours. Just when your adrenaline activates with your fight or flight response, the rat dives again. You breathe; you calm. But the calm does not remain because you know the rat is just beneath the surface, and will pop up again. You're not quite sure where or when, but he will certainly appear again.

Life with an abusive person is like that; abuse pops up at random intervals. There could be peace for ten days, and then suddenly you are delivered a physical or verbal blow. Then a few days of calm waters. This makes victims of abuse hypervigilant, always waiting for the other shoe to drop. Secretly, I hoped every episode was the last. It took me nearly 2 decades to learn that the techniques my ex-husband implemented had names. It made me scream "Now it makes sense!" That is the mantra for many victims who have endured abuse and learned there are actually names for the array of tactics thrown at them. How often did I say to myself, "What just happened?" There truly is a joyous relief in making sense of it all. For me it was diminished because I felt so frustrated and angry with myself for enduring too much too long.

Every time I recovered from one nonsensical event, there would be another, and then another. It was like the storm waves at the beach when I was a kid, cresting over my skinny body, turning me around, wiping me out, and leaving me gasping for air. Finally when I got out of the tumble, I found my bearings and firmed my feet the best I could on the shifting sand, only to find the next rogue wave pounded me, filling my swimsuit and mouth with salty sand. While I was caught in that torrent of waves, sometimes someone would see my golden hair bobbing up and down and rescue me. Other times I just had to rescue myself. In my relationship, however, I did not know how to rescue myself. I did not know how to find balance on that ever-shifting sand. Even today, it saddens me tremendously that I was never able to see that storm coming. I looked everywhere other than ahead of me.

Dear Younger Me,

Truth is an important thing. Opening the door and speaking the truth will be scary at first, but don't let fear shut the door again. Fear kept me bound in an abusive marriage, but it does not have to be that way for you. You can be someone who reveals and speaks the truth, and that truth will resonate with others. You can improve your life by taking a chance and being honest with yourself and others. Honesty can be hard, but it sets you free when you are being abused. Let me help you share the true and messy details. Feel hopeful, not hopeless.

CHAPTER 2

THE UMBRELLA

Today's technology enables us to quickly discover resources; help is on the web. Before the internet, it was harder to know how to conduct research. I was experiencing these bizarre events and I was only in my early 20s. My young tender brain could not fully process what was happening. My youth combined with my high threshold for crazy abuse, since I had endured it as a child, created so many obstacles. The bells and sirens were whispers and barely audible.

The *Diagnostic and Statistical Manual of Mental Disorders* (DSM-5), published by the American Psychiatric Association, is a reference experts use in diagnosing mental conditions. Narcissist Personality Disorder is defined as follows:

> ... a mental disorder in which people have an inflated sense of their own importance, a deep need for admiration, and a lack of empathy for others. But behind this mask of ultra-confidence lies a fragile self-esteem that's vulnerable to the slightest criticism.
>
> Some of the symptoms include:
>
> - Having an exaggerated sense of self-importance

- Expecting to be recognized as superior even without achievements that warrant it
- Exaggerating your achievements and talents
- Being preoccupied with fantasies about success, power, brilliance, beauty, or the perfect mate
- Believing that you are superior and can only be understood by or associate with equally special people
- Requiring constant admiration
- Having a sense of entitlement
- Expecting special favors and unquestioning compliance with your expectations
- Taking advantage of others to get what you want
- Having an inability or unwillingness to recognize the needs and feelings of others
- Being envious of others and believing others envy you
- Behaving in an arrogant or haughty manner

My ex-husband is eleven years older than I am. I believed this decade-plus difference in our ages equated to confidence and justified life experience, not an exaggerated sense of self-importance. But that was me looking through the lens of my dysfunctional childhood, an opportunity he was quick to take advantage of. As if the agenda of the *simple* Narcissist were not enough, there are those who have Narcissist Personality Disorder (NPD), which means the abuse to the partner escalates one hundredfold.

Experts say people with NPD are sometimes diagnosed with lesser problems first. It's a bit like a physician noting you have significant swelling in your lower legs, especially your ankles. He could diagnose *edema* of the lower extremities and prescribe a medicine called a *diuretic* that removes excess water from the body. But the truth is you have a huge cancerous tumor in your abdomen that is interfering with the circulation of your body fluids, especially to the lower limbs. Unless the tumor is removed, the edema will not go away. NPD is like that huge tumor that spawns many symptoms.

For another word picture, imagine a big, black, oversized canopy umbrella, the kind four or five people can get under to find protection from the rain. The metal rods that stretch out to hold the water-resistant material are called *ribs* or *stretchers*. These are the bars that have little points or caps at the end that will poke you if you are not careful! A big umbrella could house eight, ten, or twelve ribs or stretchers that expand on demand and create a haven.

This big, black umbrella is NPD. Dangling off every rib or stretcher is one of the labels, symptoms, weapons, or tactics the dysfunction of Narcissism presents. While swaying you can catch a glimpse of what each says: explosive anger, physical abuse, mental abuse, emotional abuse, spiritual abuse, sexual abuse, discounting, diverting, minimizing, bullying, projection, entitlement, pornography, need to win, control, power, reality perversion, put downs, you're too sensitive, OCD, and crazy-making. Crazy- making is a method an abuser uses when he does obvious or underhanded covert controlling that leaves a victim intentionally confused.

> Crazy- making is a method an abuser uses when he does obvious or underhanded covert controlling that leaves a victim intentionally confused.

While the oversized NPD umbrella is successful at creating a huge, dark, ominous covering over you, it's not a safe haven. Those symptoms can rotate, tipping the umbrella heavily depending on the tactic the abuser is using at the moment. It causes those end caps to give you a stinging poke quite regularly.

When a couple receives counseling, the counselor may observe one of the symptoms of NPD that has allowed itself to manifest and pick that low-lying fruit on the umbrella tree. The abuser may show anger toward the victim partner, so the counselor may choose and spend months on the *anger* label. Counseling can be an arduous process. Many counselors and even doctors treat only the symptoms and miss the umbrella culprit causing them. This can be due to a lack of knowledge, proper training, or as Sandy Hotchkiss notes on pages 30-31 of her book, *Why Is It Always About You? The Seven Deadly Sins of Narcissism*:

> Many of these individuals never come to the attention of mental health professionals because they are too shame intolerant to recognize their own Narcissism and more inclined to blame others for their pain. Even when they seek help they are more likely to be treated for depression, anxiety, relationship difficulties, [and] job-related stress than for NPD that lies beneath their presenting problems. Many therapists miss or ignore Narcissism because it is not amenable to the short-term approaches currently favored by insurance companies that pay for treatment. Sadly, treatment is not often effective in these cases, because the more Narcissistic people are, the more rigid and resistant they are to behavioral change.

In my case, Sandy's explanation is spot on. Our insurance did indeed want to discontinue payment for counseling and my ex-husband was highly resistant to behavioral change. A psychiatrist unearthed the low-dangling fruit of Explosive Anger Disorder and put him on medication, but his psychiatric sessions, not therapy, were required visits for medication renewal. Since my ex-husband was resistant to change, he found an excuse to stop medication and counseling sessions. My own counseling sessions continued but not without the insurance company making my counselors jump through a series of hoops so that the bills would be paid.

I am thankful my counselors were prepared for that battle. It took me a long time to find counselors who were trained to catch the nuances of the abuse, detect the serious dysfunction, and not be conned by the perversions presented by my ex-husband. It was my last counselor in the North and my first counselor in the South who helped me escape my ex-husband's tangled web. I'll tell you more about them later.

Dear Younger Me,

You are so lucky to be living in a time where resources are at your fingertips, on the computer. Use the library computer if you don't have one at home. Definitely use a library computer if you need secrecy to perform searches. Make a list of what is happening to you. Think of how the abuse starts. What he says. What he does. Find web sites about domestic violence. Use key words like Narcissist, abuser, Sociopath, mental abuse, physical abuse, emotional abuse, and spiritual abuse. Read the contents. Compare what you are experiencing to what you are reading.

Now be brave and confide in a friend, or call the national or local domestic violence hotline and share what you have discovered. They know you are afraid and will help. I too didn't know how to explain some of what was happening to me. These sites will help give you words when you have none.

When researching counselors, don't be afraid to ask for reduced rates if you feel you can't afford therapy. Some counselors will gladly take a greatly reduced rate in cash instead of waiting for an insurance company to pay. If your insurance will cover counseling, be proactive in helping your counselor get paid.

I have only been married once but I am a second wife to my ex-husband. Nearly four decades ago I joyfully jumped into being a stepparent to a boy and a girl. In one of my first meetings with my former husband's first ex-wife, she blurted, "He is a Walter-Mitty." It was a term I was unfamiliar with and too young to put any thought to. I now understand the reference. It is listed under the symptoms of the Narcissist personality. The expression *Walter Mitty* describes a person who is preoccupied with fantasies about success, power, brilliance, beauty, or the perfect mate. I don't think she knew she was naming one of labels for his NPD, though I am sure she saw glimmers of these traits during her marriage to him. I did not understand, and I surmise she did not either since she also married him at a young age due to an out-of-wedlock pregnancy, which in the late 1960s meant a quick marriage.

I had worked in the world of show business from a young age. I have acted in movies and commercials and have appeared in national print ads. It was common to see me in Sunday's newspaper, a national magazine, or on a six-foot store display dangling from the ceiling. At that time I also had a weekly gig at a major TV station. For me it was just my job; I didn't attach any glamour to it.

He was enthralled. Early in our marriage my ex-husband participated in some of my photo shoots, and a few times the shots of the two of us together caught the right look and chemistry to land a prized spot in my model portfolio. While I did not know it, this lifestyle ticked a box in his Narcissist chart.

When I left him, not only was I exposing his brutality and dysfunction, I was taking my show business life and his Narcissistic image of an ideal marriage away from him. The structure of the kingdom he had so carefully crafted tumbled down. In his mind that proved to be grounds for war. He felt the need to destroy me, my character, my reputation, and my motherhood.

> The structure of the kingdom he had so carefully crafted tumbled down. In his mind that proved to be grounds for war.

In hindsight some of his behavior was strangely familiar. I had watched him do this in a smaller degree to his first wife. She was just for practice; with me he was aiming for perfect annihilation. Until writing this book I did not fully understand he was transferring to me the disrespect and contempt he showed for his first wife, but it makes sense now. I had hoped our marriage was going to be far different from his first, but I was to learn that in both was infidelity, domestic violence, and lies.

In my research I discovered that any disrespect and contempt an abuser shows for an ex-partner should set off alarms. Simply being angry is quite different from disrespect and contempt. That is part of an abuse pattern, and I was totally oblivious to it. I should have taken note that if he was willing to try to estrange the children from his first ex-wife through false narrative, then he would do the same to me. I thought his belief in Jesus Christ, church leadership, and teaching Bible studies would preclude him from doing this, but it didn't. I was so completely unaware of the scope of his sickness.

While he would never want the full custody that was awarded to me, he was happy to alienate my children from me, just as I watched him try to accomplish with the oldest two children and their mother. It grieves me that sometimes I was an unknowing naive accomplice. Two ex-wives, same modus operandi, same pain.

His Narcissism grew exponentially over our many years of marriage, so for him the need to be perceived as perfect grew greater; therefore, he retaliated against any criticism, constructive or otherwise. Narcissists can't conceive they have faults, so they can't imagine anyone else seeing them. A second divorce would make his image look bad unless the two wives were wrong about him and they were the ones who were responsible. So that was the route he took.

More than a decade after our legal separation and subsequent divorce he still had me listed as his wife by name on his ministry and book websites. I called and ask him to remove my name, yet he intentionally left verbiage leading people to believe he is still happily married to his second wife. I have saved, dated, and archived his words. His marketing also leads visitors to believe his first wife was solely responsible for the first divorce. She just didn't want to be married. Being the cause of two failed marriages is simply unacceptable to him, so he must veil the truth to his followers.

Here are some signs and techniques abusers implement and personal examples of how my ex-husband used them in our marriage. Can you recognize these within others?

THE OVERBEARING OPINION—ANOTHER PERSON REFUSES TO CONSIDER YOUR OPINION AND FORCES YOU TO ACCEPT THEIRS

My ex-husband did not have conversations; he had conquests. He had to win. He had to be right. Years ago a good friend so aptly said to my ex-husband, "You don't listen to the person you are talking to. In your head you are always constructing an answer. You don't really listen." I thank him for that.

If he had to win in public, please consider what he was doing to me in private. I was not allowed to have my own thoughts, and not having his thoughts made him combative toward me. If he perceived my thoughts did not align with his, I could expect to have a session where he would try to undo my *wrong* thinking. He would sometimes belittle me with statements that let me know only he could be right. The words, attitude, and verbal tones were harsh, then softer, then harsh again, depending on the progress he thought he was making. There was this subtle and sometimes outright forced indoctrination to join his version because that was the only real truth.

> If he perceived my thoughts did not align with his, I could expect to have a session where he would try to undo my wrong thinking.

The Person Who Is Always Right

My former husband always pretended to possess information he didn't actually have. Showing off a self-perceived brilliance was vital. At a dinner party a gentleman in the group asked if anyone had professional knowledge about a particular subject. To garner attention, my former husband jumped in on the subject even though he knew absolutely nothing about it. Nonetheless, he offered his alleged "input" in such a grand positive fake-it-'til-you-make-it, *look-at-me* manner, anyone at the table would have thought they were hearing the long-awaited answer to a question they had been asking since the dawning of time.

Even though the pomp and circumstance in the delivery was obvious, the input still lacked professional knowledge, so one of the guys at the dinner nailed him. He took a deep breath that raised his chest, looked my ex-husband in the eye, and spoke in a strong tone that spoke of his obvious frustration: "I just asked if anyone has professional knowledge, not general information." My ex-husband stuttered and again tried for position by adding some explanation about why what he said was still important and right.

In conversations about end time events, prophecy, or the Bible, my husband told people why they were wrong and why he was right, as he expounded on his alleged great Bible knowledge, too many times to count. Somewhere along the way the conversations always turned to conquests. During the conversation at the dinner, everyone was exchanging glances…uncomfortably.

The Put-Down Artist

My former husband believed putting people down was the way to extol himself. When I expressed feelings or showed I was upset, he told me I was crazy. Put-down statements included, "You're not appreciative enough," "You made a big deal about everything," and the ultimate verbal twist, "You're too sensitive. Even your father said so." Ah, the abuser was able to recycle the words he had heard from my father, who stated to my former husband on more than one occasion, "You know, she's too sensitive."

I was taught as a child that being sensitive was a bad quality. My ex-husband quickly realized those were words he could use as part of his repertoire and did so at every opportunity. In his mind he never did anything wrong; I was just too sensitive. My father did think I was too sensitive: too sensitive to his abuse, too sensitive to his beatings that turned me black and blue, and too sensitive to strap marks.

Through a good counselor I was able to understand, however, that I was *appropriately* sensitive. I was sensitive to things I should be sensitive to. Abusers don't like that. They don't like when you learn you can reframe their lies to speak truth, get healthy, and tell them to stop the abuse.

THE ROLLERCOASTER RIDE

In the 1960s I rode the world-famous Cyclone roller coaster in Luna Park, Coney Island, Brooklyn. The Cyclone is a wooden-tracked roller coaster that opened in 1927 and became a national landmark. A carnival busker callout invited all prospective riders to "get ready to shake, rattle, and rumble" for two minutes of nerve-wracking, amusement park thrills. The heavy safety bar swung over my head and across my lap. I could hear it lock in place. That click was supposed to make me feel secure as I blazed across 2,640 feet of noisy tracks with six fan turns and twelve drops. Anyone who survived and didn't throw up or cry was KING! Surviving the ride earned respect, kudos, and a place of honor. It was the gold standard of that era. I did it. I own a piece of history!

Once was definitely enough for this queasy, gutsy girl, however, or so I thought. It appears a roller coaster ride was more than a two-minute thing for me. I didn't know those up and down motions would travel home with me and into my adulthood. The screaming, the tossing about, the hard turns, and unexpected drops are just like an abusive relationship, which sadly do not end after two minutes or 2,640 feet. I missed the opportunity to completely exit the ride. Instead I stayed in line to repeat that nauseating ride over again. I stayed locked in that seat and I barely noticed the subtle realignment to the marriage track. This left me in the very abuse I did not like as a child. I was still tossing, turning, and gripping on for dear life. It was all too familiar.

A roller coaster often goes through a steady course, giving you a false sense of security before the next big dip or loop de loop sends you into a tizzy. An abusive marriage is much like that. One day my former husband was benevolent and kind, letting me sleep in after being up all night with a sick child, or bringing home a favorite treat, or even giving me a foot massage after a long day of modeling shoes at a fashion showroom. The next day, however, I would be at the receiving end of verbal or physical abuse. I would be tossed around like a rag doll, my teeth rattling after his angry hand met my face. Sometimes the week contained no physical abuse; instead it contained a string of crazy-making, countering, discounting, joking, teasing, blocking, diverting, accusing, blaming, or trivializing. Unlike physical abuse, these things are not as obvious in their wounding. A few more rounds on the Cyclone would be preferable to the decades of loop de loops and fan turns at the hands of an abuser.

THE DR. JEKYLL AND MR. HYDE

In the very beginning of our relationship (1980) my former husband's persona was charming and agreeable. With time that changed. His concealed techniques of control grew to an intensity that forced them into the open. The arrival of our three children along with my two much-loved bonus children he brought into the marriage and the increased responsibilities appeared to bring more negative changes to his personality. I don't know if it was just the natural escalation of his Narcissism with age, the additional children, or the need to create an impervious shell of the dynamic, perfect, and knowledgeable Bible teacher after his confession of faith, but the scale of his personality swings became more noticeable after he recognized Jesus as the Jewish Messiah in 1990. Yes, my ex-husband is Jewish.

In the mid-'90s I received one of the worst physical assaults right after he taught a well-received Bible study. The upstanding Bible teacher transformed into an out-of-control maniac at my suggestion that he could have had more compassion for a woman in his Bible study who was going through a particularly rough patch in her life. I will detail the assault for you later when I begin my actual journal entries, which I am using to present a timeline of events.

In 1998 when the fact was known to friends, family, and church circles that he had sex with one of our children's babysitters, he crafted a new face to wear for a time. He was just a poor guy whose wife lacked any forgiveness for him. He focused solely on me being unforgiving, deliberately avoiding the truth of the physical and mental abuse. He was unwilling to acknowledge truth because it didn't match his story preference. It was a superb manipulation.

He garnered sympathy in the absence of honesty. For weeks I watched him stroll to the altar while I sat in my seat in the quaint church with the stained-glass windows. People gathered near to pray for him while tears streamed down his face. Witnesses waited impatiently for my reaction. One even threw me a tilt of their head, suggesting I join my husband in prayer. A friend slid down the smooth oak pew to place an arm around my shoulder. Inside I was screaming, "This is only *today's* face, one of his many masks. His fake tears will not change his sick behavior." But nothing I could have said would have changed anything, so I sat there until the charade passed. I felt so alone and judged.

> Inside I was screaming, "This is only today's face, one of his many masks. His fake tears will not change his sick behavior."

THE WRATH OF GOD–THE PERSON WHO MISUSES SCRIPTURE

While the abuser claimed a personal relationship with Jesus Christ and did indeed learn much about the Bible, his Christian character at home was fleeting. Ephesians 5:25 says to love your wife as Christ loved the Church and gave himself up for her. This would be a sacrificial love. Yet, the word *SUBMIT* was a constant in his vocabulary and more often than not delivered with a yell. "If you would just submit we wouldn't have a problem."

He would often say to me, "Sex does not stop because we are having problems" and then misuse 1 Corinthians 7:5 to back up his accusation: "Do not deprive each other except perhaps by mutual consent and for a time, so that you may devote yourselves to prayer." How did he translate that to *a wife should partake in sex with her husband even when her was beating her black and blue*? To address his sexual addiction and pornographic thoughts that had become apparent to me over the years, when the American Family Association started a ministry in the 1990s to help men with those problems, I begged him to go to one of their meetings. I even made a phone call, but was told *he* has to be the one to call. He refused to talk to them. He said he didn't need help.

The Intimidator—Using Fear, Anger, and Threats to Get His Way

Every book, medical journal, and website I consulted and every trained professional I spoke with stated the same facts. Abusive men feel powerless, so they use fear to intimidate others and inflict abuse. I had no idea his internal powerlessness was one of the causes for his external displays of control. Some of his fear tactics included telling me I would be the one arrested if I reported his abuse to the police. He also said he would make sure I had nothing if I left him, constantly insisting I could not support myself, which would mean I would have no place to live with the children.

During the times he suspected I was growing emotionally stronger and responded not in fear but in a reasonable tone of resistance, he would resort to cruel comments and threats, such as "I will go to court, say you are unfit, and take the children away from you." Once he dragged my precious bonus daughter into the argument, saying "I will bring her to court and have her say you are a bad parent."

In her innocence, she said, "Yes, I will do that."

I broke into a million pieces. I didn't think there was any way to put me back together.

Giving you examples of just these seven methods, can you see how a Narcissist abuser functions? In a public setting a Narcissist appears charming and seems to possess a sparkling wit. My ex-husband's façade was close to perfect as he was directing the roller coaster my children and I were riding. He steered it, applied the brakes, increased the speed, and chose the angles of the declines. He was the Carnie. So let's call him that.

> In a public setting a Narcissist appears charming and seems to possess a sparkling wit.

One counselor said to my ex-husband, "You are always *on*. When are you not *on*? When are you real?" It was a good observation; his habit was to speak with authority and with more grandiosity than necessary while garnering attention. I was expected to be a member of his fan club. If I didn't respond with a level of excitement, I would be challenged with "What's the matter with you? You don't enjoy anything. There's something wrong with you." The defect was never his. If I hadn't been so naïve I would have caught and understood the comment my former husband's friend and workout partner had made in 1981: "He's a peacock."

Dear Younger Me,

Narcissistic men are like peacocks. They strut. They put on a show and display plumage in an impressive manner to draw attention to themselves. Peacocks believe they are the pinnacle of creation and somehow they can draw you in to believe their fantasy. They are colorful, charming, and engaging. The confidence they exude is impressive, especially if you are young and naive. Awareness is needed. The Narcissist may be looking to throw up his feathers and gain a victim. Be on the lookout for times of disparity between meager accomplishments and grandiose fantasies or inflated self-image. Such times will cause the peacocks to force you to join their grand world or be criticized for being unable to do so.

Not every Narcissist exhibits every symptom listed under the umbrella of that disease. My ex-husband seems to leave nearly none untouched, which explains the constant confusion I swirled in. When I first met him, he proudly shared a pornographic novel he had started writing. I could tell he was anticipating an affirming response to it and perhaps even sexual arousal. He was surprised when I did not give him accolades. I found the topic vile and inappropriate for a father, especially for a man with his daytime occupation.

I was sorely lacking the understanding experts had already discovered: Narcissists can suffer excessive or erotic interest in themselves and their physical appearance. Prior to meeting me, my ex-husband had entered the then-trendy world of the male exotic review: male strippers. Hordes of women attended the restaurants and clubs for bachelorette parties, girls' nights out, and an erotic night of men dancing in G-strings. The venues were packed. I attended some. Sometimes I assisted by collecting abandoned costume parts, those once torn away through the magic of Velcro and tossed dramatically into the audience.

It was all business for me. I considered this line of work just to make extra money. We were saving for a down payment on a house. Some of those tips thrown at him and tucked in his G-string were spent at the supermarket the next day. The cashiers often asked why I used single dollar bills. At times I obliged with the truth and was rewarded with expressions of disgust at the thought of where the bills once sat. Once, one of the dollar bills had a note on it that said "Get rid of the blonde." If only I had acted on that message.

I had no inclination I was watching a Narcissist fill his self-love tank and not just his wallet. Yes, I was that unaware. Nearly forty years later, my southern senior citizen self (over fifty-five) sees this as naivety and stupidity, as I'm sure you do as you sit reading about my past. But my reason, and not my excuse, is that most twenty-somethings don't know about NPD.

This evening side job enabled him to fill his attention tank before returning to his less-exciting and unrewarding day job. Today he fills his love tank sometimes by competing with his sons at the health club. When their dad invites them to work out with him, the competitive muscle bearing social media pictures ensue. Some of the children share with me that they receive subtle put downs if they don't show the same enthusiasm as their dad does in their bodies or his.

Observant Self is a big concept I learned in the late '90s. My understanding came about as I questioned how a human being could be a serial abuser. Abusing, apologizing, doing it again, killing people with actions and words over and over and over. Those without an observant self never look at themselves in reflection. So my husband would never stop to observe, truly contemplate, admit, and most importantly correct his destructive actions and words. He could fake sorrow, give a gift, or write a repentant letter, but these things were done because he had been caught in his lies or abuse.

Any form of apology was simply to regain his image in the eyes of those who observed his deception. A verbal apology had significance because it gave the Carnie a defense. He could say to me and others, "I did apologize" even if his *but* negated the apology. The Narcissist kept me in control by having me believe he was perfect and I was not, that he was to be trusted and I was not. Because of his lack of observant self, he believed his own lies and it was vital that I did too.

> Any form of apology was simply to regain his image in the eyes of those who observed his deception.

There was so much unseen faulty wiring in his mind. It was like buying a house that looks good during the walk through: the new front door, shiny counters, new blinds, custom tile work, and fresh paint. But after you move in you discover there is a short in the bedroom wiring, so you can't turn on the overhead light and the floor lamp at the same time. The washing machine won't work when the oven is on and someone jimmy-rigged a few electrical outlets to work, even though they constitute a fire hazard. After I had bought the house, the problems began to slowly reveal themselves.

My Carnie had me adapting to his intentionally incrementally confusing world. I spent too much time defending myself, and not enough time grasping that everything was all about him. Narcissists are inordinately sensitive and take offense at simple criticisms. It is one of the reasons I was on the receiving end of critical manipulative verbiage or a physical attack. It's called Narcissist rage. It was his reaction to anything that hinted at his imperfections.

Much like a friend pointing out a cut on your leg, you might say, "I didn't see that. Thanks. I'll get a Band-Aid." But the Carnie internally always placed a benign observation into the highly charged column of criticism. On one occasion he kissed me, and with a smile and no malice, I said, "Honey, I think you need to brush your teeth." He did have impeccable mouth hygiene, so this was surprising. When that unpleasant breath continued, I suggested, "You might need that checked."

Instead of a simple "Thanks" and a promise to make a dental appointment, however, my suggestion sent him into defense and denial mode. "I don't have a problem. I take very good care of my teeth." And it was true.

"But I think there might be a problem," I said.

"I don't have a problem," he started. "You do! You're too sensitive! Sensitive to perfumes, sensitive to garlic, sensitive to all kinds of things! You are always complaining about something!"

The roller coaster had dropped fifty feet without warning. This example may seem insignificant on its own, but when this was thrown

> Narcissists use a ceaseless stream of small, nearly insignificant degrading comments that form a foundation to build on. Confuse. Belittle. Degrade.

at me every day, it became frightening and humiliating. Narcissists use a ceaseless stream of small, nearly insignificant degrading comments that form a foundation to build on. Confuse. Belittle. Degrade. It's how they begin to exert control over their victims. The covert message being crafted is "You are flawed; you need me."

My reaction was an internal bombardment.

What? Look left; look right.

Tight chest.

Confusion.

Where did that come from?

What just happened?

I'm disoriented.

He successfully shifted any fault to me. My character was bad, not his breath. And being blasted with this tactic so often made me wonder if I truly was bad.

Not long after that attack, the Carnie attended his regular dental checkup. He had periodontal disease and was referred to a specialist for ongoing treatment.

CHAPTER 3

THE BOOK THAT HELPED SAVED MY LIFE

*I*n 2000 a woman who went to church and Bible study with me started me on my path to freedom. Let's call her "Lindy." Lindy held out a book and said, "I know you love to read. I think you will like this book, *The Verbally Abusive Relationship* by Patricia Evans." My face revealed a questioning look, to which she gifted me a reassuring glance. I tucked the book in the *Women of Faith* lavender tote bag I had embroidered with my name. The book joined my Bible, notes, and papers I always stored in it.

All the way home I thought about that book. I felt nervous, my stomach unsettled. When I got home I added the book to my "before bed" reading pile on my night stand. I didn't even know there was a book about verbal abuse. Though I had other books in progress, this one took precedence. Only a few pages in I had to stop and grab my highlighter. Soon the book had an abundance of yellow lines and sidebar notes. I was writing things like *YES! This is my husband. WOW! This is my life! This is all true,* and *He does this all the time.*

I devoured that book. It spoke to me about my life. The one exclusion was the physical abuse I had also suffered. After I finished the book I waited for an appropriate private moment with my friend.

"How did you know?" I asked.

"Oh, I saw it," she said.

Lindy told me her first husband was an abuser so she recognized it in my husband.

I didn't hide the book. I was so excited about its contents I encouraged my husband to read it. And he did. He didn't even say anything about all my sidebar notes and comments. He said, "You're right. I do see myself when reading this." In my ill-informed early learning stage, I thought if he recognized his behavior, changes would quickly and gladly follow.

> "How did you know?" I asked. "Oh, I saw it," she said.

Within a year of receiving that book we moved one thousand miles south. I never got to tell Lindy that book changed the direction of my life. I think it took courage on her part to give me that book. We were not very close friends; we did not spent time together outside of church or Bible study. My kids were small; hers were much older. She chose the gateway of my love of reading to get me the insights I desperately needed. I am sure she prayed about how to give me this book. No challenge. No admission. No explanation. It's just another book for a woman who loves to read.

When I was well into writing this book, I decided to search for Lindy. I had not talked to her in more than fifteen years, so there was a lot to catch up on. She told me all those years ago my ex-husband had confronted her after a church service. "How dare you interfere in my marriage?" he had said to her. What he really meant was, by giving me that book she was exposing him and empowering me. He could not allow that. He needed to change the focus. Blame her for interfering in his marriage. I now understand this diversion tactic. He implied she did something wrong rather than label his behavior as wrong.

Lindy, having already endured an abusive marriage, said she knew he was trying to keep her from conversing with me. "I was too smart for that and I knew he would be back for a second round," she said, "so I made the pastor aware of the situation." He did indeed return for another round of bullying and insisted she had no right to interfere in his marriage. She called the pastor over immediately. When my ex-husband realized she had enlisted help, he didn't come back for a third round.

One of my relatives told me she had also observed the type of person my ex-husband truly was. "I thought maybe you liked being controlled," she told me.

> When my ex-husband realized she had enlisted help, he didn't come back for a third round.

I was taken back by her comment. Had I become accustomed to his control? I felt ashamed. I told her I did not like it, but I did not know what to do. It was so much more complex than the control she had seen many times. Later my research, reading, and counseling helped me to learn all the complexities of the abuse were wrapped up in two things: control and power. Those two overwhelming needs in a Narcissist create damage on a grand scale.

Unfortunately, she was living her own kind of crazy, and we often comforted each other. She would often ask me questions about my counseling sessions to see if she could learn something that might help her. Because she has since passed away, the few sweet notes of encouragement she gave me along my path to recovery are even more cherished. I think she would be proud of me for escaping and for writing this book. I wish she had the opportunity to know the new me, not the one tightly wrapped up in the world of a Narcissistic abuser.

CHAPTER 4

JOURNALS TELL A STORY

I have journaled for decades. Later in the book I will be using select journal entries to aid in documenting and explaining my story. There are many more than I will use here, but I have chosen entries I think clearly portray the array of methods my ex-husband used to abuse me, without losing you by reiterating events that show his habits were repeated for more than twenty years. Sharing these with you gives me a chance to explain how a Sociopath Narcissist with compulsive behavior orchestrates and covers his abuse.

My journals also contain everyday joys and tasks. Once in a while I left those words so you can know that although abuse was weaved into my daily life, I have warm, fuzzy recollections too.

I grew more consistent in my journaling after giving birth to my first child in 1987. I wanted my children to have their own journals detailing stories of their first years of life. Those journals reside in individually labeled bins stacked in the garage.

Perhaps I wanted to journal and I wanted my journals for my kids because my mom did not journal. She did not create baby books. There

> To my disappointment she could never provide concise memories or stories, something I so longed to be told as if listening to a fairytale.

were some photos, but very few. Nothing captured a continual timeline or life story. To my disappointment she could never provide concise memories or stories, something I so longed to be told as if listening to a fairytale. When did I walk? What was my first word? How did I behave on my first day of school? Was I excited? Scared? Did I cry? The few photographs told a paragraph of the story, but I wanted chapters, and then the whole book.

One photograph captured the family at Easter in the '60s. We didn't have much money, as our father was sometimes employed and sometimes not. But somehow the budget allowed for brand new fancy outfits for Easter every year. My sisters and I look adorable in the pretty, flouncy dresses with matching Easter bonnets. What would Easter in the '60s be without shiny, white, patent leather shoes? WOW! Those were my pride and joy. I felt so special when I wore them. I dreaded the first scuff mark that was bound to ruin my perfect shine.

My brothers' attire was just as fancy: sharp tailored suits topped with a gentleman's brimmed fedora. Every year my mother lined us up, in order of height, in front of our blue, two-story home. The sun was shining and all was well, though one of my brothers squinted and grimaced in the glare of the bright sun.

In the family home I have discovered other photographs in musty old boxes in the basement or the backyard shed. They're vintage Kodak snap shots or Polaroids capturing the sisters, separate from the brothers, but we were always lined up according to height. Mom insisted on that.

Even though we all dressed up every Easter, we never went anywhere and no one came to see us. We didn't even go to church. We just looked pretty for the annual pictures. Our tree-lined suburban street intersected with another street, making a *T* so cars would be required to stop at the stop sign placed at the intersection. This allowed them the privilege of seeing us in our Easter best. They would be the only ones to see us. I did not think it odd. I just liked my new pretty dress.

Mom tells me we did the traditional coloring of hard boiled eggs in our elementary-aged years. While I don't remember this, I do know after photograph time, we joyfully returned to our Easter baskets full of marshmallow peeps, malted milk balls, chocolate bunnies, jelly beans and Brach's chocolate eggs.

Dinner time in my childhood home was 5 p.m. sharp, and Easter Sunday did not change that. The scents were different on Easter Day than on other days of the year, however. Sweet honey ham wafted in the air as it simmered in the oven. The side dishes were green beans, corn, and mashed potatoes. I hated mashed potatoes and still do. But my dad made me eat them, even after gagging to the point of heaving to vomit.

Dad wasn't one to show mercy. Occasionally I could sneak a forkful to the dogs waiting patiently under the table. The dogs not only shared my mashed potatoes; they also shared my pain. Whether I was shedding tears after a beating at the hands of my father, or in utter frustration of living under his dictatorship, I could be assured the dogs would lick the salty tears from my face. I found comfort in putting my head on their bodies, in the soft part, just above their back legs. I could hear their stomachs gurgling. Sometimes I would make their hair wet with my tears. They knew I needed them.

> Dad wasn't one to show mercy.

Over the years we had different dogs, always mutts. Dogs that were a little bit of everything, never pure breeds. I don't have a favorite; I loved them all. Once when I was in elementary school we got a new dog, an ever-so-cute puppy! All the kids got to have a say in the potential name.

Even all these years later I can still distinctly remember being in the backyard, sitting under a tree, and then pacing back and forth on a bright sunny day. Pacing was helping my creativity. I was playing with names in my head, then saying them out loud to hear how they sounded. The puppy was half German Shepherd and half Collie. So I came up with *Tinassie* in honor of Rin Tin Tin and Lassie, which were popular television shows at the time. I presented the new name at the family dog-naming meeting, and *Tinassie* was chosen. I was so proud.

Cocoa and Jinksey were other dogs that gave me love therapy. Jinksey was big, black, and fluffy. She lived a really long time, so she took to the grave a myriad of secrets I had whispered in her ear. Cocoa was the dog I said goodbye to when I moved out when I was eighteen, and I have always felt as if I didn't say "thank you" or "goodbye" well enough. Cocoa was a bit smaller. Sometimes I felt my head was too heavy on her little body, so I would just have her curl up into the curve of my body and hug her. That felt like love.

In addition to journaling, I spent thousands of dollars capturing my children in photos and videos. I was never without my camera, which did not always make my children happy, especially as they grew older. My mom's retelling of childhood stories often ended with, "Wait! Maybe that was not you. Maybe it was your sister. Well, it was *one* of you!" For her, over the years, her children's experiences had all melded together.

While I understood that sometimes we forget, I did not want to forget. So I made glorious, detailed scrapbooks before scrapbooking companies became popular. When I reached a total of one hundred, I decided to switch to photo boxes. One of my special enjoyments was creating the kids' special-event school parties and being chosen to chaperone class trips. I remember traveling into the city to take one child's class to a history museum. For another child I made a homemade sheet cake and, using my huge selection of decorating tips, made it bakery perfect including hand-piping every single child's name on the cake. The kids giggled as they searched the cake for their very own name. For another I successfully spearheaded the eighth-grade trip to Washington, DC, and I still have the coffee table book I was presented with as a thank you.

Backyard birthday parties included creative games. One game the kids loved was a relay race I created. It's a fun activity that always produced lots of laughs, a little friendly competition, and some exercise. Using a big sharpie marker, I labeled two sets of twenty-six tennis balls with the letters A through Z. The kids lined up in two rows and I placed a bin with the A-Z balls in front of them. Then I positioned an empty bin at a distance away. The first person on each team had to rummage through the balls to find the letter A, then run that ball down to the empty bin, drop it in, run back like lightning, and tag the next person in line, who had to rummage through and find the letter B. Each member of the winning team received a prize. Sometimes the prize was fifty cents or a dollar. Sometimes it was a special candy bar or a toy.

Birthday parties also included a creative sign-in board. My children's dad had a knack for drawing and made some cute sign-in boards. All these are in a big, tall box in my garage, waiting for the day my kids take these mementos to their houses! I think with today's digital technology, though, they might capture shots on their phones, catalog them, and then dispose of the boards. In some ways, that will be a sad day for this momma.

Their dad often contributed to the parties with his knack for pantomime and even magic tricks. Exceptionally long paper coils would unfurl from his mouth and coins appeared from behind guests' ears. But just under the surface of the fun and smiles I could always feel the underlying current of the controlling behavior of my ex-husband. Parties mean messes and things in disarray; this doesn't sit well with a man who has OCD, along with a need to control and to be *in* control. In the midst of the parties I could always count on a small form of control or abuse, perhaps a mean word or facial expression meant to make me feel as if I was inadequate or wasn't keeping things neat enough. He received many positive comments about his participation during parties, and he often turned those comments into ammunition. "You don't appreciate me enough," he would complain.

> In the midst of the parties I could always count on a small form of control or abuse

On the rare occasions these events did not include abuse, he ended the day with, "I did good today; didn't I?" That was a strange backhanded admittance of his control and abuse. This momma spent a lot of time running around taking pictures of all those precious party moments. I scribed on the back of each photo details of the image: whom, when, and where. You would be forgiven if you did not recognize the heartache and confusion in those thousands of 4" x 6" images.

Many have said to me, "You seem so smart. How in the world did this happen to you?"

Abused women don't always have a particular look. Sometimes things in our lives help us to be more susceptible to accepting or not understanding the behavior. I have a friend who has endured an abusive husband but came from a great family. She said her parents were kind and there was no abuse, so she was not sure why she so readily accepted the abuse in her marriage. There was abuse in my family, so I will be sharing the rocky foundation of my childhood, which might help you understand why I endured the abuse so long in my marriage and did not escape sooner.

> "You seem so smart. How in the world did this happen to you?"

The following words may assist your walk alongside me through this journey. I found it so helpful that I have this printed and hung on my prayer wall. It is from Max Lucado's book *You'll Get Through This: Hope and Help for Your Turbulent Times* (Thomas Nelson 2015). One of my counselors suggested I read it.

> You'll get through this. It won't be painless. It won't be quick. But God will use this mess for good. In the meantime, don't be foolish or naive. But don't despair either. With God's help, you will get through this. Don't equate the presence of God with a good mood or a pleasant temperament. God is near whether you are happy or not. Cling to God's character. He is sovereign. He knows your name. Angels still respond to his call. God is faithful. I need you to hold onto everything you know of who God is because I have some really tough news to tell you.

Dear Younger Me,

Discover the strength of being brave. Pray out loud, even if you don't believe in God, because talking out loud helps you process. Turn the energy you use for despair into energy for direction and decisions. I believe your story. I believe in you.

> Discover the strength of being brave.

CHAPTER 5

How Did I Get Here?

My mother and father met at a park in Brooklyn, New York, when my mom was thirteen years old. Dad was her senior by eight years. She was there to play on the swings. He was there to hustle money, playing handball. Much of their dating was spent at the Coney Island handball courts. When he won on the court he took his babe to the movies and had an egg cream or a root beer float. In my entire life, I have never heard my dad call my mom by her first name. She was always referred to as *babe*.

My father honed his skills and became a legendary handball player in the early '50s, and his name is listed in the many records from that era. His sport acumen did not win over his future father-in-law, however. He was not permitted to marry the girl of his dreams until she graduated high school.

Mom graduated. There was a September wedding in the cooler weather of early fall. She made for a stunning bride in flowing white satin and he looked quite handsome in his tux. The black-and-white wedding pictures on the streets of Brooklyn in the poodle skirt era are iconic. But that is where the beauty ends.

> The control my mother tolerated as a teenager escalated in her twenties, and she endured abuse into her late seventies.

The control my mother tolerated as a teenager escalated in her twenties, and she endured abuse into her late seventies. She did not know how to escape. She lacked a support system. Her mother was deceased, and in her place stood a mean and unlikable stepmother, and all the siblings had become disconnected. My mother's mom died when my mother was just thirteen. Mysteriously, she was found on a park bench in Staten Island. A picture of her in the local newspaper, posted by the police, alerted the family to her passing. While very little has been said about the incident, I am sure the trauma of losing a mother while marking the milestone of reaching the teen years was emotionally disastrous, and left her vulnerable to the wiles of a controlling man.

My father grew up in abuse dealt at the hands of his mother, and he continued the pattern, entrapping his wife and his seven children in the same existence. His mother's favorite tool of punishment was an iron frypan that not only caused great pain but made a frightening sound on impact.

I grew up in a suburban four-bedroom house with a big back yard and lots of pets: dogs (as I have previously mentioned), cats, turtles, squirrels, and whatever any one of us came home with on any given day, perhaps found while out delivering newspapers on an early morning route or rescued from the lake in our favorite park.

While the location of my bedroom changed over the years, sometimes on the first floor and sometimes on the upper level, I always remember my bedroom as being lavender and blue. It had subtle, pretty, floral wallpaper, and a crocheted lavender and blue blanket, handcrafted by my mother that kept us warm on chilly nights in the twin-sized bed.

While we all went to school and smiled to our classmates, our home was one of competition and conditional or nonexistent love with extraordinary physical abuse. We were beaten with a belt, a ruler, or his large hands. Sometimes it was an open-handed

> Our home was one of competition and conditional or nonexistent love with extraordinary physical abuse.

slap and sometimes a fist. We were brutally beaten for simple childhood mistakes that needed nothing except an explanation, a kind word, and an apology.

The grandness of the physical brutality for such simple things made no sense to me. We could rarely be prepared, not knowing what would set him off. One sure offense was not being at the dinner table at 5 p.m. I think all seven of us were late at one time or another and can remember running like the wind from a friend's house or an afterschool event to make it to the dinner table before the clock ticked to 5:01. My older brothers used my fear of my father's rage. "If you don't do this chore for me, I will tell Daddy you took fifteen cents off the counter." For a young girl living in such injustice, this added to the terror of the already-evil empire that was my home.

We were often pummeled, and made to kneel on the hard oak floor in front of our father while he perched himself on the edge of the couch. From there the assault was launched. First a punch to one arm, and then the other. Then a massive blow to the thigh. I was a skinny kid. The pain was excruciating. We were not allowed to voice the pain. If I cried, he said, "Stop it. It doesn't hurt that bad. You are just too sensitive."

Eventually the power of one of the blows would make me tumble over. And like an inflatable bounce bag, as quickly as I went down, he demanded I come right back up to the kneeling position so he could continue. It progressed to hits to the face, though at times I escaped those. Why? I was a child model. I appeared in print ads, catalogs, and commercials.

"And why are you being punished?" he would demand, after predetermining the required response. My desire to tell the truth was met with a punch. I was to repeat what he had told me to say. The answer was to be what he wanted.

I remember being punched while his favorite TV shows played in the background: *Bonanza*; *Gun*

> My desire to tell the truth was met with a punch. I was to repeat what he had told me to say. The answer was to be what he wanted.

Smoke; *Wild, Wild West;* or *Big Valley*. Sometimes I was punched as the Mets played, but only during the commercial breaks. Sometimes more than one child was in trouble. He would line up one, two, even three kids at once, and beat us all while we were on our knees. If it was perceived we turned our heads to catch a glimpse of the T.V, his fist would turn our heads in the direction he demanded. Not missing a beat, as soon as the commercial break arrived, my father would then continue the beating.

We did not have central heating or air conditioning, so in the spring and summer the windows would be open. I could hear the neighbors mowing their lawns, or kids playing on the street. I wondered if they could hear the hits, the cries of pain, and the Mets baseball games. When finished, he would check my body for the results of the beating. He was proud if he broke blood vessels, but at minimum we all sported lashings of black and blue or welts with red swelling.

If I had gym at school the following day, he rewarded me with a day off. We wore little one-piece blue uniforms with short sleeves and short balloon bottoms. It would have done no good for the teachers to see his version of fun. Then to complete the process he would demand a kiss on the cheek, and say to me, "I love you."

No one dared rescue another sibling from his rage. We knew what to expect if we interfered, and I wanted to, especially for my

> He pushed my brother's head through the kitchen wall, and my brother pretended it was nothing. He had to. We were all helpless

youngest sister. Sometimes the beatings were not on our knees. I stood before him, my arms outstretched and my hands straight. His wooden ruler hit and hit and hit my hands, over and over again, harder each time, for what seemed like an eternity. He pushed my brother's head through the kitchen wall, and my brother pretended it was nothing. He had to. We were all helpless. My very handy mother was in charge of all the wall repairs, even the ones caused by a fist that was meant for her head.

I was about thirteen years old. All seven of us had an equal share of candy we had collected at an event. I wanted to make the sweets last and enjoy them over the weeks rather than eat them all at once. My siblings did the opposite. They badgered me, then told my father I was not sharing. I was beaten. It was a beating of a lifetime. Some of my siblings were sometimes evil like that.

> My father marched in, saw the fuss, and ordered us to our hands and knees. "Lick the salt off the floor," he barked.

We were doing the dishes, being silly with the bubbles in the sink, giggling as kids do. We were wiping down the salt and pepper shakers when one sibling, known for their troublesome antics, thought it would be funny to shake salt over my head. I returned the favor. It went back and forth for a bit. We laughed and laughed. Salt landed all over the floor.

My father marched in, saw the fuss, and ordered us to our hands and knees. "Lick the salt off the floor," he barked. As our tongues did the work, gathering dust and dirt as well as the salt, he gave each of us a kick, and then another.

Once I visited my parents in their new home on the West Coast. I was there to work at the convention center for a huge trade show. I was excited about seeing my baby sister eleven years my junior. I am the oldest daughter and she is the youngest. We have a sister connection, but we also have a mother-daughter connection because of the age difference and the fact that I cared for her a lot when she was a baby and a toddler.

She was standing in the living room attired in the dress I had given her earlier that morning. It was a one-piece white dress with black polka dots and belted with a shiny, thin, black belt. The bottom was puffy layers as was the trend of the time. She looked adorable.

My father decided to show me he was still in control. He began punching my sister. He punched her legs. He punched her arms. She had done nothing at all to cause his ire. My father firmly said to my younger sister, "Don't you look at your sister. She can't help you."

"Why are you doing this?" I pleaded.

He lifted his chin, gave me a threatening, haughty look, then said, "What are you going to do about it?"

I considered the options. Attack him? Grab my sister and run? Call the police? If I called the police and gave the story, they might put him in jail, but he would get out, and I would be back in my home state. He would probably beat my sister severely, perhaps my mother too. If I took her and ran and did not take my mother, he would beat her or kill her. If I attacked him, I could go to jail, or he could go to jail but get out while I was gone. I would have to attack him and kill him to make anyone safe. Though I had not verbalized my thoughts, he said, "Go ahead and try."

I cried. He had won. He gave my sister a few more punches and stopped.

I still can feel the intense internal pain of that day. My sister and I have talked about it. I have apologized. She understands. We both know we lived with a sick tyrant and what he did was psychological warfare, sinister and calculated. He needed me to see his power and he needed to see my fear. When this sister had children, she threatened jail if he ever touched any of his grandchildren. Somehow he honored that, though sometimes his words were rough or unkind.

My brothers through the years have denied the extent of what we endured. They repeat my father's words: "It wasn't that bad. You're too sensitive."

"Did your head go through the wall?" I asked once in reply.

"Yes."

"Were we ever so black and blue we couldn't go to school?"

"Yes. But still, it wasn't that bad."

My sisters never minimize the abuse. One sister sees an imbalance in the symmetry of her face. The left droops a little. My sister suspects it was from the years of abuse. My father was right handed and the impact was primarily to the left side of the face.

Dear Younger Me,

What you experienced was hard. You knew it was bad, you knew it made you feel horrible, but like many young women, you didn't have a name for it. If you need to cry now, go ahead. Before, it was a cry of frustration. Now you get to cry with understanding. The tears taste different.

I was my father's *trophy daughter*. It was a burden and a curse. He rarely gave me a compliment but lots of criticisms. He would talk to others about me with pride, but never to me. He expected perfection from me, something I could not live up to. Though it granted me no grace from beatings, my siblings perceived I got off easy if I was not punched in the face, or if my beating ended two minutes sooner than theirs. This caused a form of competition, which resulted in the permanent damage to our relationships.

> I was my father's trophy daughter. It was a burden and a curse.

You may ask where my mother was during this. She knew, she heard, sometimes from another room and sometimes the same room. Sometimes with great fear on her face she would tell my father, "You're hitting her too hard" or "That's enough."

"Babe, don't you interfere, or …" he would yell back at her.

Mom once announced she was leaving. He calmly responded, "Okay, but I will get a gun, find you, and shoot you." Mom was just as controlled and abused as we kids. He was her Carnie. She tells me he once strangled her to unconsciousness. I asked her why she didn't leave him. "I was overwhelmed at the thought of seven kids to take care of." Abuse and fear work. I know firsthand.

> He calmly responded, "Okay, but I will get a gun, find you, and shoot you."

Age did not deteriorate my father's violence, even into his eighties. He commanded my mother to sit in one of the matching Lazy Boy chairs next to him at all times, except for some occasional gardening.

She never shopped alone; he went with her. If she read a book it was in the chair next to him. On the occasion she was permitted time in the garden, it would not be long before she would be summoned. "Babe, that's enough. Come in." He decided when she was done, not her.

When all seven children were adults, he proclaimed, "I must have done a pretty good job of raising all of you. None of you are drug addicts and none of you are in jail."

My mother worked until she was seventy-five; his excessive spending habits saw to that. In his younger years, he gambled on the horse races. In his older years, he formed a penchant for expensive clothes. Upon his death, we discovered a plethora of clothes in the closet, many unworn with tags still attached. At eighty-five my father died of dementia and my very simple and emotionless statement was, "The reign of terror is over."

> At eighty-five my father died and my very simple, emotionless statement was, "The reign of terror is over."

A statement revealed my mother's indoctrination: "Don't talk bad about the dead."

I replied, "I didn't talk bad. I spoke truth."

She looked at me with an empty stare. She knew she could not argue with my point. I offered that statement without emotion because I had worked through any un-forgiveness decades prior. Bible study, mentoring from others, and understanding the heart of God helped me do that. I also came to understand he was a product of his upbringing and that he repeated the only actions he'd been shown. Because of my strong faith, years before his death I made sure to share Jesus with my father and the forgiveness He offers. He wanted no part. My mother asked me to stay with my father for what would surely be the last night of his life. I did, as did one of my siblings.

I talked to my dad about who had visited him that day and I told him I forgave him. I sang "Amazing Grace" to him. He might be angry at me for that, since I can't carry a tune, but that hymn I love so dearly flowed from my lips as I prayed he would seek God in his last hours on earth. We watched him exit this world in the early hours of that morning in his palliative care setting, and then called the other siblings and our mother. They arrived. There were hugs, a few tears, and everyone stayed for a time, mostly talking about the cremation plans.

My father left my mother no money, no insurance policy, and a large mortgage. Repairs or some extra cash flow was always attained by refinance. He had told her many times, "I am not leaving you any money so you can go off and have a life with some other guy."

I recently treated my mom to a professional pedicure. She was eighty-three years of age. I asked her how she liked it. She said, "It's nice but I don't have anything to compare it to. It's the first time I have ever had one." I was so pleased to make this mother-daughter memory with her. I took pictures and posted them to my siblings' social media pages. I was hoping these years of living without his control would bring total freedom. But I was not seeing this *free* woman I had envisioned.

It confirmed what my counselor had explained to me long ago. After sixty years of riding my father's roller coaster, she didn't know what anything else felt like. The counselor told me not to expect my mother to suddenly become a woman who jumped at the thrill of freedom and blossomed into a new person. It would be the first time her Carnie was not at the controls, and like her first time having a pedicure she had nothing to compare it to. Sometimes it feels as if her Carnie controls her from the grave. It breaks my heart.

Dear Younger Me,

Parents are not supposed to wound their children. Your father is a bully. Just like bullies at school, your father bullies his family. Not all parents are loving, just like many people are not loving. But don't give up. There exist people who will care about you and help you. Your teachers did not understand that being introverted resulted from fear. You are shy from fear of punishment and assume every adult is just waiting to pounce. I wish someone would spend time with you, and see that you gravely need help. Your age and fear kept you from knowing how to find help. Talk to a teacher. Call a domestic violence hotline. Living with a bully breaks blood vessels and the spirit. Forgive yourself and seek the help you need now.

CHAPTER 6

MEETING THE ABUSER

I escaped the madness of my childhood home around my eighteenth birthday, and moved a few hours away, trying out my newly acquired nurse's license at a recently opened hospital. At my mother's encouragement, I was taking nursing courses while still in high school. At seventeen years old I not only graduated high school, but a few months later I also passed the state nursing boards. I never lived at my childhood home again.

> I escaped the madness of my childhood home around my eighteenth birthday

I was twenty years old when I met my former husband, and had just returned to my hometown after a two-year absence. I was invited to a Bar Mitzvah celebration at my neighbor's house a few doors down and was busy readying when a knock came at the door. Standing there against the backdrop of the sparkling water view that was my backyard was the man I would marry two years later. He wasn't tall but the dark and handsome part was accounted for. He was Jewish. I was Protestant. A difference that did not faze me. I had dated Jewish guys before.

When our relationship was in its infancy, I visited him at the club where he danced. He said with all seriousness, "Well, it's a good thing you came tonight because if you didn't I was going to go home with one of the girls here." The naïve me missed that first sign of trouble. But sure enough the charm and gifts won out. He assured me he was to be my knight in shining armor. I saw his very charming and confident side. I did not know there was another.

Within six months we were engaged. We lived together and saved to pay for our wedding. In the beginning there was no direct physical abuse but definitely Narcissism, a bit of controlling, and some OCD traits, all of which I failed to label correctly. Any problems noted I packed into the bag of normal issues. Of course my gauge for normal was broken.

The popular hit *I Need A Hero* was often brought up in conversation. "I'm going to be your hero," he would often say, and I believed him. Superman is mentioned in the lyrics. He had purchased himself a pendant with a Superman insignia with a sparkling S. If you are a fan of the series, my next sentence will make perfect sense. He said he would be my Superman but he turned out to be my Doomsday.

Dear Younger Me,

Men, old or young, who want your attention, will be on their best behavior in the beginning. Some people are like car salesmen. They make you see how shiny the car is, but the engine is what matters. A wiser mentor knows how to ask appropriate questions and knows where to look for issues. Do not get stuck in a relationship. Ask for help and other people's perspectives. To find a good car, you need to know cars, or find someone who understands cars.

The same is true for your partner. Abusers, like salespeople, make you feel as if they are 100 percent trustworthy, so there is no need to look further to gain more advice. It's not true. Do not be afraid to talk to other people. A good car can take you anywhere for years. A bad car will give you pain every time you use it.

From about 1979 to 1982 I did a weekly short production at a TV station in one of the most popular cities in the world. Over the years I had a close friendship with my co-host and his wife, who was very sweet and had a good sense of humor.

After our engagement, I invited my fiancé's parents to the production studio. I thought it would be a treat for them. We met on the bustling street that had been dotted with the signature city food carts just a few hours earlier. There remained a scent from the hot dogs and chili they served, which was barely discernable next to the exhaust from the stream of cars passing by.

I took them past the security team that guarded the entrance. I was a familiar face so we passed with a welcome nod; then we went into the elevator and pushed the big dial to take us to the floor where I did the weekly show. I gave them a mini-tour. My green room and the studio with the cameras, then I was off to dress and touch up my makeup. That left them to look around with my fiancé, who had already been there a few times. My darling friend said to me later that evening, "Are you sure you want to do this? His mother is extremely jealous of you and she will destroy you and you marriage." Oh her wisdom, which was lost on the twenty-two-year-old. More than twenty-five years later I called her and told her she was right.

Dear Younger Me,

When someone says something you don't understand, or makes a statement that needs to be spelled out a bit better, don't be embarrassed and don't be afraid! Even though it might feel scary, ask that person, "Can we talk about that some more? Can you tell me what you mean?" If you can't do that at the moment, take the person's phone number and talk another time. Don't be afraid to ask. Helpful people are an alien concept to you at this stage of your life, but I assure you these people exist.

Every Friday his mother called our home and spoke to her only son. *How sweet,* I thought. *She calls her son to see how his week was. She is so caring.* Much later I found out the phone calls had a sinister purpose, to plant seeds of deception and hate. My ex-husband kept their secret, but revealed all to me two decades later. His mother was constantly criticizing me. Sometimes it was something that seemed petty, like I didn't treat his sister right, or something more serious, like I stole something from their house. He knew his mom had disparaged his first wife too, but he just could not make sense of it. No one wants to believe a parent is capable of such intentional manipulation.

Through the years I started to hear stories, watched this unfold with my own eyes and learned she was a verbal and physical abuser too. She was known to be cruel. Once she told me, "I put a spell on someone so they would get hurt. It worked; the person fell off the roof and broke their leg." She told her son she was a witch, the noun not the adjective. He didn't tell me these things earlier because he didn't know how to process them himself. But in hindsight after those Friday phone calls, he developed a short temper and became easily irritated.

In truth, I had been kind to his siblings. The youngest wrote me a tender note when she began to see through her family's dysfunction. She told me she saw things differently due to some life experience and becoming a mom herself. She thanked me for a few of the nice things I did for her. I will share this letter later.

> On her death bed, his mother confessed to her manipulation. She told her son she was jealous of me and that all the stories she had created over the years were indeed lies.

On her death bed, his mother confessed to her manipulation. She told her son she was jealous of me and that all the stories she had created over the years were indeed lies. I actually felt a sense of satisfaction. Vindication. There was a certain relief and comfort that with her last hours of life she chose to speak truth, allowing my character and reputation to be restored.

He spoke to me about sharing his mother's confession with his cousin. He purposely omitted that it wasn't only his mother's lies that destroyed our marriage so he could keep an untarnished image to his cousin, which caused her to offer, "I hope you can find your way back to each other." His omission was a reminder of his unscrupulous behavior and that I needed to reinforce my safe boundaries.

Dear Younger Me,

What does a good mother or good mother-in-law look like? Let me help you. Good mothers want their kids to enjoy a healthy marriage and not try to sabotage it. Good mothers cut their apron strings and realize their son's wife is the primary influence in their lives. A good mother-in-law does not fight for position by grasping for her son's emotion, presence, and time. A good mother-in-law does not make up lies about her daughter-in-law; rather she honors her, especially in the presence of her son. A good mother-in-law lets her daughter-in-law begin to make her own family traditions without staging a pity party. A good mother-in-law doesn't make her daughter-in-law feel as if she doesn't measure up. Good mothers are sensitive about how and when they offer advice.

How I wish this more mature and wiser me could help you. You would have chosen differently! No one taught you how to discern or analyze situations or people. Examine potential in-laws. Observe. Ask yourself if the woman will perceive you as competition or a complement to the family. Do you see controlling behaviors that will tiptoe their way into your marriage? Do you see any signs of intentional meanness, intentional desire to hurt people, mental illness, or physical abuse to any members of the family?

You need help seeing the gravity of these things. You did not put enough credence in the fact that your in-laws, very obviously, physically hurt each other on more than one occasion. If you could have processed that fully, you would have understood this is what was emulated to your future husband. Then you would have been able to give proper weight to the fact that the same could happen to you.

Don't disregard these things! And read about the relationship between Ruth and Naomi in the Bible. It provides a wonderful example of love to think about. (Ruth 1:6).

CHAPTER 7

NOT HAPPILY EVER AFTER

The first incident of physical abuse came during the honeymoon. I later learned this to be typical for abusers. A grooming period exists. Grooming is the predatory act of maneuvering another individual into a position that makes that individual vulnerable. For me it was an exhilarating time of fancy restaurants, museum visits, gifts, romantic notes, and special adventures. The gravity of my nativity and stupidity came years later, followed by feelings of confusion, shame, guilt, remorse, and disgust, because I fell for it.

> The gravity of my nativity and stupidity came years later, followed by feelings of confusion, shame, guilt, remorse, and disgust, because I fell for it.

We honeymooned on one of those Caribbean islands where the subtropical temperature stays at a pleasurable 80 degrees. We were at an all-inclusive resort with twenty-four-hour gourmet dining, ice sculpture displays, evening entertainment, and blue-green waters as far the eye could see. The authentic tropical flavors of the Caribbean in the fresh seafood, filet mignon, and artistic roasted vegetables were bliss. All dishes were presented at our table as if being photographed for the cover of a food magazine.

We floated on rafts in the beautiful crystal waters under sunny skies, watching big and little colorful fish swim by. We stood beneath rushing waterfalls and had our photo taken. In the evenings we lay in the resort hammocks and watched the sun lower to the horizon and glisten on the water. We wore matching outfits that told everyone we were a couple. A favorite was our classic black-and-white-striped, button-down shirts with matching white shorts.

One night, poolside, we danced to reggae music. We had not conquered the skills and rhythm, but we were having fun. A dance contest was announced. I was keen to sit it out as reggae was proving difficult. My new husband was not. He wanted to win. I conceded, and did my best, but we were simply quite ordinary, if not awkward.

My husband said, "Follow me!" I gave a questioning look because he was angry. Then he pushed me, hard. He already had me by the arms as we were dancing, so it was easy to add some force, let his fingers dig into my skin and take control. He began a combination of lindy and swing, something he could ace on a bad day. He was all smiles and enjoying his own showmanship.

I whispered in his ear, "This is a reggae contest."

"Just follow," he spat.

He suffered a moment of disappointment when we were not offered one of the top three awards. And I suffered a moment of fear, then questioning, then fear again. That was the first time I had felt real fear in his presence. I brushed the doubts away and told myself it was a one-time thing.

> That was the first time I had felt real fear in his presence. I brushed the doubts away and told myself it was a one-time thing.

Dear Younger Me,

Most teens and young twenty-somethings have no idea what a good relationship looks like, so ask for help. Your father, family, and husband did not value you, but guess what?

You have value! I know it was easy to slide into living together and excuse it as a way to save money. It wasn't your first time.

I am older and wiser and can say without reservation, it's a poor excuse. Please do not live with a man before marriage. I had heard it was like taking a car for a test drive. You are not a commodity to be bought and sold. You are a precious human being made to be loved and cared for.

You are a gift. Sex is a gift of oneself to another person. Sex is meant for marriage and marriage is what God planned since the beginning of time. It's timeless and it's the right way to go, even if a marriage does not work out as it should. Please read Hooked: New Science on How Casual Sex Is Affecting Our Children, by Joe S. McIlhaney, Jr., M.D., and Freda McKissic Bush, M.D., published by Moody in 2008. I do wish I had read such resources before making some of my decisions.

Do not let men use you for their sexual needs. Very often men think with their penises rather than their brains. Even though people often say this in jest, don't ignore the advice. Men who push for sex are not valuing you. They are valuing themselves. This selfishness is not the sign of a good man. Your body and your virginity are special. A real man knows this.

It's OK to cease a relationship even if you think you have invested so much. This is what I did wrong. I was afraid because I had invested so much. I was afraid to back out. I don't want you to be afraid. Change can be good. The task I set before you is to learn what a healthy and wonderful marriage looks like. Learn the characteristics of a man who lives with integrity and character. Make a list and revisit it often. Study the real thing and you will recognize the counterfeit.

Let a woman who understands the traits of a quality man and a good marriage help you. Some women like to mentor. A mentor is an experienced and trusted advisor. Ensure this type of person is in your circle of friends. If you have had a dysfunctional childhood, you can't make decisions in a vacuum. This I have learned the hard way.

I want to go back and make different choices. Many of them. Ninety-nine percent of my current friends have real regrets and sorrows about living with men, having sex outside marriage, and not understanding about valuing themselves. Many feel shame. I do. Trust this advice.

After the wedding, traits of obsessive behavior appeared. His habit of being overly neat and clean became excessive. His need to control the home environment grew to acts of pushing and shoving me to win. Some instances he deliriously excused as accidents; others he played down. "It was just a push. Why are you making a big deal out of it?"

At times I'd place his teacup in the wrong place. He complained, "If you'd put it in the right place we would not have a problem." I never did discover the correct positioning of a teacup. At times our children's Legos had to be grouped in piles of like pieces, not spread out across the floor, and at times two dishes in the sink were two dishes too much. These incidents left me confused. My chest tightened. My mind would grow foggy and I would convince myself things would be better if I only did as he demanded.

> "It was just a push. Why are you making a big deal out of it?"

In the early years we had some really nice times: pleasant conversations at the dinner table, snuggling on the couch, and watching an episode of MASH with a cup of tea and Social Tea cookies. A cruise with port stops at San Juan, Venezuela, Grenada, Barbados, Martinique, and St. Thomas. A holiday in Hawaii. These are occasions I can recall when I felt loved and cared for, when I did not fear my husband, when I did not anxiously watch for the next explosive mood. Lacing the hits, shoves, or unkind words with some good times gave windows of hope. Just when I thought I couldn't take any more, there would be peace and tokens of love and generosity. *This version of my husband is okay*, I would think to myself. *I hope he will stay.*

In the times I appropriately recognized abuse, these pleasant events were summoned as evidence in his allegations that I did not appreciate all we had and all we had done. "You don't appreciate all the things we do." His allegation conveniently diverted focus. He had abused me in some

> Just when I thought I couldn't take any more, there would be peace and tokens of love and generosity.

way, shape, or form and I was pointing it out. He did not want to focus on that. It should be no surprise that this constant manipulation tarnished the nice memories I did have.

After one particular week where he was busy bombarding me with verbal put-downs and control tactics, it was time for my birthday. My ex-husband arranged a limo to transport us to a Broadway play. The play was enjoyable. The company not so much! I was spending time with a man who had displayed controlling behavior that had been wreaking havoc in my soul all week. I was emotionally exhausted, but my Carnie wanted me to ignore this, put on my happy face, and pretend all was really wonderful.

The façade of pretending wonderfulness is attached to one of his Narcissistic traits, and it was on display in all its glory that night. I just did not know it had a name back then and I could not fake it that well. So to this day, at every opportunity, he uses this as one of his stories to show others how unappreciative I am. "You just can't please her!" he says to disparage me to our friends and even our children.

One of my sons said he had heard this story many times and with great remorse confessed he believed it. He recalls times he treated me with disrespect because of things his father relayed to him in a purposefully twisted unfavorable light. I do too. Blame is like anger in that it dulls a person's sense of empathy. Empathy is one of the things a Sociopath Narcissist is lacking. Not possessing it allows a person to act in a hurtful way to others.

I often wondered if anyone had ever asked him, "Have you ever hurt your wife?" One might think this a good question. It's not. No one can ask an abuser if he has ever *hurt* the victim. Abusers redefine the meaning of hurt. The times I pointed out a black-and-blue bruise on my arm or face or a broken bathroom window, or the times I spoke of feelings of despair or told him his pinch to my arm hurts, he would respond with, "I would never hurt you!"

So someone could have asked him, "Have you ever hit your wife?" but he would just deny it or minimize it.

"Well, I pushed her, but it was not a big deal. I said I was sorry."

The redefining of *hurt* happened with the children too, because it makes his actions acceptable and suggests he does not deserve the blame. His mindset, driven by his fragile Narcissistic ego protection quickly disowns his actions and adopts blaming others as a defense.

I know my Carnie repeats this verbiage to bolster his "It's not me; it's your mom" deception to the children. He believes his wall of deception is airtight, but there is mortar falling away and some bricks have been shaken loose with time. Some light of truth is peeking through those cracks. I want the whole wall dismantled.

Dear Younger Me,

Narcissists have an inner story; it does not have to match truth. They are slaves to the inner Narcissistic voice.

My former husband did not assault me in public, careful to avoid witnesses, but his restraint in this rule faltered on occasion. For a decade we were performers for a high-end dance troupe, dancing at corporate affairs, major charity fundraisers, weddings, and lavish bar and bat mitzvahs. At one event, staff wheeled a table with an extravagant dessert into our dressing and prep area. It was a beautiful assortment of chocolates, cookies, mini cakes, candy, and fruits in a finely tuned elaborate and elegant display. I sneakily removed one strawberry. His hand grabbed me and spun me around. He screamed, "What are you doing?" He threw me against the wall and my head bounced. He held me there, his grip tight at my chest. "You can't touch that! No one gave you permission to touch that!"

My feet dangled; I barely touched the ground. His brain didn't cope well with disorder, so had I taken a piece of fruit from something so orderly? Was he saying that he chooses what I can and cannot do? Co-performers watched and said nothing. I could see shock and horror in their looks, but still none

> He threw me against the wall and my head bounced. He held me there, his grip tight at my chest.

of them told him to stop. There existed the perfect opportunity for someone to tell the Carnie what he was doing was wrong in so many ways. But it did not come.

He let go after what felt like an eternity, and left me to prepare for our show while I was burdened by shame, belittling, and fear. I struggled to regain my composure. There were five sets of dance productions to be performed. *But the show must go on.* The audience enjoyed a flawless performance.

On the way home in the car I asked, "How could you do that?

He simply replied, "You should not have touched the dessert table."

He was unable to see the act of taking one strawberry and his actions of throwing me up against the wall were disproportionate. While he was under the care of a psychiatrist, this behavior was named: Explosive Anger Disorder, and Explosive Anger Disorder does not go by any rules. The volcano erupts when it feels like it. I now understand what happened that day and many times since then. Abusers internally fill with tension and then at unpredictable intervals the need to let that tension out is uncontrollable, so they explode. No one knows when it's coming, but a huge outburst releases that internal pressure. Internally the abuser is relieved while the victim is the recipient of what feels like a tornado that has touched down. Spun around, confused, hurt, and fearful. Then the tension tank starts to refill and the cycle continues.

Dear Younger Me,

It is a tragedy that abuse is revisiting your life. Please, don't make up an excuse for why it happened. Any hit, pinch, push, or shove is unacceptable. Do not accept any rationalizations. Leave. Find a center that helps abused women. Do not tell him when or why you are leaving because he will minimize the abuse so that you doubt yourself. He will tell you they won't believe you. I promise; they will believe you. He is trying to make you lose courage. Don't try to figure it all out before you go; just leave and accept the help. Don't let embarrassment stop you; you are not the first and you will not be the last to need help. I know you feel alone. I know it is hard. Do it anyway. You have the strength.

In the late '80s my first child, a precious son, was born to us, my much anticipated and loved son, who received a name that means "my love." The arrival of this precious child became a trigger for intensified dysfunctional behavior. Children mean stuff! Tons of toys, diaper bags, walkers, play mats, puppet theaters, and more. They require time, cost money, and create noise. It was compounding and expanding pressure in my ex-husband's brain. Enter my second, then third child.

"Stop paying so much attention to the baby and pay more to me!" he yelled at me.

I have read that some men often feel this way when babies arrive, so I rationalized it to mean just that. Actually, as time went on, I knew this was one of his Narcissistic traits blooming in the face of the newly arrived competition for my attention and affection.

> "Stop paying so much attention to the baby and pay more to me!" he yelled at me.

There were many instances of control on an everyday basis. If he could not control with his words, it would escalate to physical. On one occasion, we were discussing something minor as I applied my makeup in front of the mirror in the bathroom. I was very pregnant and taking up more room than usual. I was not agreeing with his view. Suddenly, he raised both his muscular arms and sent me flying into the window and then walked away into the nearby bedroom.

I called to him, "You pushed me so hard the impact broke the window. You could have hurt me or the baby."

Incredulous at the accusation he boasted, "I would never hurt you." He offered, "Wasn't that window already cracked?" then complained about the cost to fix it.

For most abusers, it's necessary to weave some good into the mix; it's needed for the Narcissist's self-image and contrived evidence they are actually good people. On occasion, the Carnie would bestow some jewelry or trinket, sure to let others see it, to remind me, "Look at all I give you; you are so unappreciative."

A few times after a beating or belittling he bought me pretty flowers. Sometimes he bought them on the day we hosted our Bible study. That evening there would be fifteen or twenty people gathered in our home. The group enjoyed my baking efforts. I tried to vary what I made, sometimes a moist chocolate cake, some nutty muffins, gooey monkey bread, my famous braided challah bread, or creamy cheesecake. All of it got washed down with gourmet-flavored coffees or hot herbal tea.

When Bible study guests admired the flowers they would point out, "What a great guy you are married to!"

Lacking true repentance or humility, he would throw me a glaring look as if to say, "See, everyone else thinks I am a great guy. You are the problem!"

There were occasional short-lived positive highlights when he grasped what he was doing and consequently connected his behavior to his dysfunctional upbringing.

"I saw pornography at a young age in the beach bath houses; that's why I have a sex problem."

"I was very young and my mother left me with my baby sister. I wasn't old enough to babysit and I was really scared."

"I saw my parents hit each other when I was little."

"My mother was compulsive; she would wipe the table around us while we were still eating and pick up little crumbs with her finger while we sat there speaking. I barely finished my meal and she had picked up my plate. She was cleaning up around me."

I thought these insights illustrated a willingness to process these things for a better outcome. It's how we change. But it wasn't. I never saw change. A few times he acknowledged, "When I feel out of control inside, I need to control the outside world." The revelation became like smoke through his fingers. Gone before it had time to settle. Even though he recognized himself in *The Verbally Abusive Relationship* by Patricia Evans, he could not change. He was a serial abuser. The occasions I received an apology were followed by the same abuse the next day.

The very popular Christian men's conference, Promise Keepers, arrived in our area. The Carnie returned home, very excited. "I wish I had done this sooner. I want to implement these precepts of being a man of God, being faithful, and being a good father. I'm sorry I haven't been a good husband." My hope soared, but not for long. Nothing changed.

In the '90s I watched a movie called *Sling Blade*. A man buys his girlfriend flowers after each time he threatens, intimidates, or belts her. He offers her a two-word apology and belts her again the next day. I was watching it at a friend's house. "This is my life" I blurted out. My friends missed the comment. The movie kept replaying in my mind. I could be in a conversation but not really be present because I was replaying the scenes I found disturbingly like my life. I wanted it to leave me alone but it wouldn't. The discomfort kept reminding me of my own sad and disturbed existence.

Dear Younger Me,

Movies can hold messages. Use them as springboards for discussion. Don't keep the reaction inside. If a man hurts you even once, leave. Do not listen to excuses or apologies. Do not engage in trying to fix someone. It is very common for abusers to plead, "But I would never hurt you." Those words tip your natural thought processes. Those people want you to ignore the evidence and believe the abuse they dealt did not actually hurt you.

This is nothing short of a mind game made to confuse you, to make you doubt yourself. Don't doubt and don't be confused. The hurt is real. Stand in truth. Don't even consider entertaining the nonsense he dribbles. Abusers keep you off balance. It is intentional. You are too young to know this is a high level of abuse.

Listen to my words of wisdom. If you are hit, slapped, pinched, pushed, spat on, belittled, put down, told you are worthless, constantly criticized, or told you have no value, you were just HURT.

When my firstborn was about two years old, I yearned to go to church. I wanted to be able to teach him about God. I joined an evening Bible study at a Protestant church. It was a lovely group of people and the older ladies were particularly sweet to me. I became passionate about the study immediately and loved reading, learning, and growing in my understanding.

Bible studies led to attending Sunday church services and enrolling children in Sunday school. Soon I was volunteering in the nursery and attending special seminars and women's retreats. My growth brought a life-changing and amazing relationship with Jesus. There came welcome internal and external changes for me.

After a time, I discovered nondenominational evangelical churches were home for me, though my search caused some challenges to my then-husband. He was Jewish. It's a common misconception that a Jewish person is no longer Jewish after accepting Jesus as Messiah. At that point, such a person may choose to attend worship in a Christian church or in a Messianic Jewish synagogue. They are followers of Jesus Christ, the long-awaited Jewish Messiah, but their lineage or heritage has not changed. Some of the common lingo for a Jew who accepts Jesus is, "completed Jew," "a Jewish believer," "a Messianic Jew, or "a Christian," which means a Christ follower. Jews were the first to recognize Jesus as Messiah and become believers and followers. I have Jewish friends who follow Jesus and they simply call themselves "Christians." It's all nuances of being a follower of Christ.

When I came home from Bible study, excited about what I was learning, I naturally wanted to share this information with my husband. He was a cultural Jew; did not attend synagogue, which is also called "temple" or "Shul"; but was proud of his Jewish culture and heritage. He began to challenge me about what I was learning. He thought much of what I shared was interesting, but "Jesus could not be the Messiah."

I requested, "Write down your ten hardest questions and come with me."

He had no interest as he considered himself smarter than those I was attending Bible study with. Eventually pride brought him to the church meeting so he could tell everyone there that they were wrong. I was just as interested in those answers as he was. He coldly voiced, "I have no desire to talk about the New Testament." They obliged and returned kindness to his arrogance. All answers came from the Old Testament.

I was embarrassed at his attitude. He went home and went to the library to relentlessly research the Bible, history, and the Tanakh (what the Christians call the Old Testament). He created ten harder questions. So he *had* to go back. He got his answers and the Bible study group continued to be kind and informative in response to his high-horse attitude. Now he felt it was time to go see a Rabbi and ask him questions. He was not satisfied with the Rabbi's answers or evasiveness on some of the content of the Tanakh that talked about the Messiah that was to come. More research. More questions. A few more visits to the Bible study group to challenge them. He was taking copious notes, and probably undertook more Biblical study than he did for his Bar Mitzvah. One day he announced, "Jesus is the Messiah. Why don't my people know?"

He returned to the Bible study group a bit softer, but still with great fervor. Then he started going to that church. We enjoyed good conversations during this journey. On one Sunday, I was unable to attend church. The Carnie announced that evening, "I went to church alone and made a profession that I wanted to make Jesus my Lord and Savior."

I issued a funny response in a silly tone. "You can't do that because I didn't do that yet and I was supposedly the Christian first!"

Over the years we laughed many times about my lighthearted response and God's timing for our commitment to Christ.

While visiting a local church for a special Easter service a few weeks later, I committed my life to Christ as well. That was the spring 1990. A friend explained, "Don't you see that God was protecting you? His Jewish family is going to blame you. But you can say with all truth you were not even here. It was truly his decision." Sounded optimistic. But that did not stop his family from laying blame at my feet.

The only son in a Jewish family believing in Jesus draws ferocious ire. The curious thing is he is more Jewish now than he was before he knew Jesus. He knows more of the Tanakh, participates in more Jewish festivals

> The only son in a Jewish family believing in Jesus draws ferocious ire.

and traditions, and knows more Hebrew. Our children were dedicated in the temple (and in the church) and my daughter even had a naming in the Messianic temple, which means she was given a Hebrew name even though she kept her given name that was on her birth certificate. His family did not know or see these intricacies because within a year of coming to know Jesus as Lord and Savior we were disowned. My husband's immediate family disowned all of us, their son, his wife, and all five children.

We enjoyed the church where we first went to the Bible study, but my husband also wanted to explore worshiping with other Jews who believe in Jesus in a Messianic synagogue. I learned much about Jewish tradition and Old Testament festivals. I also learned to recite the Hebrew blessings and took lessons in Hebrew for a while. I also made some pretty awesome challah bread and matzo ball soup! For five years we went to the Messianic synagogue on Saturdays and church on Sundays. Then we just went to church. I will use the term *Christian* going forth, but I am pleased to have used this opportunity to illustrate what happens when a Jewish person accepts Jesus.

He began to take on the look of a *good* Christian. In-depth Bible study, attending seminars, prayer, teaching the kids about God, and eventually becoming a Bible teacher. He has an amazing memory, so quoting and teaching the Bible came easily. The Carnie knows much scripture; he can quote it from memory, open the Bible, and find something in a blink. He quotes the precepts for others to hear and be impressed, for his own benefit and gratification.

> A sense of entitlement places the Narcissist above the law, even God's laws.

But rules don't apply to him. He is permitted to give false testimony, commit adultery, curse, spit in his wife's face, manipulate, be prideful, control, show disrespect, and tell bold lies to his children, friends, family, and church. A sense of entitlement places the Narcissist above the law, even God's laws.

Character changes that usually follow a confession of faith have never happened to him. None of his hits, pushes, belittling, meanness,

OCD, diverting, manipulation, or control ceased, and to his delight, he discovered something new: spiritual abuse. He slid the Spiritual Narcissist title on like a well-fitted glove. Scripture tells us not to seek our own glory and to let our work stand on its own, but a Spiritual Narcissist raises a baton and commands his orchestra to follow. Proverbs 27:2 says: "Let someone else praise you, and not your own mouth; an outsider, and not your own lips."

I have witnessed the Spiritual Narcissist flaunt anything he believes might bring him praise, and he is adept at twisting scripture with ease. In one discussion I made valid points with great merit. Lacking the upper hand, his anger boiled. Knowing that continuing the discussion would cause him to rethink his position or possibly agree, he screamed, "Submit! Why don't you just submit?" Just one of the many times I had that line screamed at me.

Spiritual Narcissists have a knack for constantly referencing their own achievements, a trait I witnessed when one of our grandchildren graduated high school. We both attended the celebration. My former husband walked into the living room and asked our grandson, "How are you?" Barely leaving time for his answer, he quickly leaped into a soliloquy listing all the things he was doing. He rambled off the number of churches he was speaking at, he bragged that the people thought he was such a good teacher, and he told of the money he had received for his organization and how many radio interviews he had done for his addiction ministry.

> Spiritual Narcissists have a knack for constantly referencing their own achievements

Part of his dysfunction is this speech was delivered for my benefit. Every conversation is an opportunity to share his perceived superiority and prove to me, "I can't be as bad as you say I am." This crazy behavior does not affect me anymore. It gives me peace to be able to identify his actions. The Carnie always calls what he does something else, paints himself as a victim or a saint, and then blames me.

Soon after his new faith began, he founded a ministry that emphasizes prayer in helping people stop substance abuse and addictive behavior. He launched press releases, hoping for some media coverage.

A national Christian TV station bit. The story of a Jewish guy who was once an exotic dancer, but held a straightlaced day job and realized Jesus was the Jewish Messiah made for good TV. Camera crews arrived at our home to produce a segment that included re-creating events leading up to and including the salvation moment. They also captured family activities and interviews. Honestly, there is a lot of *gold* in that story. It's no wonder they wanted to cover it. But it is his cover.

> The Carnie always calls what he does something else, paints himself as a victim or a saint, and then blames me

The Carnie was frustrated that I wasn't as hyped as he was. I acted my part, smiled, provided appropriate words in our joint interview, and prepared the kids for their scene. But that wasn't enough. "What's the matter with you? This is a great opportunity. Why aren't you as excited as I am?" he challenged. "You don't know how to appreciate anything. You have to support me in this." He wanted me to ignore his abusive character, dominating control, and just appreciate this thing that was so good for him. Internally he needed to avoid any shame that his status was not as high as he thought it should be and me not conforming to his expectation was a hindrance to that.

A few years after my salvation, I had an occasion to meet the mother of a pastor's wife, who at the time was visiting from another country. She was a lifelong follower of Christ and we chatted about the changes we make when creating a personal relationship with Jesus. Specifically we were talking about husbands. I said, "What happens if they don't change?" She missed my veiled call for help. Of course that was probably my missed opportunity; I never admitted his abuse to anyone, never mind the severity.

In my time in the church, I listened when others spoke of problems in marriages. I considered it advice to me in many ways, perhaps guidance, perhaps a framework of repair. But I was equating money problems and arguments with someone leaving the cap off the toothpaste to my life: the beatings, the threats, the mockery, and the belittling. I read in the Bible that God hates divorce and that always weighed heavy on me. It was much later that I came to understand that He hates abuse of His creation, His daughter, His child, His beloved, and my husband was not following any instructions that God gives husbands regarding the care of their wives, and that was equally important. He ignored 1 Peter 3:7 "… be considerate as you live with your wives, and treat them with respect."

> I never admitted his abuse to anyone, never mind the severity.

In the '90s, as Christians eager to learn and grow, we attended many conferences. I wondered if what he heard would cause an end to responding to perceived criticism with a verbal attack or if a few well-chosen words would stop him from transferring work pressure to compulsive behavior at home. Would just the right concept be explained to stop the need to control and have power over me? Would a quote see him treat me with the kindness the Bible commands him to do? Would some locution make him shriek "Eureka, I got it!" I kept hoping.

We attended the Gary Smalley series on *Hidden Keys to Loving Relationships*. Excited about the great concepts, he said he wanted to implement some of them. He felt the seminar was a mountaintop experience. For a week he was considerate and kind, and things were peaceful. The descent was rapid, however; a week later the same verbal put downs and spiritual abuse reappeared, and then a few pushes. My hopes were dashed once again.

Family Life, another great organization, speaks of the *oneness covenant*. It stresses we are to mirror God's image with a focus on the typical marriage vows: love, honor, and cherish. Again great information and precepts presented with promises made to be a better husband: more patient and kind, and not verbally or physically abusive. Promises not kept, once again.

We also participated in Marriage Ministry International's *30 Days to A Great Wife or Husband*. This program caused some conversation but no change in his destructive behavior.

All these seminars just became talking points on his resume. Bragging rights. We trained to become counselors for the Billy Graham crusades, attended *Walk Thru the Bible*, and listened intently at *Answers in Genesis* seminars. None of these efforts resulted in him being a safe person to live with, or a man of integrity or character.

> None of these efforts resulted in him being a safe person to live with, or a man of integrity or character

Biblical submission may be a difficult concept for some. Submission never means abuse. When I received my first Bible I wrote something that will either make you laugh or make you feel offended. Please laugh with me. I did then and still do. Of course now I understand the context and refuse to take it out of context like many do.

Ephesians 5:22-33 New International Version (NIV)

"22 Wives, submit yourselves to your own husbands as you do to the Lord. 23 For the husband is the head of the wife as Christ is the head of the church, his body, of which he is the Savior. 24 Now as the church submits to Christ, so also wives should submit to their husbands in everything.

25 Husbands, love your wives, just as Christ loved the church and gave himself up for her 26 to make her holy, cleansing her by the washing with water through the word, 27 and to present her to himself as a radiant church, without stain or wrinkle or any other blemish, but holy and blameless. 28 In this same way, husbands ought to love their wives as their own bodies. He who loves his wife loves himself. 29 After all, no one ever hated their own body, but they feed and care for their body, just as Christ does the church— 30 for we are members of his body. 31

For this reason a man will leave his father and mother and be united to his wife, and the two will become one flesh. 32 This is a profound mystery—but I am talking about Christ and the church. 33 However, each one of you also must love his wife as he loves himself, and the wife must respect her husband."

Next to verse 22 in my Bible I wrote, "What is this crap?" I was working from no Biblical knowledge or understanding, nor did I the read the "part 2" to this scripture. If I had, I would have had no problem being under and with a man who is submitted to the LORD.

The husband is supposed to be a leader. He is to love his wife like Jesus loves the church. Jesus was sacrificial; He gave His life for me. I should have a husband who would die for me, a protector, not a man I need protection from.

A husband should feed and care for his wife. It's an above, but equal, thing. Jesus calls me His brother. He says we are friends. The husband should place his wife in an esteemed position, caring for her needs with love, showing compassion, and keeping her safe.

> Jesus was sacrificial; He gave His life for me. I should have a husband who would die for me, a protector, not a man I need protection from.

We become one flesh. I didn't see my husband giving himself a black eye or bruises on his body. I shouldn't have those either.

The word *submission* is not limited to only wives. Christians are to submit themselves to each other (Ephesians 5:21), to government (Romans 13:1), and unto God (James 4:7). This is a frequently seen concept. Self-sacrifice is required in each circumstance. Submission is never glossed over as easy or always convenient. Instead, it is viewed as a service unto God.

Submission should not be confused with a person, especially a woman, being weak. When I compared my husband's actions to what God really wanted, I found great disparity. When I pointed out scriptures that should craft who he is, he kept assuring me he was working on changing, so I shouldn't and can't betray him and tell all. His growth in spiritual head knowledge reinforced his Narcissism, however. It never traveled eighteen inches down to his heart to change his actions or character. He believed he had divine insights.

Often it was in his view of end times events and prophecy that he felt he had the upper hand. He stated those who did not hold the same view or understanding would not stand in truth in the end times. He enjoys heavily debating the placement of the rapture, but the goal is to ensure that others adopt his position. He alienated two congregations with what he felt he knew better. He felt those in the Messianic temple were being legalistic and disagreed with the doctrines of a certain church denomination that had been around since the nineteenth century, but he wanted to take on the doctrine and the pastor. Instead of just moving along, he evoked doctrinal battle, which brought about dissention and hard feelings. That need to win is linked to his Narcissism.

Of course my name was linked to his. We were a couple. If the husband has a strong opinion, people assume the wife has the same. While I also disagreed with the doctrine, I do not have that competitive spirit in this area. I just knew that meant there were other churches to choose from and I should seek them. I had taught a tightly knitted weekly women's Bible study group through that church for seven years. That did not change. There were women in my group much further ahead in their walks with God, and they showed me how doctrinal battles have gone on for centuries and how to let them go.

Finances in the late '90s were tight. Our children attended a Christian school, an expense we weathered year to year. My youngest was in Christian school but transitioned to home schooling for the sixth through twelfth grades. The weathering included cashing in the one and only deposit I made to an Individual Retirement Account (IRA), at the order of my ex-husband. It was one we created using a few thousand dollars in our savings before my first child was born. I pleaded, "Please don't touch this. It's all I have. I have no retirement or pension. What about a low-interest loan?"

But he pushed further. Scare tactics. "If we don't do this, we could lose the house." Losing the house was not going to happen, but being behind on bill payments does not sit well with a person who has compulsive behaviors.

"But this IRA pays an incredibly high rate" I explained, "one we were lucky enough to get during a boom window. The rates are not even half that now. We'll have to pay penalties if we touch it now." It was the only financial security I had for my older years. I didn't want to end up like my mother.

I guess he saw it as a way of controlling me. He tried to assure me, "You will be with me and we have my pension, so you don't need anything extra. I will always take care of you."

I gave in even though I knew it was wrong. At the end of the year when we filed our taxes, our CPA (Certified Public Accountant) said, "I wished you had talked to me first."

> Narcissists don't ask for opinions.

Narcissists don't ask for opinions.

Dear Younger Me,

Some wisdom does come with age and from mistakes made. Always have your own savings account whether you're single or married. Drop in small amounts at regular intervals. Have a cushion for surprise gifts, surprise expenses, or a security blanket. It's yours, no one else's. And NEVER let it be used for any other reason. Choose a husband who will support this process.

Don't be afraid to talk to a financial counselor if tough periods appear. If you are being bullied into using money that is earmarked for retirement, don't stay silent; talk to a friend about it. Don't let it remain your secret. Let someone know and help.

The bully will try to talk you out of that. Don't listen. He will tell you no one can help or that no one cares. It's not true; go ahead and ask for help.

Journal, July 31, 1997

My husband has been gone all week in Hawaii with the dance troupe. It is Thursday night at 8:30, and all is in order.

The sad thing is I can't really say I miss him. It is very relaxing not to have him here. I do the dishes when I feel like it. I have no pressure or expectations, no one to make me feel inadequate, no one buzzing around me being compulsive.

When I go to sleep I can sprawl out on the bed and there's no one expecting to use my body after I've felt everyone pulling at me all day. I calmly did some normal and appropriate discipline with the children. I haven't lost my patience with the children.

I'm enjoying peace and quiet with no fights, no confrontations, no one challenging the how and the why of things. I did housework, took out the garbage, and separated the trash for recycling. I have been the taxi service all week, place to place. I am not behind on anything (laundry etc.).

I did not like what he said during one of his phone calls: "How's the gas in the van?" I am perfectly capable of putting gas in the van and perfectly capable of noticing when it needs gas.

I am not sure if anything will change when he gets home. He sent an upbeat, "I'm trying" letter from Hawaii. More promises? Can he keep them? None so far. I feel empty. It's a very sad and terrible place to be. Our anniversary is in two weeks. That makes me sad; there is nothing to celebrate.

Dear Younger Me,

You are capable and smart, despite being caught in this bad relationship that makes it seem far from the truth. It's not all your fault. It's not. Your brokenness is not the same as his sickness. Fix your brokenness and get away from his sickness. You can't fix his sickness. There is a difference between the two.

The times my husband left for travel were times of relief. It meant I could have some peace to air out my brain. His constant undermining of my perceptions was tiring. Eventually I came to the conclusion that when I spoke to my husband to plan days, complete chores, and nurture children, that is not what he was doing. Unbeknownst to me we were on two different pages. The goals of his conversations were to preserve control over me and promote his selfish needs. It's like we were working in two different realities. I kept accepting my ex-husband's reality of power over me without understanding the severity and depth of that control. Even though I sometimes struggled against it, I mostly responded to his abuse and control as it was valid. I had learned to tolerate the control and the abuse without realizing it.

> The goals of his conversations were to preserve control over me and promote his selfish needs.

Once he stole a kiss on my cheek. By stole, I mean it was unwanted, unasked for, and unexpected. While my face clearly showed strong disapproval, I didn't make a fuss; I thought my expression was enough. When he followed with an attempted kiss on my lips, I objected. He said, "Well you *let* me kiss you on the cheek, so what's the big deal? After all, I am your husband." This was not the only time he twisted facts to fit his fancy and then looked at me with disbelief that I did not see it exactly as he just delivered it.

Journal, August 18, 1997

My husband and I have not been getting along at all. It was our anniversary on Friday the 15th, our 15th wedding anniversary, and it was meaningless. He wanted to act as if it was something to celebrate; I refused to say everything is good, because it's not. But he wanted me to. I would not just smile, be romantic, or ignore his abuse because of the date on the calendar. My husband called me horrible names, really mean, mean things. I am tired mentally, physically, and emotionally.

My ex-husband *needed* me to join him in his false reality, at least on our actual anniversary date. By not pretending for him I was interfering in his sincerely held belief that he was a great husband, which riled him so deeply he let loose his vile, disgusting rant.

At first he tried kind cajoling, knowing special events were something I enjoyed marking with great fanfare.

Early anniversaries were planned and decorated for. On our first four anniversaries, for example, we returned to the venue where we married. I wore my wedding dress and he wore his tux. My dress was a classic 1950s style with long sleeves and a fitted lace bodice that had a V at the waist. The bottom was full with a slight train that was easily bustled and had a touch of pearls and rhinestones that shimmered as I walked. It was a thrift-shop find: $50.00.

In the early anniversary years, we took pictures by a glistening lake, where white geese and multicolored mallard ducks paddled. In that exact place is where we stood under a Huppah with a rabbi and a minister and pronounced our traditional wedding vows. The ceremony ended with the ritual of the shattering of the glass under the foot of the groom. With time, what was being shattered was my inner spirit.

Dear Younger Me,

Narcissists live in a false reality. Don't play in their pretend world. Refuse the invitation. Playing even only once will result in you being reminded you partook, and that action permits a repeat action. Don't go there, ever. I am proud of you for not joining him there this time.

Journal, December 14, 1997

My marriage is in the pits. I hate it. My husband's OCD and a multitude of other things are causing a stressful time. To top it off, for some reason my husband thought it would be a good time to reach out to his mother, who has not talked to us for eight years, because he is Jewish and believes in Jesus. He was rejected again. She said to him, "You have done so many wrong things, plus you have *her* for a wife. Maybe I'll talk to you when your wife is dead and buried." He wanted to get kicked one more time and let her hurtful words reach my ears too? I am angry with him for doing that.

Journal, April 28, 1998

Tuesday night after teaching our Bible study, (my husband) was talking to me. I was lying in bed, reading the book *Israel my Beloved*. We talked about the Bible study and how he felt it went. I compassionately offered, "I think you could have been kinder to (a woman at the study) – she is having such a hard time right now and needs extra patience." Instantly he accused me of criticizing him. He raised his voice and told me I was a piece of s**t and a string of other expletives, then accused me of always complaining. He continued on the rampage.

I responded with "You are a jerk!" As soon as I did that, he seized my arms with all his might. He wrenched me from left to right over and over again like a rag doll. I was catapulted back and forth. He grabbed my chest and bounced me hard into the bed. I yelled for him to stop and screamed in pain. He screamed at me, "Go to hell" and then followed with a stream of expletives. I yelled for him to stop and screamed in pain. Then he spit in my face. My wrists were sore and red, my chest hurt, my heart was racing, and I wiped the spit from my face.

Totally out of control, foaming at the mouth, my husband continued to scream and rage just inches from my face. Spittle landed randomly on my face. I was able to push his face away but that made him even angrier.

When I screamed it woke our son up. He came to our bedroom to see me being beaten. He said, "I am going to call 911." He ran downstairs. When our son did that, my husband stopped.

I followed my son and said, "Wait; don't do that." Though I am thrilled he knows that is what he should do, I was scared to have him call and scared to have him not call. I was crushed that he had to be awakened to violence and vile language.

My husband has hit me before, but this episode was really bad. Each time in the past I swore if it ever happened again I would leave and yet I have not. I am scared. I need to do something.

His OCD has been bad. I do not want to be married to him anymore. I do not want to live like this. I did go to the doctor to have at least one of the abuse results recorded. I don't want to be married to someone who would spit in my face or who would call me such vile things.

I really want to separate, but I am very worried about the children. OH GOD how could I have made such a big mistake? I am sad. I am angry. Like the drug addict or the alcoholic, he does it again. Oh God, please help me. I am all alone. I have no one. I have no one to tell.

Though I had been pushed and hit many times in the sixteen years prior to this journal entry, this time I kept my promise to myself: I would not buy into the Carnie's rhetoric of "You made me," "You deserved it," and "I'm not hurting you." I did not deserve this. I stopped my son from calling 911; my facial expression reassured him I would take care of it rather than the police. My ex-husband had never been so scarily out of control, with direct hits to the face. I now know the label for this, Narcissistic rage.

I went to the local walk-in clinic. I was embarrassed and scared. The doctor asked, "Who did this to you?"

"My husband," I confessed.

He picked up my chart and glanced at my name. "Jewish guys don't usually do this. I am sorry." He recorded the abrasions, the cuts, the swelling, the black-and-blues, and the swollen eye. Bruises were not just on my face but my chest and arms too.

I drove right over to my sister-in-law's home. We were also friends, celebrated holidays together, and had children similar in ages. It took courage, but I confided in her. Taking off my sunglasses that shielded my black eye, I showed her my face. Her eyes grew wide. "What happened?"

I told her.

She wanted to know what I was going to do.

"I have just come from the doctor and showing you is part of my not hiding it any more. More than that, I do not know."

She was very calm. "Let me know how I can help."

> Sometimes I persisted for the right reasons, sometimes the wrong reasons, but most often with the hope he would leave so I did not have to.

I am actually mortified reading my journal entry. The healthier me sitting here typing at my keyboard would not accept that. You might ask why I didn't just leave. It's a valid question. Everyone asks abused women that question. I don't have an answer that would make you satisfied. Sometimes I persisted for the right reasons, sometimes the wrong reasons, but most often with the hope he would leave so I did not have to.

I was ashamed my son saw his father's violence and saw me do nothing. I did tell my son what his father did was wrong and not acceptable. That was the extent of the conversation. My journal words were stronger than I actually was. I stayed. Our house was up for sale so I was always waiting for the right time. That didn't come for three more years.

Dear Younger Me,

You did a BRAVE thing going to the doctor! I know that was difficult. You were scared and embarrassed. But it is not for you to be embarrassed; that should be shouldered by the abuser. You have exposed the lie to the light. The more you work in truth the easier it is to stay in truth. You broke the veil that hid so much for so long. Good for you. It's going to get easier now in some ways. It will also get harder in others. Don't give up. Keep telling the truth.

In another particularly ugly physical and verbal tirade, I was left with bruises, swelling, and red marks. These usually began when I did not immediately and fully agree with him. I tried to defend myself, grabbing his arms as they flew toward me. My meager attempts caused small, insignificant scratches on his arm. His words and fists kept flying with such fury; I don't think he heard my cries to stop. Though I had not said this very often, I told him, "I am reporting you to the police."

He looked afraid for just a split second, but then his face changed to smug and haughty. "Look at this scratch on my arm. They won't believe you. I'll show them what you did to me! If I go to jail, you won't be able to pay the bills. You will have no place to live with the children. I will lose my job and that will be your fault!" He let that soak in, then returned to add one more comment: "You have no job; you can't support yourself." He did not acknowledge the harm he had caused me. The red marks and black-and-blues that were starting to show through on my fair skin were all ignored.

When doctors and therapists write about patients' stories, it is my story too. When these same experts record the abusers' techniques, excuses, and personalities, it is my former husband they describe. My ex-husband can be identified in both *The Verbally Abusive Relationship* by Patricia Evans and *Why Does He Do That? Inside the Minds of Angry and Controlling Men* by Lundy Bancroft. I read Lundy's book seventeen years after Patricia's book and was impressed with his breadth of knowledge, tremendous insight, and brilliant answers for women. It's a compelling read and all- encompassing. He covers the subject with generous compassion.

I often purchase secondhand books on this subject, and at times discover handwritten notes inside. In some ways I find the written words and notes from previous owners affirming. They tell me there are others who have walked this path. Some notes reveal a twist of other abusive techniques. Some point out when the abusers used children as weapons to hurt their victims.

Journal, April 1998

My ex-husband's family left a mean message on the voicemail. They are glad we had a little girl so she can have a hard heart and hurt us. There were multiple voices on the voicemail. His sisters and his mother. In the same voicemail my mother-in-law said to me, "I can't wait for you to die so I can dance on your grave."

Journal, May 10, 1998

My son seems to be adjusting? Healing? Letting the shock settle? What is the right word when a little boy has seen his father beat his

mother? My son has been very affectionate to me lately. My husband gave me three roses for Mother's Day. One red, one pink, one white. Tomorrow I am class mother for a trip to the Old Time Village. I baked fifty cupcakes and two cakes for the boys' classes. I still feel so empty and sad. Off to bed now.

CHAPTER 8

MOVING DAY TIMES 2

In September 1998 our house that had been on the market for a year sold about the same time my ex-husband thought he could retire. A retirement move south would be the perfect time to exit the marriage. His pension system possessed a concise retirement tiered formula, one my husband had inaccurately judged by three years. Exiting the marriage would also take three more years.

After the house sold, we lived at a friend's house. She had empty-nested and was alone. We needed a place to live and she needed the money boarders would provide. Her home had five bedrooms on three levels, a huge backyard for the kids, and children their age right across the street. We used three bedrooms.

My ex-husband found two women to criticize. One day our friend was frustrated and said, "I have had a lot of people help me out over the years as a single mom, but I have never been made to feel so bad about it. Why does he help with something and then remind me more than once? His remarks make me feel inadequate." Our friend was now feeling the OCD and the blows from the Narcissist. She just didn't know this is what I lived with. His actions distanced the friend and me. I was quietly miserable. The presence of a prospective witness, however, kept the physical abuse to a minimum. Verbal, emotional, mental, and spiritual were still accounted for.

I have read in many cases physical abuse was indeed intentional and even thought out. The fact that he was able to control the physical abuse during this window where there was a witness is interesting. Like my father, he knew what he was doing was wrong, even criminal, and a consistent witness would not be a good thing.

Before we moved into our friend's house, we talked with her about whether it was feasible to continue the Bible studies we both taught. She was a friend from church and had visited both of our studies on occasion, so she understood how they worked and what they entailed. She was on board. The Tuesday morning and Tuesday night Bible studies went on seamlessly. The Tuesday night coed class was the one my former husband taught. My group was ladies only and we usually worked through one of the popular women's studies from Kay Arthur or topical studies that applied to a woman's daily life. Tuesdays meant getting up early to set up the room and the prayer board, bake treats, and get the kids ready for their school day. The ladies arrived at 9:15 a.m. and we chatted, prayed, and worked through the questions in our guide book.

> Like my father, he knew what he was doing was wrong, even criminal, and a consistent witness would not be a good thing.

Tuesday nights ran similarly. I set up the room and baked, as well as brewed some flavored coffees and teas, but my husband led the study. I generally did not sit in on that study as I was upstairs doing homework, reading with the children, and then putting them to bed. In about 1999, a prominent professional sports figure attended one of our studies. I had a friendship with his wife during that sport season. During our visits I had confided in her about the hits, pushes, and verbal abuse. Telling the doctor of my injuries had broken my self-decided silence. She said, "Many professional sports players were known for domestic violence and they even had a spiritual counselor for the team to try curb that."

Maybe she could help me? As it is with every sport season, when it ends the athletes and their families return to their hometowns for the off-season. That was many states away and her little ones made for a busy life. She was very sweet. If we had lived closer I am sure we would have stayed friends. Knowing my ex-husband's tactics, however, I have no doubt my former husband followed his usual pattern: "She's the problem, not me. Look at how many people come to my study; I am respected."

When this sports figure heard from his wife that his Bible study leader was exhibiting abusive behavior, he said to me as I was ascending the stairs to see my children on the second floor, "You mean all this is a front? This is all a show? It's not real?" Sharing with his wife, I had just been the most real I had been in twenty years. I thought, while waiting for things to change, the changes my husband promised, I was persevering in a trial, being a servant to those who came to my home despite what I was living though. I think he perceived if the room, culinary, and Bible presentation were so perfect, I had to be too.

There could have been so many other reactions:

"I heard your husband has been hitting you. I'll get with him and have a talk. That's not acceptable."

"I heard you guys are having some problems. I'll be praying for you. Is there anything we can do to help?"

"Your husband is a good Bible study teacher, but his character is not aligned to what he is teaching. That is not good. Let's talk about this."

Though I lacked the fortitude to do it, I should have stood up at the full table and said, "Your Bible study teacher is abusing me and he has no right to be teaching you anything."

Unknowingly, this towering athlete then stepped into the arena of enabling. My husband shared with him that he had written a book and really wanted to publish but did not have the money. I guess my husband's smoothing-over process helped him to brush past any nagging thoughts that this author was abusing his wife. Somehow he warmed up to the idea of keeping that fake front that he had so loudly protested against just weeks before.

He funded the publishing of the book. It's so easy to get spun into the Narcissist's

> Super score for the abusive Narcissist, now he could be a published author.

sticky web. Super score for the abusive Narcissist, now he could be a published author. He had such an exciting story to tell! "This is wonderful; it's God's provision, a miracle, and meant to be." Part of the exciting story my ex-husband loved to spin bigger than it deserved was that the athlete had the same last name as my ex-husband's first publisher (he has since had other publishers). "Did you notice my friend and the publisher have the same name? Isn't this just such a God-incidence?"

He wrote and published his book about the Biblical timeline for the End Times while he was punching me in the face and stalking me room to room to verbally abuse me.

After a year or so of sharing living space with our friend, it was time to be in a house of our own. My former husband told me, "You know any tension or discomfort we had while living here is your fault. You just can't get along with anybody." The new rental house was in the same town

> My former husband told me, "You know any tension or discomfort we had while living here is your fault. You just can't get along with anybody."

with lots of kids on the block for ours to play with. Our acquaintances who owned the house wanted to participate in full-time mission work. Renting the house enabled them to do that.

A nice big kitchen window enabled me to watch the kids play and see the yellow school bus arrive that took them to their private Christian school. The house had two floors with the bedrooms on the upper level and the tiniest bathroom. You did not walk around in this bathroom; you barely had room to turn around! When I entered the house, the second room I saw was the dining room and it sorely needed a coat of paint. I created a layering effect I learned about in a book, using soft aqua tones with just a bit of tiny gold flecks. I replaced the non-descript wooden cabinet knobs in the kitchen with modern green marble knobs for a quick pick-me-up.

A swing set was the perfect addition to the backyard and provided hours of fun for our kids as well as the neighborhood ones. I did the legwork of searching for the perfect one at the perfect price and we bought it. My ex-husband spent hours putting it together. It had an eight-foot slide, four swings, and climbing areas. While living there we found lots of activities to indulge in and celebrated a few birthdays with grand parties.

The kids were delighted when we added a pet gerbil to the family. They named him Oreo. Watching this black-and-white creature run his squeaky exercise wheel made everyone smile. One of our kids was convinced Oreo learned to respond to his name. He escaped the gentle cuddle of one of the children on one excursion from his oversized aquarium tank, and enjoyed freedom for two days until we were able to return him to his scented bedding that occasionally sent a waft of pine through the air.

This was home for the next year and a half. During this time we visited a new church. The pastor was about the same age we were, and his contemporary church consisted of about a hundred congregants. During a prayer time he said to us, "God showed me a vision. You two are like beautiful tea cups. The front half is very attractive, beautiful, and shiny, but when you turn the cups around, they are all broken."

I struggled to keep my chin from quivering, but could not stop the tears. They welled in my eyes, then one by one fell slowly down my cheeks, and tasted salty when they touched my lips. I felt as if he was saying he had seen behind the curtain.

> I dabbled in escape plans. Letting all the scenarios percolate was too much for my brain.

Sometimes when the kids were at school, I dabbled in escape plans. Nothing ever came together. Letting all the scenarios percolate was too much for my brain. Plans to leave almost always came second, third, or fourth. In my perfect vision he would have an epiphany: he would admit he was responsible, gladly leave in peace, and happily support me and the children. So I just kept waiting. Many nights I stared at the ceiling, calculating if I could survive in this expensive area we lived in, or anywhere else for that matter. Would I be a mother on welfare?

Would he make good on his threat to go to court and take my children from me? Would I get a full-time job and not be a stay-at-home mom? No more class trips, and no time to bake cupcakes, make costumes, or cuddle in long bonding sessions. Would my children hate me? Would I lose the closeness we have? And would their father have too much alone time so he could alienate them from me? Would my intellectually bright school-aged children begin to do poorly, both academically and socially? I had already seen this happen to my exceptionally gifted bonus son when my ex-husband divorced from his first wife.

Journal, May 1998

My husband grabbed my son by the neck and pushed him. He was out of control. The force made him jolt forward. It was totally unnecessary. It hurt me to see my son's expression. He had no idea that violence was coming and he certainly didn't think it was necessary. What is wrong with this man! I am so grieved.

My husband seems to be losing control more often and more frequently. He must find the reason for his acting out in physical violence. He is seeing a counselor. This behavior makes me feel disgusting inside. He was apologetic after I talked to him and pointed out the wrongness, but then he quickly rationalized it.

In the journal note you just read, my husband is seeing a counselor. I asked him to go, and it wasn't the first time. A counseling group offered a class in Biblical counseling, meant for the lay Bible teachers in the church. I took that course. It was fairly basic, but I enjoyed it.

I suggested my husband go see one of the counselors in that group. He reluctantly went and that was the problem. He believed through his lens of Narcissism I had a problem, so he went to complain about me to people I had just taken the course with. I did not know at that time I was dealing with an abusive Narcissist, so I did not know to interview the counselor to see if she was trained to counsel someone like my husband.

When my husband shared details with me after these sessions, I knew he had told the counselor lies and half-truths. In a follow-up session I listened as the counselor minimized my husband's OCD behaviors. In a tone meant to say, "It's no big deal" with an accompanying shoulder shrug, she pronounced, "If he does the dishes and they are not clean, so what? Just rewash them." His OCD registered dishes in the sink as clutter so they must be banished to the cabinet in haste. I got the feeling that in his sessions with the counselor, he talked about *me* rather than talking about what *he* does. His deflection for his actions was often, "My wife has issues because of the abuse in her childhood." I often thought, *What does my childhood have to do with how you* act?

> He came out of that short counseling period, feeling validated that he was not the problem. And I suspect that was his plan going in.

He came out of that short counseling period, feeling validated that he was not the problem. And I suspect that was his plan going in. In the year 2000, I wrote this counselor a letter explaining my feelings about her time with my husband.

It was one of the things my new and very qualified counselor encouraged me to do, as part of my healing process. I was grateful to find her. She lovingly walked me through some of my roughest days.

When choosing any service provider, we have to do a thorough job of investigating that person or company so we receive quality service and good value for our money. That obligation remains the same, and perhaps carries a heavier weight, when choosing a health professional who will help promote improved mental health and unlock the doors that gate the way to developing the skills to understand and solve someone's issues.

Sometimes, even a recommendation from a trusted source can be sour. As part of my bonus daughter coming to live with us I had to see a counselor, he was recommended by our attorney. By the second session the counselor was asking me to divest very intimate marriage sexual history. I found that odd. I was also in a vulnerable position not wanting to do anything to disrupt the process of my bonus daughter living with us. Perhaps he was holistic in his approach? Perhaps he was a predator? The sessions ended before I had to find out. A year or so later this counselors name was splashed across the newspaper as having sexually assaulted multiple women who were in his care. At the time of the police investigation we were in the middle of writing new wills and the attorney who recommended him to me abruptly stopped returning my phone calls. That left me wondering if my attorney was complicit in the assaults by supplying woman clients to the counselor.

Dear Younger Me,

People go to school to learn their trade. That does not always make them good at their job. Like medical doctors, counselors have their expertise. You need to discover one who is conversant in the world of Narcissism. Having the support of a qualified counselor will help you exit as quickly as possible. My abuser wanted me to think if I had changed counselors it affirmed his theory that "Nothing makes her happy." Stop caring about what he thinks. His thoughts are not valid. It's OK to search for the right counselor, one trained for this battle. Did you know your abuser does not want you to have a highly trained counselor? He wants you to stay in bondage so he does not have to change. He would rather have you suffer than change himself.

Journal, March 11, 1999

I told my husband a few weeks ago I want a legal separation. He responded:

1. You are worthless.
2. You can't support yourself.
3. You are old.
4. You can't model anymore.
5. You can't do nursing.
6. You don't contribute to the house.

Add that to the punches, throws, and chairs that have been held over my head and it's no wonder I am depressed. Oh, I function. Everyone gets a lunch packed. Dinner gets made, orthodontist appointments get kept, haircuts are gotten, but there is no joy, no spark, and no love.

All abusers enjoy making their victims feel worthless. He was overreaching for details to create his big ball of insults. In his mind when he wadded it big enough he could wind it up and let it fly, dreaming it would make a meteor-sized landing that would disable me, causing me to surrender to his control. Any weakness I showed would automatically raise him up to the privileged and improved status he wanted.

> All abusers enjoy making their victims feel worthless.

Full-time mom brought me the most joy, but there were some bookings in the show business field, and occasionally a job would fall my way from a past connection. The twisted sickness of his statement is that on a different day of his flip flopping personality, the words that warmed my ears were endearing: "It is so great you can be a full-time mother. That's the way it should be. The children thrive with you being with them. It's an important job and you're a great mother!" But today's Dr. Hyde accusation is, "You are old, you have no qualifications anymore, and you contribute nothing to the household."

One afternoon we were having a discussion. The children were not yet home from school, and he had just returned from work where strength training with heavy weights was part of his day. Internal rage was bubbling because I was not reading his thoughts and agreeing without hesitation. Suddenly his expression transformed to scarily evil. He raised his hands to my chest and decked me. I tumbled to the floor and he picked

> Suddenly his expression transformed to scarily evil. He raised his hands to my chest and decked me.

up one of our substantial, solid wood-carved dining room chairs and held it over me, swinging it to within inches of my head while leaning down with uncontrolled fire in his eyes. I trembled. It was what he was hoping for. He put the chair down and walked away. He said nothing about that episode, as if it didn't happen.

Dear Younger Me,

The man you married promised to love, honor, and cherish you but has failed on every account. There is no love in harsh words, no honor in hands that hit, and no cherishing in verbal threats and lies. This is not a husband. This is a brute. This is not acceptable. You have worth, you are valuable, and you deserve to be honored and cherished.

You have reason to be depressed, but that is not what I want you to do with your emotions. I want you to rise up and be defiant to your diseased husband. I want you to GET OUT. He has a job and you can garnish his salary for your support. You did not know that? Yes, you could survive financially without him. He does not want you to know that. You will get out eventually, but it could be sooner. You will have a great job, travel, own a lovely home, and have healthy friends who stand by you.

Regrets are ahead of you if you do not heed my advice. You will regret that you did not make your home safer for your children. Some regrets are really hard to live with.

Journal, March 1999

My husband wanted to vent last night, so he did, and I made little comment. His raised voice venting was alternately mixed with kind compassion. He felt he could help me discover why I am so unhappy that I would want a separation. He was taking guesses at why, as if what I explain to him can't be right. He could not be the source of my or the children's misery. The misery of mean words, the pressure of his OCD, the physical blows. To him it was not anything he was doing. There HAD to be something else. His final determination was, "You don't appreciate things and nothing is as bad as you think."

Even as I read my journal entries, I feel sick. I tremble and sweat. My deodorant is being tested! I want to turn back the clock, choose another path, and take the advice I am giving the younger me. I have so many regrets. It's a huge burden to bear.

In the book *30 Days To Taming Your Tongue* by Deborah Smith Pegues (Harvest House 2005, page 76), Deborah states, "The intimidator counts on his victim to wilt in the face of verbal attack. That is why sometimes (when it is safe) you have to let an intimidator know you refuse to be oppressed by him and that you do indeed have God-given strength to resist his tactics." Deborah uses 1 Samuel 17:45-46 as her text for her chapter on *The Intimidating Tongue*. I appreciate the way Deborah expresses this sentiment with scriptural emphasis because my ex-husband often misused scripture to control and blame. Here scripture is used for a healthy productive purpose and in a truthful way that helped me stand up for myself, rather than using it as an excuse to endure abuse the way my ex-husband and predatory intimidators use it.

Journal, May 1999

I was on the phone, speaking with the dean of my children's school. My husband was yelling at me while I was on the phone. I asked him to stop and wait to address me when I was done. He would not. He continued to yell and try to embarrass me. He wanted me to lose control and say something out of character for the Dean to hear so any misstep could be used by him as ammunition.

We were at a friend's wedding and I was chatting with another friend when my husband came back from the bathroom. He walked right up to me. His face had a mean, twisted expression; in a demanding tone he delivered this: "You are talking too much. SHUT UP!" I was mortified.

Formerly he had enough jurisdiction over his illness to at least shelter the public put downs; now the gate was wide open and they ran freely. Pronouncing his decree, SHUT UP! is a control mechanism and there will be a few more journal entries that record this rank. He did not put these words into play until my talks of separation were expressed so I would not be surprised if there was an internal battle and what he really meant was, "Shut up about the idea of separating; I can't stand to lose control or power!"

His internal tornado previously ebbed and flowed but now I was living in tornado alley. It spun faster and harder, leaving him no ability to show restraint, here and in many other areas. He hoped it would scare me enough to allow him to regain command of his castle. The more it happened the more I recognized it not just as an isolated incident but a tool in his tool box he strategically moved forward for better access.

> Formerly he had enough jurisdiction over his illness to at least shelter the public put downs; now the gate was wide open and they ran freely.

Journal, September 15, 1999

Tonight my husband told me his sneakers have holes. I said, "Then throw them away. Why are you telling me? You can throw them away."

With great thought and obvious internal burden he said, "Well, [pause]... I am going to leave them here on the floor."

I said, "Put them in the garbage."

He said, "No, I just changed the garbage bag."

One time I put some garbage in the garbage pail and he raised his voice to me: "What? Are you stupid? Why did you just do that?"

Being confused about what he was saying I responded, "Do what?" Then I got it. I could not use the garbage pail if he had just changed the bag. When I told him he should think about what he had just said, he let the put-downs begin: "You are an idiot; there is nothing wrong with me; it's you!"

Not wanting to hear any more of his blame I changed the subject. I asked him, "Please begin to put the kids to bed so I can cover schoolbooks the kids need for the morning."

He flippantly answered, "You use me."

Dear Younger Me,

Narcissists who have OCD have an inability to change. His rigidity is confining and causes him to vomit abuse on you for not understanding his limitations and adapting to his sickness.

Do not question yourself or your actions; rather acknowledge that his words and actions are not normal. Don't let him wiggle you away from your correct assessments.

Obsessive Compulsive Personality Disorder is characterized by a preoccupation with orderliness, perfectionism, and mental and interpersonal control, at the expense of flexibility, openness, and efficiency. In the 1990s my ex-husband was forced to admit what family, friends, and workmates had already observed. He had OCD. We brought one of our children to a psychiatrist for suddenly displaying OCD traits, which turned out to be a reaction from the tension in our home. Thankfully this resolved quickly.

The doctor asked, "Does anyone else in the family have obsessive behavior?" I looked at my husband, waiting for him to confess. He did. In the previous journal note you see his mental struggle. Because of his OCD he was prone to become angry in circumstances where he was not able to preserve control of his physical or personal environment. OCD married to Narcissistic behavior created an environment where he ruminated about any perceived lack in his mantle of control, which led to explosive anger.

About this time, my ex-husband decided everything he did as a natural part of being a father and running a home together was now to be considered a favor. He wanted me to feel the struggle of single motherhood to hinder me from leaving. Occasionally and just to prove to me I needed him, he became resistant to parental obligations: putting the children to bed, driving the children, covering books, or helping with homework.

He was also punishing me for being resistant to his sexual advances. In his mental filter, since I was resistant to keeping what he considered my marital obligation, he could freely change his parental obligations. This kind of distortion was added to his repertoire once I started, even on a small level, initiating healthy thinking and creating boundaries. One such boundary was, "I have no obligation to have sex with a man who holds a chair over my head."

> "She is always playing the victim" is one of his well-used tag lines to excuse his own bad behavior.

Bravely or stupidly, I called out his bad behavior more often. My ex-husband stayed with his *go to* response. He deflected the blame. Positioning me in that seat allowed him to maintain his positive image of himself. "She is always playing the victim" is one of his well-used tag lines to excuse his own bad behavior. If he could convince the children or any other listening ear that I often complained, then it could deflect what I was saying was true.

My sons, unaware their father was indoctrinating them, would then wait for the right moment to repeat that parlance to me. One of my sons, who went through particularly rebellious teenage years, screamed those exact words at me more than once. I understood these were his father's words, not his. It hurt very badly to have my sons be so ignorantly callous, but like the title of a Michael Jackson song, they had just been used by a *Smooth Criminal*.

CHAPTER 9

SECRETS REVEALED

Journal, February 2000

Saturday morning, February 12th, my husband decided it was time to tell me a secret he's held for 10 years. This occurred because we had been taking a thirteen-week marriage seminar, and in week twelve they suggest you offer up any confessions you may have. So on Saturday morning after our Friday night course, he told me he had been having sex with our barely nineteen-year-old babysitter in the late 1980s. He had sex in our house and in our car.

I am devastated. I feel betrayed. He even lied with a straight face at first, insisting it was only once. But I pressed on because I knew it had to be many, many times. He thinks life revolves around his penis. He confessed to getting her drunk the first time. He said he seduced her on purpose. This was an act of selfish gratification on his part, as always. Issues with his penis have been lifelong. He said, "I eat three times a day. Why can't I orgasm three times a day?"

A few weeks ago, I was in bed with three icepacks on my head, trying to find relief from a migraine. I had already set a boundary of no sexual activity, but my diminished capacity caused him to think that would be a good opportunity to take advantage of me. When unwanted sexual intercourse happens, when you are incapacitated, I call it rape. That happened to me.

Constantly wavering between "This all lays at his feet" and "There might be something I could do," I agreed to attend this multi-week marriage seminar hosted by a local church. When he revealed this decade-old secret, I became visibly upset. He challenged me: "I thought you were Christian enough to handle this." My deficiency was the problem, not his actions. This showed his true objective: "I am going to say something and if you can't handle it, that's your problem." Instead of comfort and repentance he was in attack mode. Continuing in his condescending tone he added, "It's not like she was a virgin. She probably wasn't a virgin."

My response to his justification was, "You have hurt this child who came to our home and was assured safety, security, and comfort. You think what matters is whether she was a virgin?"

He threw back, "Well, you know, I was just fulfilling my fantasy of having sex with a babysitter." His face and tone suggested his fantasy took over and I should sympathize with that.

I never blamed the young girl. She too was a victim, and for that I am deeply saddened. She was taken advantage of by a Sociopath Narcissist who thought everyone would welcome his sexual advances. It is incredibly sad a teenager's life was forever changed, and in my home, and that the man I shared a life with was the perpetrator.

As was his habit, he swung yet another diversionary tactic. Assuming his mother would even break from our banishment for his sister's upcoming wedding he launched this: "This is why YOU are not invited to my sister's wedding. You are a terrible person. You just don't know how to forgive." I did not recoil and accept I was to blame for his actions, so he quickly rotated his accusation to, "YOU caused me to have sex with her."

Just like an automatic ball pitcher at a batting cage, these *flips of blame* kept launching repeatedly in our marriage. He began to tell as many as would listen that he did indeed have sex with the babysitter, but the worst thing in the scenario was I was unforgiving. Friends approached me to discuss how sad and repentant he seemed, and how I should forgive him.

He told my son of the adultery, and the version weighed heavily on the diversion that I was not forgiving. He even asked my son to pray with him, "Dear God, help Mom become forgiving." My son's thought processes followed that I didn't forgive, so I was bad and his actions toward me coincided.

For the next six months, close friends listened to my husband's version of my non-forgiveness. They were confident they had the magic pill that would make everything copasetic. They decided to surprise us with tickets to a popular traveling weekend marriage seminar as a present for our birthdays. They even watched our kids so we could attend the weekend event. In grandiose words and pleading, my husband said, "We should go; they already paid for the tickets. Let's see what GOD does during the weekend."

When we came back from the weekend seminar my former husband rushed to our friends with this report: "In one of the breakout sessions we were supposed to say something nice about each other. Do you know she could not think of one nice thing to say about me?" I can still see his face as he pleaded with me to be *honest* and find all the good things about him. He waited, then offered, "I can see I am the mature Christian, not you."

In my February journal writings I note my former husband raped me. Strong words, I know. I had drawn the line in the sand months prior; I was no longer having any kind of intimate relationship with him. He knew my history: migraines that incapacitated me, off-the-chart pain, vomiting, tears, and definitely the inability to consent to anything. Stillness, a dim room, and the ice packs that sat at all sides of my head only dulled the pain from a ten to a nine. The tiniest movements were excruciating.

Suddenly I heard my name called. I gingerly lifted my head and squinted to focus my eyes. There before me was my husband in full erection. He told me, "I took a Viagra just in case." The little blue pill called Viagra was the latest hype, so he had to indulge.

I barely had the strength to address him. But I managed to ask, "In case of what?"

With confidence he offered, "In case you change your mind." He smiled at me weirdly. I was scared. I recognized his Narcissistic sense of entitlement speaking to him: "Sex is your privilege. You have the right to have sex with her whether she wants it or not." A cold shower does not satisfy a rape mentality.

He understood that my incapacity created limitations to resistance. Just like a rape victim trapped in an elevator, I was trapped by my illness. To him it was a perfect time to take what was rightfully his. I had a jack hammer in my head and one on my body. Both were uninvited and unwelcome. Crying more would only make my head pound worse, so I just laid there hoping the pain of being raped by my husband and the pain of the migraine would pass.

His sexual dysfunction was not just something that rose up at home; it rolled into his workplace as well. He had a forty-five-minute midday rest period. He told me he normally used this time to take a nap but not before pleasuring himself on almost a daily basis.

In counseling we discussed his apparent addiction. The final answer seemed to lie with the fact that the body's natural production of dopamine is at its highest during orgasm and addiction to the chemical change is similar to experiencing a heroin rush.

Journal, February 16, 2000

Since my husband told me the news on Saturday, there has been a cloud hovering over me. I could not move. I stared at the walls for hours. I laid anywhere, sat anywhere. I fell over with no strength. I did not shower. I could barely move.

My mind told me to unpack the boxes that surrounded me, but my body would not obey. Do something. My body would not obey. It would not move. Death sounded very good.

My husband told me, "You make a big deal about everything. What kind of Christian are you if you can't forgive me? You have to. You are a Christian."

This infidelity, hidden for a decade, and marring a young girl's life really bothered me. It was an affront on every side. It was the proverbial match in the powder barrel. It put me into overload. Maybe it was the way he minimized it and blamed me that finally made my body collapse. But when I rose up, as hard as it was, the next steps started me on the right road, the one I should have started walking a long time ago, the road that took me to freedom.

Journal, March 2000

I was trying to show my husband a math problem for my son and he smacked my hand as I was pointing to the problem. He then denied that he did it, and then switched to, "I did it, but why are you going to make such a big deal about it?" I am tired. I am so tired of being abused and then blamed for the abuse. I feel so trapped. I've made such a big mistake.

I have been telling my husband what the terms of the separation look like. Right now I have a window where he is agreeing. But I know that can change at any minute. Verbally he has agreed to the terms. But he asked me, "Can we wait till summer, till I move out since we just moved to this house?" Then he added, "I would like some time to prove myself a changed man. But I will sleep separate from you and make no demands of any kind from you."

I said, "You can stay in the house under those conditions."

The children will be devastated, which is the only reason I am willing to hold off. My son has a very soft side. He said, "You guys fight too much." He does not understand *we* are not fighting. I am resisting his father's control. It broke my heart when he said, "You are going to get divorced and I am going to kill myself." He drew a picture about it. He was very upset. I have to stay for the children?

Journal, April 2000

I have spent three hours in prayer, on my face, begging God for relief and answers. My husband tells me, "Just get over it. You're not doing a good enough job getting over it. Submit to God; just change or just forgive." He said, "I told you my sin because I thought you were mature enough to handle it." When I mention my pain, he says, "Shut up!" He is mature enough to teach a Bible study but not enough to know he should not beat his wife? Was he mature when he smacked my hand in March? I am going to have to find a Christian counselor to talk to.

I put up four bird feeders. Squirrels, cardinals, and blue jays visit all the time. The kids love it. We went bowling; there was lots of laughter! Tomorrow we will go to Fun Zone Amusement Center. The kids will show their stellar honor roll report cards and get free coins to play with.

CHAPTER 10

BRING IN THE CAVALRY: COUNSELORS THAT GET IT – FINALLY

Journal, April 21, 2000

I used a Christian phonebook book called the *Shepherd's Guide*. I had a choice of three Christian counselors. One took our insurance, so I had a free phone consultation with her; she made me feel confident so I made an appointment. The session went okay. She had one or two great insights.

In my subsequent sessions with this counselor she led me to create boundaries, be comfortable with them, and make my Carnie know I meant them. In my early counseling sessions, I asked my counselor, as if asking permission from her, "Can I get separated from him?" This seems like a decision someone should be able to make alone but I needed confirmation.

Journal, May 25, 2000

Today my husband gave our daughter a sharp smack on her hand that made an audible noise. It was because she turned on the radio in his car and the volume was very loud. She had not touched the volume; she only turned it on. He must have previously been playing the music loudly. It was not her doing.

I told him, "You should not be smacking her hand." He went through the usual denial:

1. You make a big deal of everything.
2. I didn't do anything.
3. I did do it, but it wasn't that bad.
4. Well, maybe I did smack her.
5. Okay, I smacked her.

In 1980 George Bach and Ronald Duetsch coined the word *crazy-making*. Bach and Duetsch defined it as "a form of interpersonal interaction that results from the repression of intense aggression and which seriously impairs its victim's capacity to recognize and deal with interpersonal reality." I realized it. The reality is he left the radio on a loud volume; however, he needed to blame his daughter so he could feel in control of the circumstance. He wanted us to doubt our reality.

Journal, June 2000

With the support and strength I found in counseling, I told my husband he has to go to counseling, once again. I told him it's like he has a four-inch wound that needs to be totally healed and closed, but he keeps working on only the first quarter inch. He puts a new piece of skin over the festering wound, but pretty soon the infection eats through the healing skin and it's back full force and worse. He went through the usually denial.

1. I'm changing and that's enough.
2. I don't have time.
3. I don't need to.

Later in the day he called me from work and said he doesn't want to go because when I go for help I get sympathy. I was the victim. When he goes he is the perpetrator and the bad one so it will hurt to talk about it, get it out, and confess it and he doesn't want to – but he will.

Journal, June 26, 2000

My husband met with his male counselor for the first time today, June 26, 2000. I went to his session. It was a somewhat productive time. My husband surprised me with some honesty, but not enough. The counselor was okay. We will go back next Monday at 5:15 p.m.

Three hours later, he had a horrible outburst. Uncontrolled carnage. The usual disgusting words, curses, accusations, and threats. He always keeps up his antics in front of the kids and then the kids get upset. Then he starts crying. The kids say, "Daddy's always crying and you're not." The kids want to give advice. But they don't understand why this is going on. Their dad ropes them in to gain sympathy and it works. But I don't say anything because it's too heavy for the children to bear. I look like the bad guy. He is doing it on purpose, to have the children support him. That's sick. They are only five, nine, and twelve.

> This was not the first time the Carnie had intentionally played with the heart strings of his children by turning on the tears.

In reading the last two lines of my journal entry, specifically the ages of the children, I had an epiphany. This was not the first time the Carnie had intentionally played with the heart strings of his children by turning on the tears. Though he presented it to me as if his ex-wife was heartless as he cried about their marital troubles in front of the children, I now realize he recycled that tactic, which in both instances deeply hurt and affected his children, not his ex-wives.

This ploy was acceptable because he lacked empathy; his children were not as important as hurting the women who were choosing to end the charade of marital bliss. This entry also introduces a counselor who I will be forever grateful for because it is his ears and his eyes that caught the nuances of the Narcissist. A quick ten-minute trip from our home made sessions convenient. He shared his bottom floor office with other counselors including the small waiting room but had dedicated space for privacy with his clients. His comfy couch sat across from his own sizable chair where he used his training to help me find freedom.

Journal, June 28, 2000

We were all lying on the floor, watching *7th Heaven*. My sweet daughter was giving me a lot of affection and kissing me with such great joy and fun! The boys were snuggled with me. My husband became upset and jealous. He began making faces like *sure the kids can do that but I can't*. He leaned over and tried to kiss me, but I turned my face so he got my cheek rather than my lips.

He got mad, really, really angry. He said in a loud, commanding voice, "How long is this going to go on with you being the one in control?" The comments went on for a while so I left the room and went to the bathroom. I did not want the children to hear all his horrible comments and his attempt to make me look bad. By leaving the room I was hoping to protect the children from him and the potential for this to escalate. We were having such a sweet, sweet moment and their dad wanted to destroy it.

When he followed me, I was scared. When he stuck his foot in the door as I tried to close it, I was petrified. When the door took the punch this time instead of me, I was relieved. He made sure the punch went so close to my head I could hear the wind in my ear as his fist passed by. He resents the fact that I have a good relationship with the kids and they can give me affection and he can't. He thinks he is entitled to the same.

So much for the promise he made in March that he would make no demands of me of any kind and he would prove himself a changed man. Two days after his first counseling session, these are his actions.

Later, when my ex-husband lost control because I threw off his reins and left him, over and over his verbiage to others was, "She is controlling" or "She has all the control." It is interesting that he thought if he did not have control OVER me, then I must possess control that rightfully belongs to him. Narcissists will make accusations like this to mirror their own problems and transplant them into the beliefs of their victims and naïve, unsuspecting outsiders.

My ex-husband's new counselor was highly qualified. I could see a difference in his questions and way he ran the session. He did not allow my husband to con him. He used appropriate techniques to prevent him from being dishonest, like restating questions to ascertain what different answers would be offered, not allowing him to talk about me, trying to keep him focused on talking solely of himself, and smartly inviting me into sessions every few weeks. I was even given time alone with the counselor. "Your husband refuses to stay on topic and only wants to talk about you. I'd like you to speak of how things are going when you come to his sessions."

At the next session I did just that. "How do you think things are going?" he asked me. "Your husband says he is doing really well."

"He has hit me numerous times, he has verbally degraded me, and his need to control is over the top," I replied. Even now, I can see the counselor's enlightened and compassionate expression as he was listening to me.

"That is not what you told me," the counselor said to my husband. "Is what she's saying true?"

"Yes," he confessed.

This went on for months. It was a curious thing to watch and hear him deal his lies when he knew I was there ready to call him out on each and every one. He really believed his own narrative and felt comfortable telling it every week. "I am doing great; I am getting better." It became quite clear to the counselor that I was not safe. For the first time I had someone grasping what was going on. I was reservedly relieved. I spoke truth and was not being discounted, nor my words minimized.

CHAPTER 11

ONE BIG DYSFUNCTIONAL FAMILY – MEET HIS FAMILY

We had not seen his family for some years after my husband had accepted Jesus as his Lord and Savior. A cousin called my husband. "Your grandma died. We know you loved her. Did you want to come pay your respects?"

My husband did indeed want to attend. We knew there would be some tension so we decided together to say hello to those who were friendly and avoid those who were not. We would be kind and respectful and smile. Our youngest was just a few months old and I was breastfeeding, so she came with us. We got a babysitter for the other two children. We made the hour-plus drive, listened to the service, and then joined everyone to exchange greetings.

His mother screamed at us, "What are you doing here? This is my mother's funeral!" then looked at our infant in the carrier and added, "Look, they brought the slutty whore to the funeral." Yes, she was calling her three-month-old granddaughter a slutty whore.

I watched as there were more disapproving glances and pointing fingers from his sisters. The people gathering did not disperse even with the harsh words being thrown; they continued the casual banter. It was as if they expected my husband's mother not to act in a civil manner. Some relatives did speak with us kindly, however, and offered congratulations on the arrival of our daughter.

Our baby was in the carrier at my feet when one of my husband's three sisters marched up to me and declared, "This is for making my brother a Christian." She punched me and grabbed me and that's all I remember until I woke up on the cold, hard cement. My husband's relatives told me I was hit and thrown so hard I flew through the air and bounced on the ground.

When I woke up on the ground, there were scores of concerned faces standing over me, calling my name. My husband told me the *Christian thing* to do was not have her arrested, which I now recognize was influenced by his Narcissism. He perceived calling the police would make him look bad to the crowd; to his mother, who he was still yearning for contact with; and the police since he was related to the perpetrator.

I was unconscious on the ground with an elbow that very clearly illustrated the force I incurred when I crashed to the ground, but he was worried about his image. I did not feel strong enough at the time to argue with his decision, but I did think she deserved to be jailed and I wondered if she understood the grace she got that day. She should have a criminal record, though my husband and many relatives said my attacker minimized the events: "Maybe I hit her but she faked flying through the air and being knocked unconscious."

Over the course of days several cousins who attended the funeral called me. All reported the same thing: "We watched you fly through the air, three feet off the ground and slam on the ground." They offered condolences and added, "We knew that side of the family was crazy but we didn't know how crazy."

Later, my former mother-in-law took pictures of my children we had mailed to her the year before, put Xs over each of their faces, and wrote *Don't mail me junk mail.* She then placed them in a white envelope with her return address in the upper left corner and mailed them back to us. The boys were four and seven.

One of my children had a small strawberry mark on his forehead. It faded to nothing with age. My mother-in-law told us and everyone in her circle, "It's a mark of Satan."

My husband has three sisters. His mom was very young when she had my ex-husband; his sister quickly followed. Explaining to me she was bored when these two were graduating high school, she had two more back to back nearly twenty years later. The youngest of my ex-husband's sisters, who has since passed away, sent me a note on April 3, 2010, via social media during a time when my ex-husband had been pushing me really hard to relent on our legal separation stipulation that the children cannot see his family. Her letter seemed sincere, but I could not act on her wish to connect because she had been unaware of her mother's dysfunction for so many years and had been equally unaware of her brother's. It was too much to undertake though I was sincerely touched and tempted by her letter. Here is the note she sent after she sent me a friend request on social media. In my response to her friend request I offered condolences on the loss of her father.

Dear (Author),

Thank you for responding to my message. I sincerely appreciate your condolences. I want you to know that I have wanted to contact you for a very long time to apologize for a lot of things I said and did that hurt you. I was wrong and insensitive. I truly am sorry. This year especially after [my older sister's] death, it made me very grateful for a lot of things and helped me see things clearer. I deeply regret that I do not know your beautiful children. I regret the fact that I let myself fall into other people's issues and did not do what I wanted to do and that was to maintain a relationship with you and the kids. This is something I have thought about every day since I saw you and the boys at [my cousin's] home almost fourteen years ago. I have wanted to call you for many years, but again I regret that I did not have the courage to do so. I want you to know that I have always asked about you and the children. Although I have not been a part of their lives, I am so proud to be their aunt if only in title. Your children are amazing and that is a reflection of you. Looking back I realize how many sweet and kind things you did for me, and if I never said "thank you" before, I want to thank you now. I understand if you do not want to talk to me or acknowledge this message but I wholeheartedly apologize for all the hurtful things I said and did. No question, I was wrong, and please know I would never intentionally try to hurt anyone anymore. I hope it is not too late to rebuild or start a relationship, but if it is, I understand. If you want to call me to talk, here is the number. No matter what happens in the future, I hope you can accept my apology and know I am truly sorry. Thank you for responding and for extending your sympathy.

[my former sister-in-law]

I thanked her for the note. I accepted her apology. But I could not enter a relationship. A few years later, cancer would take her life.

Journal, August 12, 2000

We are on vacation in another state, visiting our oldest son and celebrating a coming-of-age ceremony for one of the younger sons. Today was yet another emotional, OCD, and dysfunctional day for my husband, especially in the morning. I was excited about designing a special glass mug with personalized engraving for our older son.

   I got up in a timely manner to go to the mall, but I noticed my husband was about to go out the door without me. I asked him, "Why are you leaving without me?"
   He replied, "To save time."
   I said, "We are not short on time. We are on vacation. This was part of our plan." I was dumbfounded. I said, "Please give me some words that describe how I feel about the kind of event we are celebrating."
   He said, "Sentimental, enjoy making memories, take pictures, be part of celebrations, creating ideas, and gift giving." He did well describing me.
   So I said, "Knowing this, why would you go without me?"

My husband said, "For the sake of time, and well, I am being a little selfish because then I can take an hour while the glass is being engraved to do a Bible study."

So I addressed the areas he mentioned:

- Pressure of time: we have none. That is a non-reality. We are on vacation with no time restraints.
- Why would you knowingly do something that would upset me? (Passive aggressive/subversive punishment toward me? Something else?)
- If you are going to do something for God, like a Bible study, perhaps you should first act in an appropriate manner that would be the most God-honoring. The Godly thing to do is to get your OCD, internal imagined time pressure, and selfishness under control and not to purposely do something that would deprive me of the memory of creating this gift.
- What are you running from?

He then said, "This morning I realized I have always viewed my abuse of you as occasional and only at certain times of our marriage. I am faced with the realization that it is a daily thing. I have abused you on some level every day of our marriage. This reality is making me want to go to the mall and get a chore done because that will make me feel better. I will have accomplished something. I can do some Bible work and hide."

This was very good work on his part. He was able to see that when he has to face anything hurtful he can *hide* by doing something, and then he can feel good about himself. It's how he buries his pain.

Claims of doing the laundry, dishes, or some errand has him looking good on the surface. He keeps himself busy so he does not have to keep facing the harsh reality of his behavior. He can pat himself on the back for his accomplishment and then say, "Look, I am not so bad. You just don't appreciate all I do." That is part of his diversion tactic. Counseling is helping me wade through this crazy behavior and two decades of confusion.

He then added, "I even feel this way on Sundays. That is why we often have problems on Sunday mornings; I feel pressure to be on time so I can pray with the worship team because that is something *done*."

This explains why there is so much tension on Sunday mornings when I am trying to get everyone ready! AHH, now that's a revelation. He gets mean and pushy and repeats himself, telling me things he has done multiple times. He will seek me out in another room to say, "I emptied the garbage." I am often left thinking *I do these things all day long and don't tell anyone, never mind two or three times.*

Sometimes it's so nonsensical and has so little to do with what's going on in the rest of the house. I am left dumbfounded. I now see it's the pressure in his body needing to keep busy, look for affirmation, and not face his thoughts or actions. I am glad he is analyzing it, but it still happens every day. There may be corrective work going on inside his brain, but it is not manifesting positively outward.

If he has a realization brought on by his counseling sessions, he tells me, "See I am working on the problems; it's better now." I explained to him he has to do the work for himself and be happy for himself, not because he wants me to dangle a carrot that says "good job." He believed his processing was worthy of reward. "I should have affection and normal sexual relations because everything is getting better. I'm fine."

The next day's comment was, "Oh man, every time I look at one layer to fix I see another part that is not right."

A few more days went by and he abdicated any culpability again: "You don't have a counselor telling you to forgive me, so that is holding things up. If you had a different counselor then things would be different because there must be a more Biblical perspective." Taking a deep breath, as if he had put great effort into being a partner in the process, he then said, "You must forgive me, but I understand healing is a process, but it's your fault things are not better already."

I do believe he has no clue to what he has done and destroyed. I want off this roller coaster, please.

Even in 2000 I knew it was a roller coaster! Reading the previous long journal note does make my heart race a bit. I can see the absolute dysfunction with years of separation from the emotional bondage and entanglement. I remember being proud of myself for calmly analyzing and asking pointed questions because of the skills I was learning in counseling. My ex-husband was diverting by keeping busy – *doing* something is his response to emotional or mental pain, discomfort, or lack of control. In choosing that coping mechanism he was willing to cause more hurt while he incorrectly processed his pain.

It is an exhausting cycle. Busyness allowed him escape from getting too close to his character flaws, troubled childhood, and abusive parents. Watching his parents inflict harm on each other, including two broken arms, which happened during our marriage, plus his mother's inappropriate touches and need to control were pains deeply felt. Lacking a healthy male role model due to his father's alcohol-induced rages gave him no role model to pass to our sons. Whether his father's over indulgence of alcohol was the response to his mother's overbearing control, or whether she felt the need to control because of his drunken binges was left unanswered.

> Busyness allowed him escape from getting too close to his character flaws, troubled childhood, and abusive parents.

Like my ex-husband, his mother did not welcome opinions different from hers, so she indoctrinated her youngest daughters to adopt her opinions and warped renditions. They repeated their mother's lies as if they were their own thoughts, not being able to differentiate between the two.

From 1980 to 1991, I witnessed the telling of so many of her inventive interpretations and twisted half-truths it was tiring to decipher. Many of the stories my ex-mother-in-law expounded were about her extended family. They were bad, crazy, and cheap. The treated her with disrespect, didn't invite one of her daughters to a party, thought they were high and mighty, and on and on it went. Time allowed me to see the pattern and recognize my ex-husband had learned to emulate it to near perfection.

One story of distortion revolved around a Thanksgiving meal. After celebrating a few Thanksgiving feasts at my in-laws, I wanted my home to be the one with the scents of turkey and pumpkin pie wafting in the air. My sisters-in-law dialed me up and, passing the phone back and forth amongst themselves, yelled, "How dare you want to do that? Thanksgiving is OUR mother's holiday; you are destroying the family." Then my mother-in-law took the phone and repeated the claims. Not satisfied, she phoned my mother, spreading her grievance like jam on toast, encouraging everyone to taste it.

In my journal note for August 12, 2000, the topic of discussion is a mug. I realized it would be wonderful for the oldest son to have the same personalized mug his younger brothers received during their coming-of-age ceremonies. The town we were in had the same franchise that engraved the first two mugs, so we could bestow the gift while we were there.

In preparation for these formal coming-of-age ceremonies, we both had read the book *Raising A Modern-Day Knight* by Robert Lewis and a few other sources on marking a coming of age. Then I let my creative juices flow, crafting a well-planned ceremony that was carried out in the early evening in a forest with a rough trail path lighted by torches. The candidate first picked up a backpack that contained instructions to guide him through the forest. Along the path the candidate was met by five men who had been assigned a subject to share wisdom about with the candidate. Subjects included being a man of character, using time wisely in life, praying, finding a woman to love, growing in the Lord, and chastity/sexual purity.

I had mementos for the men to give to the candidates. For sexual purity, they received white handkerchiefs to give their future wives, to say they saved themselves for her. For using their time wisely they received an engraved pocket watch. For prayer they received two Bibles, one to be signed by the five men and to be kept by the candidates, and the other to give to the first person they shared the Lord with after the ceremony, whenever that occurred. I designed a sheet with the motto from the book *Raising A Modern-Day Knight* and laminated it. They also received their tall glass mugs that incorporated a knight's crest and the engraving of "Sir," followed by their first names.

As the finale the boys were *knighted* with a sword before a roaring bonfire. The ceremony was supposed to be a reminder for our sons to act with honor all the days of their lives, but sadly they did not have a mentor to display the modeling of such honor.

I put the same effort into my youngest daughter's ceremony; her theme was Queen Esther from the book of Esther, which is memorable to many by the words *for such a time as this*. She met five women in the very same forest and received some of the same mementos, except she also received a purity ring and a plum line to remember to align her life to God. She was anointed with oil and crowned with a tiara instead of knighted with a sword while wearing her Queen Esther Tallit (prayer shawl) and Kim Hill's *For Such a Time as This* playing the background. Her path in the forest was lined with both torches and rose petals. I printed scripture on special paper, laminated each, and with special ground stakes displayed these along her path. As you can tell I like marking milestones and events in a memorable way.

Journal, August 15, 2000

We are finishing our time in [town] where our oldest son lives. The coming-of-age ceremony is over. It's been a nice vacation and visit. It's time to drive back up north to our home.

Last night, however, I could see my husband was thinking about the leaving process. I could tell it was heavy on his mind and he was getting uptight. For instance, my son was talking to his friend, who is also the son of the pastor. My son's friend asked, "Will I see you Sunday?"

My son answered, "No, not Sunday, I probably won't see you Sunday."

My husband snapped harshly, "Why did you lie and say we won't see them Sunday?"

I asked my husband, "Why did you snap and why did you call him a liar? He is not lying. We don't know when we will be home; we have a long drive. Why did you speak so meanly and strongly? Why are you so sure we will be in church on Sunday?"

He did not have an immediate answer for his unconfessed anxiety and turmoil, so I offered this explanation to him: "You feel childlike because it is the pastor's son talking to our son and you feel guilt or shame for not being in church five weeks in a row because of our traveling, so you feel pressured to say we'll be there even if we are not going to be there and you need our son to affirm that." He did not disagree.

How Exhausting!

My husband has been making comments about his *to do* list when we get back, so I know he is feeling internal pressure. He is getting ahead of himself because mentally the vacation time is over, even though we are not home yet. The truth is we may not arrive home till Sunday night or later. I know the trip home will have a lot of discomfort because he will not allow us to *stop and smell the roses* on this last leg of the trip. He will put pressure on everyone because of some image he thinks he's making or not making. This is part of his OCD and control.

My son was bewildered by his father's comment, bullied, and put down. My son said to me, "My dad called me a liar. He just listened in on my conversation and jumped on me in false accusation."

My son was just a victim of his father's many crazy scenarios. But he understood so clearly by his mature words what his father did to him, even as a teenager. Even I was amazed at his grasp of what happened and his responsive verbiage. Part of his precise response was due to his academic and intellectual gifting that included his above-grade vocabulary. Today he is an adult with an even more impressive vocabulary and resume to match.

You may notice that my journaled responses and questions to my husband here and in other places are succinct and very pointed. With eighteen years under my belt I knew his OCD habits well. I knew what he was doing, but I wanted *him* to see what he was doing. I asked things I already knew the answers to, but I wanted *him* to say them. Counseling was also illuminating dark places and changed how and what I said to him, but still, I didn't always get it right. Sometimes when

I journaled, I quickly scribbled partial thoughts; other times I carved out windows of time to write thorough and cohesive information.

My journals, like life, are sometimes neat and orderly and sometimes messy and barely together. My journal covers are all consistently stylish but my journal writing lacks that consistency. Since I am transferring my entries, you can't see the emotion I allowed on those pages. My pen leaned hard on the page when I was upset, leaving an indent and not just ink, and I am not making you suffer through ten explanation points that I placed for emphasis at times of exasperation!

During this August trip I brought my journal with me. Some of my clear and concise notations were written with kids drowsing or watching a movie in the back of the van while I sat in the passenger seat during our more than 1,000- mile trip back home. The scenario and our words were fresh in my mind so I could peacefully transfer the thoughts from my brain to the page in front of me.

Chapter 12

The Narcissist's Sense of Entitlement, Lack of Empathy, and Art of Pretend

Journal, September 2000

My husband is being pushy and mean. He said, "You are a better Christian than me so you should give in and have sex."

I responded, "My counselor said I am allowed to say no and have it respected."

He said, "Yeah? She's a counselor who knows a little about the Bible but not a Biblical counselor. The Bible doesn't say anything about staying apart sexually. You only come apart for prayer." I am tired of being pushed around, badgered, and made to feel wrong in my right judgments.

This morning while we were praying, he told me what I should pray and how to say it! I told him not to do that. He questioned me as if I was missing something important: "Don't you want that?"

I said, "You should not be telling me what I should pray."

Challenging me he said, "See, you don't want to get better."

I said, "No, I just don't want to be told what and how I should pray. It's self-serving."

He wanted me to pray we would be intimate and make love. When I did not allow his tactic to make me feel wrong about my boundary, he yelled, "Great, I get to pay the bills and be a father but no husband privileges." Such warped thinking!

Journal, October 4, 2000

My husband announced at a dinner with friends that he had not been kissed in eight months. It's such a weird thing to announce. It was very uncomfortable for our friends. Later he defended to our friends that he should get affection from me in spite of the fact that he recently revealed he had sex with the babysitter.

A strong sense of entitlement is a trait of a Narcissist; it blinded him to the inappropriateness of his comment. Objectifying me, he believed he had particular rights and I was not respecting them. In his mind he never does anything wrong that would keep him from having his needs met at all times.

Journal, November 9, 2000

In counseling with his counselor, the topic was communication. I had a perfect scenario to share. One of our sons came home from school. It was a Thursday in October. It was unusually warm for October, in the upper seventies. My son was dressed for gym in a fleece sweat suit. He came home and said, "Wow, it's hot. I have to change."

My husband ordered him to go wash his hands and get something to eat because they have to go out later.

My son said, "It's so hot. I have to go change."

My husband again ordered him to go wash and eat.

My son said, "But I'm hot."

My husband said, "What's that got to do with what I just told you? Go wash your hands and eat."

My son had communicated perfectly well. What happened in my husband's brain when he received that information was the problem. Why would he refuse to receive that my son needed to change? So I stopped and said, "Our son just told you he is hot, and it is unusually hot for October. He needs to change his clothes. Why are you not receiving that?"

My husband was unable to break from whatever details he had set in his head. He had to go out at 6:45 p.m. yet it was only 3:15 p.m. He was unable to work through and analyze that. He stated, "I am the only one who knows what hot feels like since I work in a hot room every day. So he can just suffer."

I explained he was not respecting our son. Then finally he admitted he felt pressure because they were going out on a school night. That was too much pressure for him. All this took such effort and time. It was utterly exhausting.

One of the traits of a Narcissist is lacking empathy, being unwilling to recognize or identify with the feelings and needs of others. This journaled scenario was his Narcissism working hand in hand with his OCD. Sometimes it feels like a deadly combination, sometimes just exceedingly frustrating. In hindsight it is so transparent how he displayed each of his Narcissistic traits. Here, lack of empathy has made my son an uncomfortable victim. Only the abuser knows "what hot feels like" so my son's suffering does not compare.

Dear Younger Me,

You are too inexperienced to grasp the convoluted dynamics of this sick man. You need to call in highly specialized forces to help you understand and plan for escape. Your skills of self-protection are getting better. Here you can really see what a man who lacks empathy looks like. This man cannot regulate his own stress. Instead it pours out as aggression, rage, and in this case a lack of empathy. Narcissists only care how they feel, not others. It makes for a bad friend, mate, or relationship.

Journal, November 12, 2000

This weekend we went to our favorite pizzeria with another couple. The husband is another professional football player we know. We were having a nice conversation, but at one point my husband decided he didn't want me to talk, so he raised his voice, cut me off, and then elbowed me hard as I sat next to him. This is from a man who promised he would never hit me again, never use verbal abuse. He did this in public and during the period we were in counseling.

On Monday, he called me from work, crying. He said he was so ashamed of his behavior, "If I would just forgive him, he won't do it again."

This morning my son wanted grilled cheese and his father said, "How about on raisin bread?"

My son said yes, but quickly realized raisin bread and cheese are not a good match.

I walked in at that moment and said "Raisin bread for grilled cheese is a pretty strange combination."

My husband tried to loop my son in and looked to him to tell him it was fine. He accused me, "Your comment is attacking me and you are telling me I don't do anything right."

I am so glad I don't have to endure these types of crazy conversations anymore! Pretend is a game many children play and parents play along, allowing themselves to regress to childhood too. I was the queen of the dress-up box. My children would often come home with best costume awards for themed spirit week at school. I first created these boxes for my oldest bonus daughter, which was a favorite activity for her and her friends. Boas, belts, hats, gloves, beads, and bangles began the collection, and then I added some popular movie character costumes found at garage sales and thrift shops. Glamorous gowns and beaded tops were a sharp contrast to the multiple clown costumes.

My ex-husband also embraced the art of pretend. As a new Christian he created a 501c3 not-for-profit ministry. Pretending he knew what he was doing, he gathered an eclectic group at our home and began to flesh out how this ministry should work. I knew he was in over his head when ten minutes into the gathering there was palatable dissention. Knowledge and knowhow were lacking, but his *Walter Mitty* drive needed to claim headship over this prayer-based ministry. His declaration that he helped people overcome drug, alcohol, and other addictions kept the masses focused away from the fact that he needed treatment himself. "God wouldn't have given me this ministry if I was as bad as you say" was spouted to remind me of his new stature.

We were at a conference for area ministries; many veteran ministries attended. While my husband was grandstanding at the delight of mingling with them, a pastor said to him, "Who are you married to? I have to see who God has put with you." He had observed my husband's arrogance and *know-it-all* attitude; he wondered who had to put up with it. I was embarrassed. I did not want his eyes to meet mine, but he saw me there. He read my facial expression. I was mortified my husband could not see his vanity.

CHAPTER 13

PREPARING FOR THE MOVE SOUTH

You may be asking, "Why in the world are you going to move with him?" I asked myself that too. All of us going together meant he would be paying all the expenses and I would land in a place where I could afford to live as a single mother. I felt that was a step forward. In the end, one moving truck, one car to drive, made sense. While selling off some unneeded furniture, I met a man who told me of a TV broadcast station very close to where we were moving. The casting director was his client and said he would put in a good word. I could brush up on my TV skills and audition. That gave me hope during the moving process.

As the time creeped closer for our relocation, I asked my counselor to search out a qualified counselor for me in our new hometown. She interviewed them to make sure they were trained to counsel the spouse of an abusive man and recognize the false narrative he creates. She found one. She was part of a conglomerate of both male and female counselors. The male in the group took on my ex-husband and briefly my sons.

One of the books I journaled in has a traditional floral cover with a country feel. Imprinted on the cover by the publisher is a reassuring verse, Psalm 24:1: "The earth is the Lord's and the fullness thereof." By hand, I added in bold, black marker, *A Year of Hardship and Change*.

It is dated from November 2000 to September 1, 2001. It includes the window of the preparation for the move, the signing of the legal separation papers in early June 2001, and the actual move south, which happened July 1, 2001.

Journal, November 20, 2000

My birthday just passed. This morning I can barely function. I am constantly on the verge of tears, but today I just let the tears flow. I feel stuck because of my bad choices. I see everything so much more clearly; the clarity hurts. I feel as if I have failed myself and my children. I want to rent two apartments in the South. It looks like there is a two-bedroom for $900. I would just share it with my little girl, and the boys can have the other bedroom. The second apartment is $625. My husband keeps insisting, as if to try to scare me, "We can't afford two apartments."

Journal, November 29, 2000

Today I was library mom. I read to the kindergarten, as well as the first grade and second grade classes. The time went so quickly. I think they liked it! I have all the kids down for the night after lots of homework and projects. Last night we finished a book poster and it came out great. It was one of those parent projects – I hope we get an A! ☺

Mentally I was a bit better today. My husband is still pushing for everything to be his type of normal. I would never want his version of normal again.

Tonight he commented, "I don't know how single parents do it. Look at all there is to do. We have to work together and it's busy."

So I said, "That was a subliminal comment meant to make me understand you are needed and I will have a hard time as a single mom."

He said, "Yes, it was."

These kinds of comments have been growing lately.

I said, "Don't worry, your apartment will be nearby."

That made him furious. He struck out with a mean comment that one of my sons caught. My son crawled on my lap, put his head on my chest, and cried.

Journal, December 2, 2000

My husband's counselor told me, "I cannot get him to focus during counseling and I can see there are some issues a psychiatrist should address. I would like him to see one."

Telling me after the fact, my husband said he sent a deposit for ONE three-bedroom apartment that also has a loft. It's in a brand-new, fancy apartment complex in the town we want to live in in the South.

While I was unhappy about his actions, I was too exhausted to fight when he sent the deposit for one large apartment. I reasoned, "I can fix that when we get there." We were not living together as husband and wife; we were just sharing space.

Dear Younger Me,

Your decisions have hurt your children. Not making a move for separate living arrangements will leave you with a lot of regret. If I could change your thought pattern I would tell you this: stop thinking you are staying for the children's sake, and start thinking you must leave for the children's sake. That is what God would want, not the other way around. You were fooled. Your thinking was wrong. You cannot trust the voice of an abuser. Don't be fooled anymore. Admit it, correct it, learn from it, and move on. Move forward. Move positively.

Journal, December 4, 2000

My husband has missed two counseling sessions due to illness on the counselor's part. The counselor's dad had eye surgery, so he needed to be with him, and then he got ill the second week. That delays my husband's progress, unfortunately. This morning when it was time for him to leave for work he kept pacing around me. Circling me like prey.

Around and around. Saying goodbye but not leaving. He stared at me weirdly. I told him, "I don't like what you are doing."

He said, "Well, when are we going to work on the marriage?" He was looking for a hug or a kiss goodbye; he thinks a hug or a kiss goodbye makes a marriage.

My ex-husband was always looking for cracks in my newfound armor. I was learning to say no and stick to it and identify behavior and point it out. I was getting a stronger exterior by working on my inner thought processes. He was capable of being extremely cruel, so I endured the usual onslaught of horrible and degrading name calling. He hoped I would absorb these horrible names, feel insecure, and think less of myself, allowing him to believe I needed him.

Any attempt at physical contact was his gateway manipulation to get to sex. A peck on the cheek, a hug, or any handholding he wanted before leaving for work was self-serving. He would feel better. "It's not natural to not want and like those things" was his tricky put down to convince me to break my boundary. He informed people, even my children, "You know it's not me. There is something wrong with her. She doesn't even like a peck on the check or even holding hands. She is frigid." Somehow these fabrications made it back to my ears.

I can hear my ex-husband's banter now through a brief note in my journal: "Yesterday we had such a nice time shopping together. We even agreed on the shopping list and we laughed in aisle seven. I remember his look when we chuckled; I could tell he placed more value on it than there was. The glint in his eye told me he saw nostalgia. "This is like old times; see how great this feels?"

Repeatedly my ex-husband would take one peaceful time and talk it up in a strange effort to try to get back in good graces. He believed a singular example of acceptable behavior covered up the bad. I was thinking, *A lone moment of laughter while shopping does not magically remedy our lives.* But the Carnie concretely believed this because he works in a false reality.

I can agree that *moment* was fine. But I don't need to take it further. He does. "See, we have fun times. Why don't you focus on them?"

I point out, "One brief instance of laughter while shopping does not change your abusive behavior."

Frustration mounts and the put-downs launch. "You just agreed it was fun, laughing?"

"Yes," I concur.

The Carnie questions in a harsher tone, "Then what is the problem? We can work on adding more laughter. You just admitted we had fun, but you don't want to focus on that. You have to turn everything negative; we are never going to have a better marriage if you don't change. I just said everything will be OKAY!" He believes his words stand as undeniable proof.

The Carnie ached for me to agree, but I don't. I have made a new boundary. I will no longer be manipulated into agreeing with things when they are not true. This real exchange is similar to those I read in Lundy Bancroft's book *Why Does He Do That? Inside the Minds of Angry and Controlling Men*.

Dear Younger Me,

If your mate creates an atmosphere that makes you feel you have no value, do not accept or ignore that. If a partner uses putdowns to make you feel off center or confused, get some books on domestic violence, emotional and verbal abuse, and Narcissism. Make use of the library for free books, and thriftbooks.com or half.com for cheap books.

Don't wait, and don't feel bad about it. Validate what you are feeling. Even if the information you discover does not mirror what is happening to you, the learning is important. One in four men exhibits Narcissism and some own the Narcissistic Personality Disorder label. Your learning may help a friend.

In healthy marriages partners value each other. They do not intentionally control one another or make each other feel crazy.

Journal, December 5, 2000

My husband came home from work and tried to give me one of his upbeat messages: "Everything is fine; I am really recovering, even though my job is the roughest it has ever been. I am doing well. I am realizing different things."

This is usually an attempt to manipulate me in some form or another. I told him he has to stop giving these mini-speeches and do the work. Everything is not okay; he doesn't see the depth of the problem yet.

He countered with great emotion: "YES I DO! I am sad all day long and have no joy."

These emotions are okay, but they don't work on the problem. I had the perfect example two hours later. I came home from taking an older son to the orthodontist to find him helping our younger son with his homework. He was being harsh and demeaning to him. Our son was trying to explain something but his father would not let him. My husband had checked the wrong answers, so in frustration he lifted his hands to his head, yanked at his hair, and screamed.

My husband would not let go of his anger and cease yelling. He proclaimed, "I have good reason to be so mean. I have to get ready for Bible study."

I told him, "Your son is more important than getting to Bible study early to set up coffee and cake." (The Bible study had moved to the church building for a while.)

A very short time later I asked this same son to show me the project he made in a Christian boys' group. I inquired if he wanted to keep it, and he said yes. When I walked away his dad crushed it, then threw it in the garbage.

Later, I caught a glimpse of it in the garbage and fished it out. I confronted my husband. He had a look of total shock when I showed him. He clearly thought he had gotten away with it. I said, "You think you have it under control and everything is fine? Now you are going to go teach Bible study after your display of anger, destroying your son's project, and degrading him?"

He went upstairs, and then called me there. While crying he said, "Do I have to give up my Bible study? It's the only place I feel liked and the only thing I'm good at." Then he said, "Maybe I do have a problem."

If any defects dared peek through his superior self-image, the Carnie's OCD would kick into warp mode. Hungering for an admiration refill, if I did not agree with his predetermined wonderfulness, I could expect a verbal and physical slapping. Then he would head out to teach a Bible study where he would entice others to give him his injection of admiration.

Journal, December 6, 2000

I am reading Patricia Evans's book *The Verbally Abusive Relationship*. This book IS all about my husband; it's amazing! I finished the last chapter, called "Underlying Dynamics – Some Reasons Why." My husband covers his feelings. He justifies his behavior and compulsions – all the time! His childhood pain has to be denied.

Journal, December 11, 2000

My husband has read the first one hundred pages of Patricia Evans's book *The Verbally Abusive Relationship*. He clearly sees himself and acknowledges everything he has read is true for him. He is not discounting anything. We will wait and see what happens.

I find comfort in a good book more so than a room full of strangers, so in my collection of interesting titles I would advocate my ex-husband read an offering, usually a Biblical or self-help topic. Resistance was his usual response, but once in a while I knew he gave in because he had moved his bookmark to page 50, and sometimes my colored sticky notes tickled his interest. I knew his inner Narcissist voice won out if I heard, "I don't need any advice." He told me he had stopped reading a book on codependence because "It was hitting too many nerves."

People do that in counseling too. They stop when the topic gets too painful, which is the precipice of when they might have a breakthrough.

The next time someone tells you he or she is in counseling, think of it in a positive light, not a poor light. The brave people who hang in there and learn about themselves are to be commended.

Journal, December 15, 2000

My husband had a physical today at his primary care doctor's office. The MD cleared him to see the psychiatrist for an evaluation.

The psychiatrist required a medical exam with a primary care physician before beginning treatment with him. The primary care physician needs to be aware of the care and any new medications that might be prescribed, to check for contraindications and potential reactions. So he had to wait for an appointment with his regular physician and then wait for an appointment to see the psychiatrist, which was a disappointing delay, if not for him, definitely for me.

Journal, December 29, 2000

Things with my husband are very difficult. Tonight, Friday, he lost total control. He was threatening me face-to-face while foaming at his mouth. He could not hear my words of defense, he was too wrapped in his frenzy. Screaming, cursing, and saying hurtful, mean things.

> My husband had a terror tank that needed emptying, and the kids had a love tank that needed filling.

When tirades erupt, he never acknowledges them or apologizes. He walks away and acts as if nothing happened. He has unleashed his terror tank and he feels relieved. I wish I had a recording so the doctors and others can see what explosive anger looks like up close and personal. The technology was not as readily or as cheaply available when I was enduring my rollercoaster ride, but it is now, and I hope many women avail themselves of this recording process.

My husband had a terror tank that needed emptying, and the kids had a love tank that needed filling. "Love tank" was an expression I used a lot when the kids were little. If I noticed they were grumpy, had a bad day, or were feeling insecure, I was sure to say, "Do you need your love tank filled up?" It meant a time of hugs and kisses, some snuggles, words of affirmation and assurance.

They felt so comfortable with the concept they could tell me, "I need my love tank filled up!" unaware that filling their love tanks filled mine too.

CHAPTER 14

MEDICINE, MISERY, AND A MOVE

Journal, January 10, 2001

My husband wants to know, "Can we just call a truce and hug or hold hands for a half hour?" as if we are at war. He wants a truce from the safe boundaries in place to try to meet his selfish needs. His reality is so warped. With a whine in his voice he keeps repeating, "This is the price I have to pay" as if I am punishing him rather than acknowledging that his behavior has consequences. A few days later in a serious but very soft drawl, he tells me, "I think I have a word from the Lord: 'Hand in hand, come before me.'" I am getting very sharp to his contrived misuse of God and the Bible in his abuse.

Journal, January 10, 2001

Today I packed boxes, stripped beds, did laundry, sewed, ironed, and made spaghetti and meatballs for dinner. My husband has been leaving me alone most of the time the last few days. Once in while he is fishing for a validation, but it's been a tiny bit better.

Tonight we had a little thing, but it was resolved in a calm way. I left the boys clean sheets on their beds so they could make their own beds as part of their responsibilities. My husband made their beds and admitted he did it to make up for going on the computer for his needs in the middle of family homework time when he had committed to help the boys. His excuse was, "Going on the computer, looking for ministry opportunities, is a place I feel important and get value from since I get none from you."

He said in counseling he was exploring the idea that he puts too much weight on everything I say and do. I agree with that. It's something I have been talking to my counselor about as well. I was not happy with his actions or the rationalization, though his "excuse" was at least an admittance of the problem. All in all, it's the same thing I always go through. He does a bad thing to cover up another bad thing. The only thing different this time was he managed to stay in control.

I have begun to fill out the applications for the kids' school in the South. I called some moving companies for prices. Five months to go.

The boys are trying new things with their hair, lemon to make it lighter, hair gel, and spending more time in the bathroom. They are maturing! One of my sons has taken an interest in magic tricks, card tricks, and sleight of hand. He has been doing tricks for me all night. He is so proud. I am too!

Journal, January 24, 2001

The psychiatrist diagnosed my husband with Explosive Anger Disorder and prescribed medicine. Today he took his first dose of medicine for this disorder. This is a day I have waited for, but I am not as excited as I would have been in the past. Perhaps ten to fifteen years ago I would have thought a label and a medicine would have been the answer. Now I know there is more to uncover. It's more than Explosive Anger Disorder.

My husband had a phone conversation with his counselor today in my presence. He said, "I think you or my wife's counselor should tell my wife how horrible her idea is, and how she will hurt the kids. Now that I am working on this, she wants to separate. Why is she doing this?"

Both of our counselors think a separation is a wise decision. The horrible abuse the kids see and hear is worse than the bad example of a divorce. I can't constantly be carrying his emotions and have him explode at me all the time.

My husband had not stopped to consider that his abuse never ceased during the seven months spent in counseling. When his psychiatrist had diagnosed him with Explosive Anger Disorder, he actually liked having a name for his problem. *It's not my fault. It's something else.* The counselor explained, "You need the medicine because your mind is not working correctly." He also could not concentrate and receive during sessions. He had monthly visits with the psychiatrist in addition to his regular weekly counseling sessions. The medicine did help a bit. I noted he concentrated better and his OCD was slightly lessened. He said, "I am amazed at how much better I feel."

Explosive Anger Disorder is also called Intermittent Explosive Disorder (sometimes abbreviated as IED) and is a behavioral disorder characterized by explosive outbursts of anger and violence, often to the point of rage, that are disproportionate to the situation at hand. My ex-husband is not the only family member with IED; I have personally watched my bonus son explode and rage. My daughter-in-law and grandchildren confirm they endure his rages. Sadly IED is present in two generations, both refusing treatment.

Dear Younger Me,

If you are exposed to explosive rages, be aware this symptom may be part of a bigger issue. It is a symptom of Narcissistic Personality Disorder. NPD will not respond to medication, though medicine may control some of the rages.

Journal, January 31, 2001

This morning was a bit difficult, though manageable. I knew it as soon as my husband came downstairs and immediately cleaned the *few* dishes that were left after breakfast before doing anything else. I thought *uh oh*. This was to be an OCD day.

My husband began to take issue with my son. It was spirit week at school and my son was picking ideas for Wacky Wednesday. My very creative son wanted to wrap his legs in toilet paper, but he needed to learn for himself it might not be practical because the toilet paper would rip before he got to school. My husband immediately started yelling. A messy toilet paper costume and a few dishes in the sink was overload. He spoke to our son as if he were stupid. "You can't do that; don't you know this won't work? You are making a mess and wasting toilet paper."

My son was not discouraged. He tried wrapping it another way and he thought perhaps a thicker layer would work better. Thicker layer meant more waste and more toilet paper to break into pieces. I didn't care. I liked when the kids tried something and learned that some things have limitations. Then it was more real to them.

Everything my son did was met with his father's frustration and mean words. "Look, you are making a mess and it's time to go to school so we can't clean it up. You are wasting our time."

Then he began to yell at me. I told him he is not allowed to do that, which made him even angrier. He yelled, "You are interfering with me being a father."

I said, "No, I am just not allowing your OCD to rule and abuse."

I told him to examine his behavior. He left the room to do that and returned to say, "Today is my worst day at work and I feel uptight. I don't want any tension or battles." I requested he go out for breakfast and straight to work. He called about 1:40 p.m. to say, "I am trying and I see there is more work to be done."

During this period of constant mental, emotional, and physical abuse at home, one day my husband came home particularly tired with great concern and fear on his face. He confided, "If one of the people I am in charge of complains and reports me to the police, I will go to jail." His abusive behavior was overflowing to innocent people who were entrusted to him. I secretly hoped someone would report him. Perhaps I should have reported him to his superiors. I knew he would discount it. "She misunderstood what I said" might be his cover.

Journal, February 12, 2001

It is one year since my husband told me he had been having sex with the teenage babysitter, a mere two years older than his daughter.

I have headed up a fun carnival day at my church. The entire parking lot will be one big carnival for all the kids in the neighborhood. Lots to do. But inside I am sad beyond measure.

Journal, February 23, 2001

Today I saw my counselor. I had to cancel yesterday because of the kids' party invitations, but she didn't want to me to miss since I was so despondent. She talked me through it. She helps me to focus on health and freedom. She helps me make sure I am responding in a healthy, proper way to all manipulations thrown at me by my husband. I need help seeing clearly after years of abuse and his constant attempts at gaining control over me…journaling interrupted by a phone call from the professional athlete who funded the publishing of my husband's book.

Journal, February 24, 2001

My husband has no impulse control today. He is trying to manipulate me, and is disparaging my counselor. "She is not a qualified Christian counselor. If she was any good, our marriage would be better, you are not working on our marriage." After meeting my resistance to his accusations, he stopped to admit, "Yes, I am trying to break boundaries. I am angry with you."

The boundaries are:

- He may not hit me.
- He may not verbally abuse me.
- He may not manipulate me.
- He may not have physical contact with me.

- He may not display obsessive behaviors or he will be called out on them.
- He may not verbally or physically abuse the children.

I am no longer readily accepting his physical hits, verbal put downs, emotional ploys, twisting of scripture, and mental games, which is why he is angry with me. He is meeting resistance in every instance. I called his counselor. The more I practiced healthy thinking the angrier and more hostile my ex-husband became. I had to work harder to protect myself. It's interesting that I actually had to heighten and tighten my protection mode as I established healthy boundaries. Bullies don't like boundaries. If I took a stethoscope to his body, I swear I would hear every cell screaming, "Just get back under my control! I don't want to change! I want you to accept my abuse and control!"

Journal, March 14, 2001

My son drew for a Spanish project today – he is a really good artist! Things are a bit calmer; my husband decided to leave me alone about two weeks ago. I feel more peaceful not being harassed all the time.

Journal, March 22, 2001

My son made the basketball team. He tried out yesterday and today he found out he made it! I baked him a "congratulations" cake with a basketball on it. When he arrived home late due to a rainstorm, he saw the cake. I was not feeling well so I was lying in bed. He came in to see me. "You made this cake for me even though you were not feeling well? Thank you!" He was beaming, holding up his team uniform to show me.

Journal, March 23, 2001

I have cleaned, laundered, and packed boxes. I feel so sad. I have just been thinking how much like my mother I am. I allowed twenty years of abuse and I criticized her, yet I have done the very same thing. I stayed with an abusive man. I am so angry with myself!

All five of us went into the city via the railroad to see a Christian performer. There was a lone guy sitting with his feet up in a block of five seats. My husband abruptly raised his voice and in a weirdly arrogant manner told him, "Maybe you should move over there," pointing to the opposite block of four seats, "so we can be together." Zero politeness or even a *please*. We could have sat across from each other, no big deal.

The man shot back, "Well I want the leg room," so he took down his legs but stayed there.

My husband continued in a rude, controlling tone, "Fine, if you want to separate my family." It was so uncomfortable that when the conductor came over to take the tickets, she commented on it. My husband quickly backtracked, "Oh, you know, I was just kidding."

She said, "Yes," but her face very clearly said no. It was so uncomfortable.

People who have OCD get angry and express righteous indignation over seemingly minor matters. We were often left to guess the culprit. Dirty feet on bench where people sit dressed in clean clothes? A stranger not reading his mind and immediately recognizing the need to relinquish his seat? An internalized frustration to something that happened early in the day? His internal frenzy compelling him to control the external? Clear or honest explanations were never offered; like you, I was left to kick around the possibilities.

Journal, March 26, 2001

My husband shared a moment of revelation about his sexual behavior, and then offered a big sigh, as if it was a relief. . He continued on in a sincere warm tone, "See, everything is going to be all right; I am working on things." The pep talk rolled on, nothing I had not heard, but things I have not seen happen.

I explained, "You should not be trying to convince me everything will be all right, but should walk it out and let me see, not just today but every day."

At that moment he immediately switched to verbal abuse. His expression and demeanor changed. Standing over me, in a mean and threatening tone meant to frighten me he said, "You have all the control and you think I am controlling. But YOU have all the control because YOU are making all the boundaries."

I explained these are normal, healthy boundaries.

Then he switched gears: "You know, when you talk about divorce, you are abusing me! Every time you mention divorce, you are abusing me. You should not talk about divorce because God hates divorce." He rotated so quickly between each form of abuse it was staggering.

Truly, I felt as if I were playing some kind of carnival game where I had to be alert and catch the balls coming from every direction. But I did catch and stop every one. He did not observe himself or monitor himself after the first abuse tactic. He switched modes so quickly as if to see which one would stick, break me, give me doubt, or have me debate him.

Instead I immediately named the form of abuse, explained it in one sentence, and left it at that. But all the while the next form of abuse was coming. In just fifteen or twenty minutes, he used every kind of abuse except physical. Verbal, mental, emotional, spiritual.

After I calmly stood my ground and labeled all abuse vomited my way, he got so frustrated, he threw himself on the floor. He stayed there and let out painful moans, wailing and crying. He rocked back and forth. Then he picked up a five-pound weight that was within arm's reach. I told him to put that down. I asked, "Were you going to hit me with that?"

He said, "No, I was going to hit myself." Exhausting. But not like before. Because I recognized every assault, I was not emotionally wasted. He was.

My ability to correctly recognize and resist what was being perpetrated on me was the result of working with a trained and aware counselor. Beginning in the year 2000, even though it was at a turtle's pace, I applied healthier thought patterns that did not allow me to submerge under his waterline.

In the past, I had surrendered to his sometimes nonsensical accusations, defending myself as if his allegations were true. I stayed wound in the corkscrew conversation meant to make me slink away after submitting to his low and broken version of me.

My ex-husband throwing himself on the ground and picking up the weight is actually monumental. The vexation was so enormous that like a frustrated overtired toddler, he threw himself on the floor because he was not getting what he wanted and more importantly *needed*. He *needed* me to stay under his control. He was accustomed to hitting me when his body arrived at this plateau of internal overload. He would prefer to have me in pain, but this time I would not accommodate. In emotional angst that he could not hurt me, he was going to hurt himself.

In the past, my habit was to surrender soon into the first act. My ease of relent never caused him to spawn this kind of demonstrable anguish. Prior to this, the curtain closed with me in defeat.

Journal, March 26, 2001

Today, I free myself from all the things my husband said were my fault. The list is huge! But I am free and almost none of it is my fault! What freedom to understand his tactics were intentionally meant to keep me unstable believing I was flawed. He wanted me to believe my shortcomings were to blame for his actions. I did not fathom the degree of manipulation. I was methodically broken down. I wish I could have gotten healthier sooner.

In my journal I wrote the words methodically broken down. Recently it was suggested I try a popular herbal supplement. Its dosage was minimal at first. I would start at 25 mg, then progress to 50 mg, then 75 mg, and then 100 mg, though 500 mg would provide the best effect. Many abusers use the same process. By the time you are at the abuser's best effect, you wonder how you got there. I certainly did. Some days I beat myself up for not refusing the next dose. I made excuses, and he asked for more chances.

In the Narcissist flip, blame lies at anyone's door but theirs. Narcissists tend to internalize failure as shame, something they avoid at all costs. In the beginning of my marriage, immaturity and naivety kept me unaware. Fear and control let it continue unchecked. It was research and learning that gradually brought understanding about Narcissistic traits. This knowledge enabled me to analyze and properly discard the blame campaign. Narcissists are very tricky and not always obvious to see. I once saw a suggestion from another victim that abusers should have to wear a big letter A on their shirt. I realize it is not practical, but it certainly would keep others from suffering unnecessarily.

Journal, April 2, 2001

I went to my husband's counseling session to tell him I wanted to file for separation now. I had dabbled in this conversation, but it was time to make the formal request at his counseling session. My counselor advised I do this at his session because this way he would be held accountable for his behavior and reaction. As soon as the words left my mouth, he sprang up from his seat on the couch with great frustration, his face contorted; he paced up and down a few times, then went to the door as if to leave but then turned and came back.

His counselor knew I wanted a legal separation in place before we moved south in July, so he said to my husband, "You have told me you are going to be God's man; rise up and get well. You know you should not be abusing your wife and have told me you want to do the right thing. You should have no problem allowing the legal separation because you won't have to use it; there will be no divorce. It will just be a temporary thing. You said you want to make your wife happy and this will make her happy. So why not do this?"

My husband said, "Yes, I will sign it."

I thank God for this counselor. He appealed to his Narcissism! Prior to this, my husband had told me in threatening terms he would not do this. He knew it would mean losing control, but the counselor

presented the separation in such a way that my husband felt he was still in the driver's seat.

I went to see an attorney. I kept the financial part of the agreement to whatever the state statutes allowed. I told him, "There will be a clause that stipulates there will be no contact whatsoever with any member of your family since they have proven themselves to be violent, aggressive, inappropriate, and dangerous."

He unreservedly agreed. He made it seem as if the addition of that was not a bone of contention, so I didn't need it in writing, but I did not trust him.

The legal separation was drawn up and signed June 8, 2001. My female counselor is turning out to be excellent; she is full of compassion and I feel her support at every level. She has been instrumental in making the separation obtainable.

At one point in the conversation regarding his family's contact with the children, my ex-husband said, "I agree with that you on that point, so you don't have to put it in writing." It was so convincing and heartfelt. Showing he was fully on board in front of the counselor, he wanted me to acquiesce on putting that request in writing. I did not cave in to his con.

Journal, April 2001

We were at my friend's mom's 65th birthday party. Two things happened that disturbed me. We had agreed the food at this restaurant was not great, hardly worth eating. I took some salad and bread. But I stopped eating the bread; it just wasn't worth eating and I love bread! He asked, "What's wrong?"

I said, "It wasn't good."

He snapped at me in a peculiar way and said, "I knew it!" This distinctly said, "Nothing makes you happy; the meal is not perfect and it's YOUR fault." It was totally weird. I challenged him. He acquiesced. "Yes, I was just mean to you and I used force and accusation behind my words."

At the end of the party when I was looking to say goodbye to the birthday girl, he eyed her before me and gave me a powerful push toward her. So much for the boundary that he can't touch me.

Conversations laced with accusation were an easy daily abuse method. For him they seemed to take no effort. Some hurtful or underhanded comments were obvious, but sometimes they smacked me in the face thirty minutes later. He threw out statements that caused insecurity, doubt, or acceptance of blame for even the most insignificant circumstances.

Dear Younger Me,

Your likes, dislikes, and personality make you, YOU! Just because your likes and dislikes are different from someone else's, that does not make you difficult or less of a person. Everyone is different. Your "different" is just fine! You are not perfect and do not have to pretend to be. Your abuser wanted everything to be "perfect" in his fantasy. You don't have to be part of the fantasy. Your imperfection is fine, so be honest; be comfortable with imperfection.

Journal, April 2001

Earlier in the day I put some tissues in the garbage pail. He followed me, took them out, put them in a plastic baggie, and then placed the bag back in the pail. The garbage can't even have garbage.

He could not relax with the thought of a used tissue in the freshly placed garbage bag. Placing it in another bag, isolating it, somehow made it acceptable so he could inwardly rest.

Journal, June 11, 2001

We had an appointment with my husband's counselor. During the session my husband acted like a maniac, tearing me apart over really weird and unfounded things. It was bizarre. I was hoping the counselor

noted and understood what went on. When my husband and I got to talk about the portion of time he had alone with his counselor, he told me his counselor said, "You sabotage your own marriage." Okay, the counselor got that part. A great word, "sabotage."

The counselor recognized that part of my ex-husband's dysfunctional behavior is to sabotage his own marriage by slandering me with nonsensical information. My ex-husband did not recognize it as sabotage because *put downs* are an intrinsic part of his Narcissistic disorder. He used and got away with it in his family and circle of influence. His self-deception was so cemented that he was confident the counselor would be unwaveringly committed to his assessment. These words would in essence be a memorable parting gift to me from this counselor. I received much help from his counselor even if my ex-husband did not. He was a positive part and partner in my road to freedom.

Dear Younger Me,

For this period of time, you had not one but two counselors who really saw and understood your husband's true self. I know you feel this was a gift from God; I want you to know that I feel the same way so many years later! You did not give up, even though that was your husband's goal. You recognized he tried to disparage the counselors because he felt he was losing ground.

It is not just you he attacks. He attacks anyone who threatens his fragile self-esteem or can expose his deception and sin. These two counselors saw the sickness. Oh, it felt so good, didn't it? I wonder if a list exists of competent counselors experienced in this level of abuse and the complexities of the Narcissist Personality Disorder.

You can say goodbye to the North now. But know that in the South it won't be easy or pain free. You have made progress, but you have not arrived.

CHAPTER 15

THE SUNSHINE OF THE SOUTH AWAITS

Legal separation papers were signed in June 2001. Every state in the USA has slightly different rules and options for couples seeking to dissolve a marriage. In the state where we resided, legal separation was the most viable and thorough option. All assets were divided and provisions for the children and me were made. I could also keep myself as a spouse dependent on his health insurance until the divorce was final. Most people get a legal separation and then live apart until the divorce can be finalized, but there were many moving parts and flying emotions to the relocation process, so we ended up sharing space the first few months.

We left our home in the North the first week in July in the comfort of our much-loved conversion van. The kids loved the seats that converted into a big bed, and the TV that played their favorite movies. While we were packing the van with the last of our treasured items for the long haul south, my five-year-old daughter closed the van door on her thumb. I felt the need to have it checked at the hospital emergency room before we got on the road, so the last thing we did before leaving was visit the hospital emergency room. Thankfully her thumb was not broken. Our memorable exit included a splint and some Tylenol, but not a cast.

Journal, July 1, 2001

When we began our trip to the South, I told him we would share the driving. I asked him to tell me when he got tired so I could take over or we'd stop at a rest area.

Along the way in my drowsy state, I felt the van swerve, but he swore he was okay. Then the unthinkable happened. He fell asleep at the wheel. He went from the center lane to the left and then off the side of the road. He overcorrected and went across three lanes into a huge spin and slide. Smoke surrounded us as the tires burned. The smell of rubber was overwhelming.

At one point we were skidding on two wheels. I thought we would tip over. We slipped sideways for a long scary stretch. We came to a stop, facing oncoming traffic. The van stalled. We were facing three lanes of oncoming traffic. A tractor trailer was coming right at us.

I was about to order the kids out of the van before impact when the van started up again. Somehow he maneuvered to the shoulder, still facing the opposite direction of traffic. His stubbornness would not allow him to admit he was tired. What did he have to prove by pushing forward? I was so angry.

We got out and inspected the van. Except for being covered with a whole lot of dirt and grass, the van seemed to be okay. I took over the driving.

A curious noise sounded. I found the mud flap bent into the tire. I bent it back and prayed it was the only problem.

I got back in the driver's seat and tried to settle my nerves. I drove a couple of exits, found a restaurant for breakfast, and then a motel with a vacancy. Graciously, they let us register even though it was 7 a.m. and check-in was not till 3. I signed the paperwork while my little ones clutched my legs and eyed the outdoor pool they begged to go swim in.

This journal note was nice and neat. I got to jot down a solid train of thought while the kids played in that pool! I talked to my children about the incident then and many years later; thankfully it wasn't as traumatic for them as it was for me. They said they were asleep so they didn't understand something very dangerous happened; they just knew something happened but everything was okay.

Journal, July 10, 2001

We arrived the first week in July and I began to see my new counselor. She turned out to be another well-informed and trained counselor. My counselor in the North did a great job vetting her for me. I think I will benefit from this counselor's experience. She had an abusive husband at one point. She is an LCSW- Licensed Clinical Social Worker.

I am so glad I was able to have a vetted counseling group already prepared because soon after arriving I realized my son needed to talk to someone too. He is angry. He is beginning to talk to me with disrespect and unkindness – continually. He watched his father do it and now he is trying it out.

Plus, I think his dad is poisoning him with lies. I also believe he is angry about his parents getting divorced. All the kids hate when the word is even mentioned. I did not tell them the separation papers were signed. They need to be kids. They don't need to know this adult stuff.

This counselor's biography said that she is a psychotherapist and a counselor with a psychodynamic approach to healing broken souls by integrating Biblical principles with a deep understanding of human development and behavior. Her well-seasoned experience and belief in the power of prayer and restoration was not lost on me, and I needed any help she offered.

It was becoming supremely obvious their father maintained a kettle of simmering lies that he added to weekly and whirled in our children's direction: "Your mom has issues." His "It's not me" narrative was done with ninja subtlety and malicious malevolence. His wafting trail of evil was breathed by adults too, who treated me with pity for lacking certain Christian attributes. He had an art form mastered, developed over the years and instilled as a child, which permitted ease in delivery with no guilt aftertaste. 10% percent truth and 90% lie was a good formula allowing anyone, especially children who don't know any better, to believe the lies.

I could feel it; the kids were treating me as if I was a failure, I was wrong, I was stupid, and I was not to be trusted. It was a constant battle. I previously had pleasant and kind responses to natural requests, now I had antagonism. Nasty arrogant answers. The boys' relationship with one another did not change much, but their relationship with me changed.

Sometimes my daughter's intentional antics caused trouble for the boys and I tried to figure out if this was a natural childhood occurrence or inner turmoil sired by the lies of her father. Constant vigilance was needed to figure out if what I saw needed to be addressed, how to address it, and to whom it needed to be addressed. Some of this might seem to be normal parenting, but in my case I was parenting with a partner whose main intention was to control, abuse, inflict pain, and lie. Normal was not a card in his deck.

Journal, July 18, 2001

My second counseling session. My counselor is trying to help me understand that my ex-husband's imprints have been in his soul for more than fifty years and he may not ever be able to control himself.

The realization that the legal separation cut his control has him feeling crazy. He is setting fires all the time, constant digs and comments. Today at the kids' school while he was sitting in the principal's office, he let his arm drop to his side and then swung it out to hit my leg. At the same time, he threw me a glance that meant, "Shut up." He waited for just the right moment so the principal would be distracted and maybe not catch it, though I think he got an uncomfortable feeling for a second as he returned his glance to us.

My husband was telling me through violence I was not allowed to have things explained to my satisfaction, that HE should be in control. He is getting daring in his violence—this was a public display. I answered his action with one word, STOP, and continued my conversation.

After this meeting he ignored his violence and said, "You can have the afternoon to do your chores and get your new driver's license."

As if I needed his permission! He added "I put gas in the car and it is running good so you can do those things." Brownie points? Control? It is not what he is supposed to do.

It was nice to start with a new counselor, but I did miss the security and relationship I had built with my counselor in the North. My new counselor had a great word picture for me as we started our time together. She said she once knew someone who lived in a very poor and depressed part of town. She had very little and she lived in a small, dirty home. It was what she was used to. She didn't know anything else. Dirt and poverty had been constants in her life. She was grateful to have her small gray bathtub that did have hot water most times.

Later she moved out of poverty and for the first time saw a white bathtub. She did not know white bathtubs existed. She thought they were all dingy gray. She did not know her dirty gray bathtub was white underneath. This woman thought all bathtubs were dirty gray. My counselor told me my bathtub was gray. She was right. I was raised with a gray bath (abuse) and married into a gray bath (abuse). I never knew that with life's dirt (abuse) removed, there could be a shiny white tub. I never knew life without abuse.

Journal, August 5, 2001

We set up a computer in the new apartment and my son and his dad worked on it together. Suddenly in frustration and for no reason he punched my son twice. My husband has had many bad episodes. My counselor said I have to stop correcting my husband because then I become his *enabler hero*.

This *enabler hero* concept was new. I had to really understand it and assimilate it into my thinking. If I was the hero helping my ex-husband to understand his illness then he would be able to keep me continually engaged in his dysfunction. As part of my wrong thinking I thought if I tried to impart this new healthy information I was learning, I could help him. I needed to understand that wouldn't happen. Enabling is different than helping when actual benefit can be realized. The abuser wants access to his victim and being the enabler hero gives him access under the cover of helping.

It's a lot to grasp; I had to let it soak in. It seems such an abnormal thing to have to do but I am in a very abnormal circumstance. Maybe you need to let this soak in too? It could save you time and pain. A strong woman will generally stay with an abusive man too long. Strong women think they can fix the abuser. They think they can make him understand the wrong he is doing and make him better. Sadly that is not true and I stayed too long.

Journal, August 13, 2001

My husband grabbed me and pushed me. It made me lose balance, misstep but not fall. I could not believe he did it. Unbelievable since he is in counseling and tells his counselor and me he'll never do it again. There is no hope for him.

Do you find it strange that I wrote in my journal "I could not believe he did it"? It seems so obvious he would do that, doesn't it? Notes like this make me realize just how abused I was. Do these words penned more than a decade and a half ago reflect my utter frustration, or am I really amazed? Both? There were sprinklings of days when decorous convention sprang out and was quickly followed by his craving for me to praise him. He used any coerced praise to prove to me he was indeed on the mend. If I tried to tame his statement to reality he would seemingly erase what he had just stated and launch into the same tirade of put downs he had just claimed victory over.

My ex-husband's retirement system had two payment options. He could take a greater monthly payment immediately with no spousal life benefit upon his death or he could take a lower monthly payment but leave me with a spousal benefit upon his death. It was pointed out that it was more cost effective to take a life insurance policy for the spouse than to take the lesser monthly amount. While the advice given to me was that my ex-husband should be required to maintain a policy for my entire life, I acquiesced and accepted one for twenty years while I had the support of my counsel team to stand against his threats and resistance. The twenty-year policy would certainly see me through raising the kids and college should he die.

After six weeks we went to work choosing a company for the policy. His diagnosis and medication pushed the cost of the policy higher than expected. The unforeseen consequence made him irate. The process included a home visit by a nurse to interview the applicant and record a medical history. Those off-premise archived forms verify his medications, his psychiatrist, as well as his lab results and reflect one company denying coverage due to the results. Denial is part of the Carnie disorder; proof stands in the wings.

Journal, August 29, 2001

I went to the health club that is part of the apartment complex we live in and came home to a blinking light on the answering machine. A photo and resume should have landed on the casting director's desk by now, so I was anxious to hear the message on the machine. The casting director wants to see me! The appointment is for September 12, 2001, at 3 PM. This is very exciting because I would have a job in my field and the hours might work so I can also be with the kids.

I am so glad they called. I was just about to give up hope since it had been a few weeks since I sent in my picture. What a lift to my day! Please, Lord, let me have a good interview, and give me the best place to work! Please, Amen! I have to work. I have to begin to get on my feet, have income, be self-sufficient, and save for retirement.

Hope rose on the horizon on this special day! I had an opportunity to attain all the things my abuser told me I could not.

The next entries were found in an oversized, hardbound, dark-green, linen journal dated September 2001 to August 1, 2008.

Journal, September 8, 2001

It is a Saturday. My husband got frustrated and angry with my son. They were working on the computer together. My husband went from zero to one hundred in a split second, for no reason. I watched as, without warning, he grabbed my son by the shoulders and headbutted him. Just like football players do. My husband has been told by his counselor he cannot use his hands to inflict pain, so instead he headbutts.

He quickly tried to rationalize his behavior. I stopped him. He began to talk about our son's behavior instead of his. Three physical abuse episodes in exactly two months. That does not count the other kinds of abuse. One son got punched, another got headbutted, and I was on the receiving end of a punch and a push.

After recording the last physical abuse, the counselor said she will call social services if there is another. My husband went absolutely hysterical. He said, "This means I would have supervised visitation and probably couldn't get a job because I work with kids."

I said, "Then you are willing to get your own apartment?"

He contorted his face, lowed his voice, and delivered these words in the most evil, threatening tone that was almost a low scream: "That's just what you want, isn't it? You want to throw me out."

Narcissists do not believe their actions have consequences. Blame always lies at the doorstep of others; this was a prime example. Two months in our new town and he was not able to do what he had promised. The excuses offered by a father who claimed innocence were, "He wasn't listening. He was distracted. Why wouldn't he just listen to me?" He needed me and the children to bandwagon to his blameless reality. I did not go there, which drew a huff of exasperation from him. Later he told me he had a talk with our son, which I am sure gravitated between, "I am sorry" and "It was your fault." In the evening, during our routine bedtime talk, I emphasized to my son what happened was wrong and his dad has serious problems.

Journal September 9, 2001

Today at church [husband] came up to me after watching me hug and affirm our son. "You know I just realized when you do that to our son it makes me think of my mother and the way she rejected my father and gave me attention meant for him and the inappropriate stuff, so you should watch that around me."

I saw through this. I told him, "You have to deal with that. I am not going to stop affirming and hugging my son because of your problems. You have to properly process this. Instead you are asking me to process for you. What I am doing is normal. What is not normal is your reaction and control." When the kids are hugging and kissing me, he stands there, intently, staring oddly. He makes faces expressing his dismay that he can't do the same.

I told him, "Your actions and attitude are why there are problems and I think we should not be living together. Get your own apartment." He dramatically placed his hands on his hips, leaned into my personal space, trying to intimidate me, and spoke these words: "Sure, go ahead and call the police because I'm NOT leaving. You will have to get the police to get me out."

It is clear he is not going to honor or protect us by leaving on his own. As disturbing as that is, his days are numbered because I feel our counselors will help move him out. I feel it coming and I need their help.

Journal, September 11, 2001

Terrorists crashed planes into the World Trade Center. Two planes into two NYC buildings. Another in Pennsylvania. Another hits the Pentagon. The World Trade Center collapsed as well as an adjacent building. #7 World Trade Center. The entire United States is in mourning. It's so unbelievable.

I watched the second plane hit on a TV in Walmart. I had dropped the kids at school and was trying to check a few things off my to-do list. Walmart shoppers and employees had gathered in front of the TV in the electronics department after the breaking news of the first plane. It was about 8:45 AM. Cameras were on the World Trade Center when the second plane hit and we all watched it in disbelief. I wanted it not to be real. People were crying, me too. The loss of life is incredible.

I tried to make some phone calls to friends and family, but phones were down due to the high volume of people trying to reach loved ones. My phone calls would have to wait.

Journal September 12, 2001

My interview at the TV station went well. They are having me back for an on-camera audition.

Journal, September 20, 2001

9 AM, first on-camera audition at the TV station

After the audition I quickly drove to my daughter's school in time for lunch to deliver homemade cupcakes for her entire class for her seventh birthday! At home my baby girl got a birthday cake with the number seven on it, made by her momma. She was so happy! We had a late celebration for her birthday because the boys had an away soccer game and needed to be picked up.

Journal, September 27, 2001

We traveled via plane to a family event. The event went fine but my husband was problematic. During the course of the weekend he spoke to me rudely, gave me a push, and interrupted a conversation he had not been part of. I was bent over talking to my brother, who was sitting in a chair. My husband pushed my arm, forcing me to fall or stand up and face him. Now, face-to-face he commanded, "You should not be talking to him."

My sister-in-law heard him speak to me rudely and say something condescending. She said she was astounded. This is the sister-in-law I had confided in about the doctor's visit and she viewed my wounds. She said, "I was expecting him to treat you like GOLD this weekend. I am not seeing that." Great observation.

Journal, September 26, 2001

12 noon, second on-camera audition, I am hired!

I was elated! My whole being was full of gratitude and optimism about the future.

Journal, September 29, 2001

A dog just joined our family. We went to a Messianic Jewish Conference a few towns away. We were not planning on buying our very first dog, but there she was, a miniature dachshund, honey-colored and adorable. She was part of a litter brought by a family hoping people would purchase them. The kids are over the top excited and in love. My youngest daughter's birthday just passed, so she says this is her birthday present.

Journal, October 22, 2001

It's been a tumultuous three weeks. Always riding a storm. My husband's behavior is erratic and irrational.

Journal, November 8, 2001

I have begun my career. I was live on national TV today. It went well. This job is ideal. I don't work every day. I just work as needed but still steady. It's a unique position; it seems to be made for me, especially at this time of my life.

Journal, November 9, 2001

This morning I dropped the kids off at school. On the way out the door my husband said with a strange look on his face, "Mom will get everything you need for the youth group lock-in tonight." It was an intentional passive-aggressive tactic. He wanted me to feel overstretched by work and meeting the kids' needs. He was perfectly capable of getting the items.

This morning my daughter said to me with excitement, "Oh, you don't have to work today?"

"No," I replied.

She let out a loud, excited, "YES!" with an accompanying air fist pump, as if she had just won a million bucks.

I said, "Why? Do you miss me?"

She said, "Yes, I miss you a lot when you are not here."

That confirmed to me I made the right choice between the two positions offered to me at the TV station.

The dog is doing great! Everyone is enjoying her. It warms my heart.

Journal, October 21, 2001

We were making a trip to our oldest son's house and my husband was speaking sharply, being unkind and uncooperative. On the day we were traveling it was his birthday and the kids were off from school. In the morning he was on the computer and I was busy packing for the kids for a weekend trip. He was stewing an ornery attitude, unbeknownst to us, which is usually the case. But soon it boiled over. His brain was marinating a pity party because he felt he had not gotten enough attention for his birthday. He started whining out loud, "Oh, I have no family, and I have no wife, and my kids don't remember my birthday."

I asked him why he wasn't helping pack the car.

His excuse delivered with arrogance: "It's my birthday and I can do anything I want, so I can be on the computer if I want to."

CHAPTER 16

THE ABUSER MOVES OUT

Journal, November 19, 2001

On Monday, November 19, we had a crisis and now life has changed dramatically. On November 19 my (estranged) husband was at the computer with one of our sons and they were having some kind of discussion. My husband grabbed him and dug his fingers into his shoulder and my son cried out. I turned to see he was rubbing his shoulder with a look of excruciating pain, so I asked, "Did Daddy hurt you? Did Daddy grab you?"

He said, "Yes."

I told his father, "That's it; you have to move out."

He turned to our son and said, "See, now I have to move out; it's your fault."

When my other son came home and heard the news that Dad had to move out because he had hurt his brother, he went in his bedroom and put his fist through his hollow core bifold closet door. Then both boys cried. Thankfully, my daughter was not home.

I called my counselor and my husband's counselor to tell them we had a crisis. My husband's counselor told him he had to move out immediately, "If you really love your family you will leave."

My husband went hysterical, and then he threw a pity party, trying to gain sympathy. My husband's counselor had a session with each of the boys. Starting December 1, 2001, my husband rented his own apartment in the same complex. Eventually I did get the help I needed to make him move. I was not capable alone.

The boy who endured his father's brutality and harsh attempt at blame on that day told me, "Don't worry, Mom. I did not absorb that. I am okay."

In my next counseling session my therapist gave me these words with a delivery that was meant to have them sink deep into my being: "You will never be safe." Letting her know the source, these same five words were conveyed to the judge who presided over our final dissolution of marriage in 2013 when she asked, "Did we seek counseling before filing for this divorce?"

In true form, my ex-husband ignored the statement and the judge's concerned countenance, and immediately went on to comment he was to be commended for his benevolence in waiting for all the children to be over eighteen before the divorce. There, in front of the judge, he did the same thing he always did. He refused to listen to what was said. In his head he was too busy formulating words to make himself look good. He moved out of the third-floor three-bedroom apartment to a first-floor one-bedroom in the next building.

I did not mention to my youngest daughter her dad was moving. One day she said, "Where is Dad?"

"At work," I answered truthfully.

Though he had retired from his full-time career in the North, he did take employment in the South. Later that day I explained he had gotten another apartment and for her it was a non-issue. The kids had easy access to visit if they wanted.

We all had watched him run a roller coaster of emotions with no guardrails. The kids and I never knew what to expect. One time the boys asked me to walk them over to his apartment. They wanted to ask him something. I stayed back a bit in the alcove and let them ask the question. He made it clear they were bothering him. He yelled at the kids, "We are separated. There is the door. Get out."

Another time they told me they were getting comfy on his couch, but their dad barked, "Don't get comfortable, you are not welcome here." Our separation agreement gave me full custody and him typical visitation times: once during the week, some weekend time, and rotating holidays. I let the boys see him as they wished or felt safe since they were older. We had to coordinate a bit for our younger daughter. I alone juggled all the children's activities, teacher meetings, school events, sports, music lessons, and doctor appointments, plus work.

Thankfully, my new job was not 9 to 5 or Monday through Friday. The hours and the days changed every week. Occasional weekend hours left me weekdays to go on school trips. My ability to stay organized and plan well left only small windows when I needed help. One time when I asked if he would like to visit with his children while I went to the store for school supplies, he responded, "You are dumping them on me!" This rancid bold antagonism lasted four or five months, then softened but not much. Many kids take a bad turn when parents separate or divorce, so I tried to vigilantly look for signs of emotional distress. All three of the younger children were doing exceedingly well at school. The boys were obviously gifted and it seemed my young daughter was on the same path.

Journal, January 5, 2002

It's like he is schizophrenic. One morning he told me, "I had a really bad morning, thinking of all the bad things I have done to you. My whole body bubbles up in anger and emotion at just how horrible I am that I have done these things to you. You are a really great mom." Then, that very night he yelled at me, "When are you going to work on the marriage, and when are you going to forgive me? You always think you are right."

These "conversations" happened at when I was picking up or dropping off children. It got to be I didn't want to open the door when he came to get the kids. His syntax deteriorates fast and furiously. He deposits a kind word into the poison pot, hoping it will be easier to get me to swallow his toxin and kill off my growth of healthy cells of reason.

Journal February 24, 2002

As a family, we had been invited to a special celebration for our friend, who was a professional athlete. It was held in his home state. We were in the talking stages of who would go or not go. My estranged husband went ahead, without consulting me, and booked five airplane tickets. My thought was just he and the boys should go. I explained we are separated, so booking five tickets was a bit presumptuous. He yelled at me, "You are so ungrateful; after all, I am paying for the tickets, the hotel, and everything."

It dawned on me later that he wanted the whole family there so he could keep his fake front for the guy who funded his book. He needed that appearance of everything being perfect. *Look, we are all here; I am a good guy.* I went because I did not trust him with the children, but avoided him.

Journal, April 19, 2002

[Husband] said, "You know you can't count on me to help you out. I am not going to make this easy on you. Get a service and make your own arrangements when you can't pick up the kids. What's the deal with the divorce? Are you going to file or are we working on the marriage? I'm in limbo here; why should I make anything easy for you? I need to know because I have a lot to offer someone else if you are not going to work on this."

I told [husband] that to wave the word "easy" is laughable. His words and thought patterns are so acrobatic. He still thinks he is a good guy and wants to bring his abuse to yet another woman's door.

I was surprised he offered this information to me: "My psychiatrist is going to switch my medicine." This is a good idea; whatever she is giving him is definitely NOT working. His daily antics of control and verbal abusive with both me and the children are severe. The children sometimes defend him: "Well, Mom, some of the things he does are not as bad as they used to be."

Fifteen months on medicine brought no changes, and psychiatric sessions lacked my presence to be a voice of truth. News that the psychiatrist was going to try another medication meant she also saw no change. Miraculous results were absent with the next medicine. That, combined with being incensed about paying such a high rate for the required insurance policy, made him susceptible to suggestion. When an ignorant person informed him that "Christians don't take medicine," and that he should just allow God to heal him, he instantly embraced this advice. No prescription medicine meant he could quit the psychiatrist visits, alleviating any shame he felt recording those monthly visits on his calendar. I can't fully blame the person who offered that lame advice. Medicine would have perhaps only controlled the explosive anger outburst frequency, not his core Narcissistic disorder.

My ex-husband's self-centeredness is very clear in this journal entry. He needs to win but I will not surrender to his invitation to meet under his big black umbrella. When my ex-husband threatened, "I am not going to make this easy on you" among other things he was saying, "I want you to fail, so you can see you need me." His Narcissistic voice fills his mind with haughty pride and it whispers, "Nothing you have done is that bad, grab the brass ring, third time's a charm. Wife number two threw off your weighty reigns of control, but you can easily re-gift them to another unsuspecting woman."

His words are a ruthless attempt to weaken me so I will let down my boundaries or be paralyzed from making additional partitions between me and him. I should restate that this paper trail of mean-spirited words was delivered by a man in ministry, with more than one Christian website and more than one publication about Biblical content.

I want to create awareness for women who may be experiencing abuse in the church; Narcissists frequently hide in churches since they see themselves as assets.

The precepts of the Bible are designed to prevent slander and perversion of justice, but even the Christian abuser will use perversion. It can mean straightforward lying, positive narratives twisted to a negative light, or lies mixed with truth. It all accomplishes his goal. The Carnie wants both my bonus and birth children to see me in a bad light. He did this to his first wife too. He told me his first ex-wife was leaving that marriage to *do her own thing*. I suspect her wanting to do that was to escape from his control she might have been waking up to, or couldn't correctly label at the time. While I was in his ex-wife's presence she labeled herself, "a crazy single mom," and I did see her live that for a time; however, in hindsight our mutual ex-husband made many statements that were highly exaggerated to convince me she was unfit.

Journal, June 6, 2002

The kids did super-well in school. The older son got an award and pin for highest grade point average in Physical Science, and one for being the best in the whole state for Algebra. The other son got pins for highest grade point average in History and Bible. Both got letters for soccer. My daughter made the High Honor Roll and got a ribbon for Bible memorization, plus a certificate for Violin. I could not be more proud!

Journal, May 4, 2002

I took my daughter up in a helicopter at a local airpark during a ministry event that happens every year. These were missionary helicopters so there were no doors! She was a bit nervous about that but loved it anyway! My daughter and I have been having some nice talks and I can tell I will have to be attentive and on top of things when she reaches adolescence. Our talks lately are about character molding, and she admits she has a hard time not being first, or fully appreciating others joys and accomplishments. Our talk about that was very good.

Journal, July 18, 2002

I bought a second car, used. Immediately I saw my oldest son's sense of entitlement, which has been showing itself more frequently, rise up. In all sincerity and in a tone of pure confidence, he told me this was "his car." He began to list all the modifications he was going to make to it, including getting a new stereo for it. He would use his income from the job he had at a local food store.

This was not childhood dreaming he was dishing out or something he said with a smile. It was clearly a bit of his father's non-reality conversation he had adapted. Many times he tried out the precepts he had heard his father portray. With conviction he apprised me, "I can do anything I want with the car." It was very much like talking to my abusive husband.

Earlier in the week he was lighting fireworks inside our apartment and then throwing them out the window. I said he had to write me an apology letter for endangering our home, and he had to wash all the woodwork. He scoffed at my request and told me I was "harassing him."

In 2002 my estranged husband found a church he liked and made it his home. A new church with few in attendance, it had a Messianic service on Friday nights and a typical contemporary church service on Sunday. A few churches have a service that embraces components of the way Jesus would have worshiped in as much as He was Jewish as were all of His first followers. Shabbat services, Torah reading, prayers in Hebrew, kissing the Torah, and scripture reading following the Hebrew calendar would be expected. Messianic synagogues normally use the same format as other synagogues, except they include acknowledging Jesus with His Jewish name, Yeshua, as the Jewish Messiah. Messianic congregations embrace Jews and Gentiles who desire to worship the Lord together with a distinct Jewish flavor.

The relationship was christened in blood on June 28, 2003, at 3:30 p.m. when the pastor's son walloped my son on the head with a broom, creating a wound that needed a trip to an emergency room and staples to close the laceration. Those two boys are best buddies to this day. That two-inch scar is a permanent, noticeable reminder of their friendship. I learned to love that broom-wielding boy, who now stands 6'5".

Journal, March 17, 2003

My daughter wants to see my counselor. She saw her brother visit a counselor, so she wants in. I asked her what she wanted to talk about. She said, "My sadness about the divorce and the kids at school who think they are *all that*." So my counselor met with her. My counselor doesn't think there is anything to be concerned about, but she will let her come a few times every other week. I drive three people to counseling every week.

I made the kids a candlelight dinner tonight, consisting of lemon chicken over angel hair pasta, steak, pork loin, and fish. Then I took them out for ice cream cones. I made a little memory! Picked the kids up at 3 PM, ate by 4:15, ice cream at 5, and then back for homework.

Journal, April 21, 2003

My son is in Spain on a mission trip.

Journal, October 14, 2003

I helped out in my daughter's class today. It's been a while since I wrote; sometimes I am too tired, sometimes I am too busy, and sometimes I am too depressed to rehash life. This past summer, swimming lessons kept my daughter busy. She is also taking singing and violin lessons. She is nine.

My son is taking golf lessons at school. One son scored a 99% on the ASVAB, which is the military test all the kids have to take, and he takes his driver's license test this week. The youngest son has his coming-of-age knighthood ceremony next month!

I am house hunting. My new career, along with a favorable mortgage and housing market, are allowing me to do that. A $2,000 down payment is all that is needed.

My daughter picks on her brothers terribly! The boys don't do that among themselves, so it's weird to see her provoke her brothers. Maybe she needs attention?

My daughter is going through a *daddy stage*; she defends her father and wants to go over and do homework with him. She feels sorry for him. I let the kids float freely between houses when necessary. He is indoctrinating her and that is why she is defending him. I don't know what to do. I can spend my time correcting her many wrong statements, but it will confuse her.

Journal, June 29, 2003

My thirty-year-old bonus daughter is visiting. She sees how difficult her brothers are being, specifically her teenage brother. She comforted me with, "I am so sorry for how difficult I was as a kid." Just as I was ready to collapse under the weight of all of this, a kind word swoops in and undergirds me from buckling.

A brief break in writing occurred; I drove the older boy to the grocery store he has been working at for a year and a half. At a recent staff luncheon my son was awarded a coveted Managers Award, which was accompanied by a certificate and a gift card.

A bit of disparity in work and home behavior, but I am happy he is excelling at work.

Journal, November 24, 2003

I bought a house near the kids' school so they could walk there if needed. Three-bedroom, two-bath, two-car garage, and a big fenced backyard for the dog.

My estranged husband took a new apartment near my new home. Along the way I learned he started using my CPA for his tax needs (Certified Public Accountant), and seeing the same dentist I use. Stalking behavior? Much like my sister-in-law expected, my husband would treat me like gold when she saw him with me at the family gathering. I somehow deceived myself into that same expectation if I offered him an invitation for a holiday dinner. My rationalization was the children would not have to feel divided, producing less trauma. They expressed happiness in having the meal together and thanked me.

I also deluded myself into believing since he had no pressure of dirty dishes weighing heavy to tilt his OCD and no daily grind of kid care, he should be able to maintain himself for a two-hour-or-less holiday dinner.

In 2003 I was still blind to the fact there was nothing I could do to change his behavior. A year or so before, my counselor had warned me against this kind of decision. After multiple failed attempts at trying to create a normal and safe family event, I had to humbly confess, she was right. Every time I invited him I was subjected to his covert attempts at participation in his fake reality. He whispered, "Look, we are all together. This is great; we can have this all the time." I brought lots of food to the table and he brought snide comments, strange, uncomfortable glances, repetitive corny jokes, and a bunch of self-serving talk.

Soon I discerned he was incapable of reeling himself in, so I would serve dinner and then disappear into a bedroom while the kids visited. For the most part I was not missed. Once in a while one of the kids would come into the bedroom and query, "What are you doing here? Come out and be with us." They didn't know I was protecting myself. I finally put an end to my graciousness and ignorance. He *still* tells the same corny jokes at family gatherings. When he does, guests give each other a knowing look. We silently acknowledge the stupidity and his lack of observant self.

Dear Younger Me,

I don't care if it seems unchristian or unkind; do not allow an abuser into your house. Not even for birthdays. Let him do his own thing. Absolutely no contact. It's important to understand this. He does not get to come over or into your house – ever!

Walk the children to his car at the curb. Do not let him have any more contact than the divorce agreement allows. Do not acknowledge any comments or compliments he makes. They are a trap to engage you. He considers any engagement a win. Don't engage.

While I was kindly inviting him to holiday dinners and allowing flexibility with the visitation schedule, he used his visitation time to plant false and malicious statements about me. He was relentless. If the kids bellyached about chores or guidelines, he told them, "Your mom always was whiney, even with me; you're right." (The children reported these exact words to me.)

My son, emboldened by his dad's disparaging remarks, proclaimed, "I am tired of your freakin' whining, go get a job that keeps you busier," when I requested he clean the bathroom. Thankfully, this son was able to escape his father's face-to-face daily innuendos and indoctrination when he went to college in 2005, which left two instead of three children at home to wade through the emotional mess their father cooked up.

Journal, May 7, 2004

The boys had a sports banquet. Baseball, basketball, and soccer are their sports right now. Both won awards, letters, and pins. One got a trophy for best defensive player. The academic banquet followed shortly after. Recognitions included ribbons, a medallion for ACSI first place, and a Pre-Algebra regional champion! Highest grade point in Bible class and Economics were also acknowledged.

My son needed ten dollars to go out with friends in a few hours, so he decided the way to get that was to cut the grass – two days early. He mowed the lawn in record time, put out his hand to receive the ten-dollar bill, and he was off.

Journal, July 5, 2004

Three years since we moved to the South. It was a good move for me. I have a job, my own house, and no more physical violence. Now, to work on separating myself from the emotional, verbal, mental, and spiritual abuse he delivers anytime he is in my company.

Journal, August 4, 2004

First day of school. One son in twelfth grade, one son in ninth grade, and one daughter in fifth grade. I can tell the kids are nervous. New Christian schools for all three of them.

Journal, November 25, 2004

It's Thanksgiving. It is also our one-year anniversary in the house. This is momentous. It is also the very first Thanksgiving I am alone. I have never been alone on a Thanksgiving. It is my first without my children. They are with their dad. I made a full Thanksgiving dinner on the 22nd. Today I will have leftovers and spend the next three days painting my house.

My daughter was cute when she left. She said, "If I die while I am away, I just want you to know I love you SO much." Then she added "I don't want to fight with you, and I want to work on being good!" Mommy melt moment!

I have been leading a women's Bible study. My friend owns a teahouse in a local town and she holds a Bible study there. She had thirty women sign up so she had me lead fifteen and she led fifteen. We did Beth Moore's study on the book of John and then we did *A Woman's Heart: God's Dwelling Place*. I'm so grateful to be able to lead a women's group again.

Journal, December 25, 2004

On Christmas Eve, the kids got to pick one present to open, and then they went to church with their dad. On Christmas morning, they got to choose one more present and then later we had a big Christmas dinner. Turkey with all the fixings. The rest of the presents are waiting because my bonus daughter is coming on January 11, 2005, and we want to have Christmas with her. She told me she wants me to make my homemade chicken soup and Challah bread for sure!

Journal, January 5, 2005

This is my older son's year! He graduates this year and we have been notified he has been accepted at a prestigious college. I got some balloons, bought some of his favorite Chinese food, baked him a cake designed with the school logo, and wrote congratulations on it. Family celebration!

Journal, January 11, 2005

My son is intentionally hurtful to me and he always offers an excuse that he feels validates his meanness. His tone and reasoning all sound very familiar; clearly their father covertly mentors them. My son told me, as a matter of fact, "I am too busy having fun to help you around the house." Later in the day he changed it up, challenging me, "How dare you ask me to help when I have school work? I have to write a bio for a scholarship, and if I don't get the scholarship, it will be your fault."

The simplest of questions are met with harsh, sarcastic answers. I asked him to do his laundry, and he said, "You do it; you don't do anything all day." He insisted I buy him something he wanted, and I said, "No, I can't do that," so he shrieked, "You are so cheap!" At my refusal to allow him and his friends to watch an R-rated movie at our house, he delivered, "You are a whiney whore; you are always up my ass." He also gave me a small push.

I shook my head no and said, "Don't you even think about doing that." With a cry in my voice I tried to get my words out: "You're, you're, INHUMAN!" I remember struggling in my mind with my words, thinking what he was doing was inhumane but it came out inhuman, which I settled in my mind also fit. I was crushed; this is my dreamed-about, long-waited-for, cherished first-born child being so hateful. No mom ever thinks this can happen when she is holding a sweet-faced newborn in her arms. I am so utterly disappointed with marriage and motherhood.

Later, he and his father, whom my son relayed his words to, would use my labeling out of context, to disparage me. *Inhuman* means "cruel, harsh, heartless, hard hearted, unfeeling, or inconsiderate." In lieu of his words and actions I thought the label fit. Cursing, yelling, or violence is not my habit, but one of those might have fit that situation.

Nonetheless my ex-husband took that opportunity to remind me of a lone instance when I acted in a manner that was violent. Many years before, I grabbed my son by the scruff of his neck pinching his hair as he attempted to descend the stairs to the playroom basement. My grasp caused him to back up the two steps he scaled, returning him to the landing where I placed him firmly against a door for his verbal scolding. I have never since repeated my less-than-stellar reaction with him or with any other child, but at the prompting of his dad, my son brought it up. His dad attempted to level the playing ground by equating my one-time action as the equivalent of his decades of mental, verbal, and bodily harm.

Journal, February 26, 2005

Last night there was no one home so I had a good cry. I am so dismayed by the boys' behavior and their dad's dysfunctional responses and behavior.

One of my estranged husband's sisters called him. I knew it would happen eventually. He told me they wanted to come see him and the kids. I absolutely refuse to allow the children to see them. It is in our separation papers that it is not permitted. I can't stop him but I can protect my children, at least for now.

I was not budging, so he quickly diverted, launching into spiritual abuse. In a raised voice booming with his superior spirituality, he said, "You are not attending church and I have a different idea about what forgiveness is. It includes reconciliation. You are not in church, which is wrong; the Bible says not to forsake the gathering of the brethren." He is quoting Hebrews 10:25, which says, "Do not giving up meeting together, as some are in the habit of doing, but encouraging one another, and all the more as you see the Day approaching."

He demands I answer for myself. I do not owe him an answer. My church attendance is not his business. He began to give me his reasons why he should see his sister and other family members. "I could be the one to bring them the gospel," while ignoring that is the exact scenario that got us disowned a decade before. He battered me with his Narcissist belief he has a special privilege, that he will be the one. He has no capability to maintain safe or smart boundaries. He is too needy and co-dependent.

I was not joining his dysfunction, so he continued to launch put-downs, attacking my character and Christianity. I simply responded, "You should have a talk with your counselor." At the end of the conversation, shifting to almost a different personality and adding it as a throwaway line, he added, "My sister still denies she hit you and knocked you unconscious."

I calmly said, "Really? With that many witnesses?"

In this conversation my ex-husband tries to make me feel inferior to him. He wants me to know his interpretation of forgiveness is the correct one. Not just for his sisters, but for him. If I have forgiven him then I should reconcile with him; therefore, I am wrong and a flawed Christian. Neither he nor his sisters were offering real or true repentance.

Journal, February 27, 2005

I am so sad. All day. It came to light that my bonus son gave his aunt his dad's phone number, which allowed contact. Though his actions were inappropriate, I have to accept and forgive his ignorance in providing it without permission. It will make my life more complicated, but there is nothing I can do.

Journal, February 28, 2005

I had a talk with my bonus son about handing out the phone number without permission. In response, he launched a rage that didn't fit the situation. I hung in there and explained his younger siblings are not seeing his aunts or grandmother. "I have to protect my children."

He said, "But I am your child too."

I agreed but reminded him he is an adult and his siblings are not. "I can explain and inform but you can make your own choice and I can't stop you."

I think he, like his dad, easily adapts to their sickness. I wonder if he will choose to acknowledge he has an anger problem and get it treated or hide, deny, and blame others like his dad.

I don't blame my son. He, like me, did not grasp the convoluted dynamics his aunts and grandparents have subjected him to. Though he displayed high levels of uncontrollable anger, he was not yet in the position to understand where his internal frustration came from. Unknowingly by reopening those decade-long estranged family connections he would be adding to his internal frustration, but not know or understand it. It's a big concept to accept that no one wants to believe the ones who say they love you would fill your love tank with poison rather than love. Though my bonus son knew the hurt of being disowned and his extended family's dysfunction, he jumped back into that cesspool rather easily. Hungry for love, he placed on horse blinders, which hindered him from understanding the scope of emotional danger.

About a year later my daughter-in-law said to me in a very serious tone, "I want you to never forget this: his sisters and mother hate you. They are dangerous. They are looking to hurt you. Do not let your children near them!" She told me she was privy to their nonstop stirring of hateful diatribe. In further visits, she told me she removed herself from the room, so they did not feel her presence was a nod to their evil.

Journal, July 29, 2005

I had a chat with my estranged husband's pastor's wife. She had released an email criticizing my boys and copied it to five people; some recipients were even unknown to me. Proper protocol would be to simply address my boys and perhaps their dad. Instead of addressing my concern she got defensive and deflected.

She raised her voice: "You are so critical; you can't even find a church because you are looking for the perfect church."

I was just tossed. Diversion.

Where did that diversion come from? She has no idea what I do on Saturdays, Sundays, or otherwise; we are not friends. She adopted my estranged husband's false narrative and used it to abuse me: "My wife has the problem, not me – see how critical she is? She can't even find a church." I have heard him say those words. He sprinkles seeds of dissention.

The pastor's wife is repeating his lies as if they are fact. She is confident there is something wrong with me, not her actions. She used false information to try to wound me. The problem is not her sending out an email meant for one person, not five, disparaging my children. The problem is I am critical. I am left wondering if I was speaking with a second abuser, if not a Narcissist.

My estranged husband had been bringing the children to this church for a few years. The pastor's wife is a talented woman who taught piano and singing and wrote music. My daughter even took lessons from her for a time. I visited their church on occasion if my daughter was singing. I once met with her and her husband, the pastor, when my estranged husband decided to join their church. They listened as I explained his dysfunction, but they did not grasp the gravity of it. Later, I made a better attempt at explaining his behavior, but they responded, "We think he is doing better." Of course they did not know they were being spun into his web of lies and false narratives. They just became of member my husband's false reality club; admission is free.

Journal, July 29, 2005

My estranged husband is presenting me with an attitude of superiority. He gets it now and has it all together. He informed me he has started meeting with his pastor once in a while for accountability. Having a private audience with the pastor is producing pride rather than humility.

Journal, August 6, 2005

It is my son's eighteenth birthday party. I made him a big two-day party. Computer cords for Halo games ran to nearly every room. Kids came and went. Some kids slept over. Food was served in shifts for the rotating appearance of his friends.

Journal, August 13, 2005

Today is my son's actual birthday. I made him yet another special meal!

My estranged husband rang the bell and said he stopped by to say "Happy Birthday" to our son. He said he wanted to bring some food since I had arranged and paid for the entire eighteenth birthday party. Rather than just greeting the birthday boy, dropping the food on the counter, and leaving, he stayed. Uninvited. Weird.

I was engaged in a discussion with my son's youth pastor, who had come over to wish our son a Happy Birthday. He interrupted us with a long exhortation about what he brought. I instructed, "Just put everything on the counter, please." Instead he began to explain every little thing he brought, blow by blow. My estranged husband told me he brought corn and described it as if I don't know what corn looks like.

The youth pastor and I exchange uncomfortable glances. He didn't know what this was about, but I did. Then he began to ask me a question but prefaced it by calling me "Mrs. [last name]." This was getting stranger by the minute. He fit that in there because our wedding anniversary date was August 15, close enough for a subtle reminder for me and the male visitor he finds threatening.

Let me explain this convoluted behavior for you. This time he felt he could not order me to "shut up" as he has done in the past, so he disrupted the conversation to exhibit control. He needed to say "Mrs." to relay an underhanded message. Our wedding anniversary was two days away and his sick, self-thought pattern needed to send a reminder.

Journal, January 28, 2006

I attended an informational meeting about homeschooling. My daughter is finishing sixth grade in her Christian school, which only goes to sixth grade, so I am going to homeschool her for grades seven through twelve. Our county is very homeschool friendly. We have more than five thousand homeschoolers with lots of events, help, supplemental classes, prom, and cap-and-gown homeschool graduation. She has always wanted to be homeschooled, so we are going to embark on this together. We will start in August of this year.

Journal, December 1, 2006

I was privy to my son's "impossible" prayer list from youth group. Two of the items show his dad's indoctrination of my innocent son:

1. Mom and Dad to get back together.
2. Mom to change for the better.

My estranged husband repeatedly told the kids with varying inflection, "We could get back together if your mom would just change." "Mom change for the better" was code for accepting my husband's abuse, not challenging or correcting it. My children had no notion they were being used. Their father had instilled confusion in them and wounded them with his nonsense. The kids carried a simmering anger; it was entirely my fault the family was broken. That anger spilled over at different moments on different days. Even my usually tenderhearted and kind son let his words and actions fly on occasion. It's an undercurrent I feel even today, one I hope my children and others can break away from after reading this book.

Journal, April 14, 2007

I arrived home after helping to supervise my son's leadership conference to find my estranged husband at my table, helping our daughter with her geography. Frustrated with her inability to grasp a concept right way, he grabbed her arm and pinched her. I was right there and saw it, yet he denied it when I confronted him. I threatened him with a police report. He began to rationalize his behavior, and when that was not embraced, he got angry at both of us.

Later I sat my daughter down and told her what her father did was unacceptable and she must tell me if anything like that happens again.

Dear Younger Me,

Sociopath Narcissists do not make good tutors. Don't fall for his claims of being there to help. He is there to look important, keep himself in your presence, and have an audience for his perceived benevolence.

Journal, July 2007

I was going over some college paperwork for our son, who started college in 2005, with my estranged husband. It showed our son's needs and expenses. His tension rose and he began to launch personal put downs. "Since you can afford a house without me, then you can pay our son's bills. We wouldn't have to be doing this review if you would just forgive me so we could live together again." He wanted to distract me from his obligation to contribute.

Then oddly, and what seemed to come out of left field, he yelled, "You tricked me into signing the separation papers and I will go to court and say that! I signed under duress!" Then he hurled this at me: "You are not the only one learning stuff about getting healthy; I am too."

He had been taking a course on childhood development for his new retirement job and he told me it was helping him be a better person. I was not seeing any proof of that as he vomited his next attack, "You have no compassion! You are willing to destroy my life by reporting me for abusing our daughter. You will make me lose my ministry, church, and new job. You will destroy everything. You are a horrible person, not me."

As a true Narcissist, he labels other people and deflects blame onto them instead of taking responsibility for his own actions. In his crazy state, he wanted to imply he signed the separation papers under duress as part of his scare tactics not to honor the agreement. Yet in my possession I have a handwritten note on an envelope he gave me after the separation agreement that was signed. It reads: "Thank you for making a potentially traumatic situation very pleasant. You are truly a woman of grace." He signed it.

Potentially traumatic? It *was* traumatic because he made it traumatic. He discounted the trauma. Even the compliment has a lie in it. This note has a place in my files, along with many others that verify my writings. I took the envelope with its paperwork contents and said "Thank you," nothing more.

Journal, September 10, 2007

My daughter is unsettled and antsy. She has not been herself in the last few days. We were talking about why and suddenly the dam broke. Buckets of huge tears rolled down her face. "I don't want to be thirteen years old. I want to be twelve years old. I want to stay your baby; I do not want to be a teenager." She cried and cried; her nose started to run as she sobbed. She crawled on my lap and we snuggled, lingering a long time. I don't know too many kids who don't look forward to being a teenager, but my baby was tender, and our relationship was so sweet and close, especially with the homeschooling. This was definitely a special moment.

Journal, May 4, 2008

It's kind of a strange feeling; the next boy is graduating high school. There will be no boys in the house. Both boys will be at the same college together. One in his first year, one in his last.

The oldest, my bonus son, was married with children, living about three hours away, and my bonus daughter was living in another state. In 2008 my youngest son left for college; he was accepted at that same prestigious college his older brother attended. This left me and my daughter at home to enjoy each other's company. We had developed a flow and balance for her homeschool learning and my work.

I homeschooled my daughter for her middle school and high school years. She flourished, obtaining her two-year Associates in Arts degree while still in high school. We not only did typical academics but as part of her economics class I taught her to run the household. When bills came in I taught her how to write checks and how to graph the electric and water usage. College commenced when she was just fourteen years old, the following month she turned fifteen. Her professors were amazed when they found out their student was just fifteen. I warmly received a compliment form one of her professors: "I would love to have more students like your daughter."

My daughter and I thoroughly enjoyed each other's company and many times giggled over our *girl's only* house. I was her willing chauffeur for the 25 or so weekly appointments and events she needed to be at. She had two loves during those years: singing and signing. She took American Sign Language (ASL) in college and loved the deaf community. God gave her a lovely voice and she was honing the gift and blessing others with it. She sang the National Anthem at many events, including professional baseball game openings, plus patriotic songs at Veteran events. One memorable activity was her participation in local and national singing contests. Sometimes we traveled by car, other times by plane. Each step of the way I kept reassured her that whatever happened she was loved and this was just for fun.

On Fridays we headed to our local mall where the deaf gathered to let newbie ASL signers practice their skills. The group encouraged me to try. I was an epic failure, but my daughter had an uncanny knack. Her fingers flowed like a perfect symphony. Watching her sign was like listening to sweet music.

Sometimes we started our mornings by putting on our favorite music, turning it up real loud and dancing like crazy till we were out of breath! Then we could begin our day including her full plate of school work and extracurricular activities like school trips, singing lessons, retreats, and seminars. While in high school she had the privilege of being chosen as an exchange student. Fortunately I already knew our Japanese host mom since the same one who hosted my son a few years earlier agreed to host my daughter. One year as a special gift I purchased her a hot air balloon ride. We had to drive about an hour to the balloon staging area and I watched as she floated up till she was barely visible, photographing the entire event from the ground. She came back with the biggest smile and she told me every minute detail about her majestic voyage during the ride home. More than once we sat side by side in a missionary helicopter at an event sponsored by a local ministry and church. The lack of a proper door did make our hearts race a bit so upon take off we grasped each other's hands ever so tightly. Giving back to the community is very important so sometimes we served Thanksgiving dinner to the less fortunate and for a few years we were stationed at a red kettle ringing the bells for the Salvation Army. We stood side by side for hours, greeting people and talking. Sometimes we brought her speaker and she would sing Christmas carols to the delight of those passing by. It was a joyful loving time except when the Narcissist was jealous and needed to trigger a rift in the atmosphere, put the focus on him, and nudge her to doubt my love and dedication to her.

Occasionally my estranged husband allowed lulls in the tumult he whipped up. At one point there seemed to be a sliver of relative peace. It turned out that was the quiet before the storm. In hindsight, I am quite sure our closeness and the place of importance I had in her life were imperial threats to the Narcissist. I am confident it was the reason he went into full-throttle attack mode. He needed to destroy what we were building.

CHAPTER 17

DESTRUCTION OF MY YOUNGEST DAUGHTER

Eight years into the marriage we had added 2 boys to the family mix and then in 1994, my bonus daughter got a sister. The shopping spree for all things pink ensued. That *deep in your spirit* stirring all my friends had told me about when having a girl was true. She brought joy. She was beautiful. She made me smile. My son's kindergarten teacher caught me on the street and exclaimed, "I saw your lawn sign announcing you had a girl! I was so happy for you. Having a girl is special." And it was so true. When a dear friend finally had a girl after four boys the whole family loaded into the van to go buy everything girly, frilly and pink! Another friend had six girls then finally a boy! There was a run on anything blue within a 10 mile radius. Each time, families rejoiced and then settled into the daily tasks of blending these tiny wonders into the family routine.

When my regularly scheduled sonogram revealed I was having a girl, the first question family asked was, "Are you going to carry on the name?" They all knew I had first dibs on the family name succession. While filling out her birth certificate at the hospital I could hear the signature song from Fiddler on the Roof playing in my mind and my lips simultaneously sang along… Tradition…Tradition!

Soon after my sweet daughters arrival my mother arrived to personally take in the beauty of our namesake. We posed for lots of pictures. Three generations of women with the same very unique name crafted by my mother's mother were immortalized in print with copies doled out as requested to close and extended family.

Tradition was strong and the bond with my daughter was too. The boys stopped nursing just after a year, she held on strong for two years and would still run to me after that for comfort when she was over tired, got a boo-boo or just because for a couple more . It wasn't often but it lingered. She would look lovingly into my eyes and reach out to curl my shoulder length strawberry blonde hair around her little finger while nursing. Those were beautiful moments. After a few scant minutes of connection her love tank was full, her emotions calm and she ran off joyfully to play. All my mom friends nursed and none of us had hard rules for when to stop. We let the child decide. Strong advocates for nursing don't necessarily have a westernized view for feeding or comforting children. Those same views had me enduring natural childbirth three times. My response to the pain after the first one was, "I am NEVER having another child!" But time passes and we forget the agonizing pain. The longing God instills in us makes those memories fade and replaces them with others.

At age two she loved the same thing I did. Shoes! I have an iconic photo with her tiny feet planted in my 7 1/2's, dangling another 6 fashion savvy footwear statements in her arms! She loved the camera, posed and smiled with ease which was great because I often wanted to capture her antics on film.

In elementary school she excelled academically and spiritually and I had the joy of being her class mom. At the playground the familiar call was, "Higher mom, push me higher!" She was a brave girl. When someone hurt her feelings, we snuggled in bed and talked about it, sometimes she cried and then we talked some more. Sometimes I had to break focus to answer the whine we heard emanating from the floor. Our honey colored miniature dachshund was telling us she wanted to be up on the bed with us and enjoy a few belly rubs while we chatted.

Like my other children she was strong willed. (There was no rest for this momma!) One time when she didn't get her way, in a huff of emotion, she sneakily escaped the playground at school but another keen eyed mom spotted her and scooped her back up before she could endanger herself. She kept me on my toes!

We were a mother daughter team. Until we were not. The *not* part came when I began to say stop and no more to the Narcissist and he decided the best tool in the tool shed to decapitate me was my youngest daughter. It was methodical, nonstop and evil. Rather than simply enjoy her company during his allowed visitation he spent his entire time reaching into her brain, remolding it like a toddler toying with bright red Jello, squishing it between his fingers. Certain areas of our brains are fine tuned for specific functions and if I had to guess, I would say he his has mangled her frontal lobe. The frontal lobe is responsible for personality and emotional intelligence, both of which took an obvious decline every time she spent time with him. Then she hit bottom.

> ...he spent his entire time reaching into her brain, remolding it like a toddler toying with bright red Jello...

The methods the Carnie has put into play have a name. It's called Parental Alienation (PA) or Parental Alienation Syndrome (PAS). Interestingly experts say most parents who institute Parental Alienation are Narcissists. In part PAS describes a child who compulsively denigrates one parent in response to consistent brainwashing by the other parent. MajorFamilyServices.com defines Parental Alienation (PA) as:

> Interestingly, experts say most parents who institute Parental Alienation are Narcissists.

> A term used to describe the attempts by one parent to undermine the relationship a child has with the other parent. Because children are suggestible, many will

eventually succumb to the relentless programming or brainwashing by an alienating parent toward a target parent. When a child aligns with a disturbed parent and becomes a representative of that parent's agenda by also behaving in aggressive and hateful ways toward the target parent, Parental Alienation Syndrome (PAS) has developed. A child with PAS becomes an alienator in his or her own right, independently creating his or her own scenarios of how horrible the target parent is. These imagined scenarios are often bizarre and bear little resemblance to the truth.

The previous paragraph is a remarkably accurate description of the skillful programming propagated on my youngest child. When I first read it, I was amazed that someone managed to spell out so accurately what was happening to my life. It was like it was written for me. I personally could not put a name to these bizarre events until reading these well documented sources. While the other four of my children were and remain occasional and sometimes intense targets of the Carnies Parental Alienation tactics, after they left the nest, he zeroed in on our youngest daughter with an obsessive zealousness. Unfortunately for my daughter, this happened at time that is already difficult for most, her teenage years. My ex-husband was trying to inflict pain on me, but was actually inflicting pain and permanent emotional and mental damage to our daughter. In the broken mind of my ex-husband, he sees our offspring as a long-term method to hurt me since he cannot do it face-to-face anymore. He watches the results of his attempts to destroy me, the woman he promised to honor and cherish, from arm's length via the children and even my grandchildren.

> My ex-husband was trying to inflict pain on me, but was actually inflicting pain and permanent emotional and mental damage to our daughter.

My decision to separate and much later divorce was experienced and internalized by my ex-husband as a Narcissistic injury. In that broken thought pattern, I wounded him, so he **has** to wound me. Every cell in his body had become committed to destroying the maternal bond between me and my youngest daughter. At the time of this writing my daughter has been estranged from me for five years with barely four sentences spoken. But she bonded to the abuser and continues to believe his lies.

At one time I was a life-sized vibrant and valuable person in my children's lives. Now I am a gray, dreary, deflated figure, duly treated with disrespect and doubt. My youngest daughter developed unjustified animosity, negative beliefs, and fears of me. In her eyes I am unworthy of her love, less important, and even mentally ill. Her father's thought reform is so set in stone; she confidently, stridently, and without guilt or filter shares her indoctrinated beliefs to anyone who will listen, even total strangers and even on social media.

She is under the command of the Carnie and he is in command of his swirling school of lies. The fermenting whirl creates ripples that evolve into Narcissistic wave trains that inch to the shore gaining height, billowing high before cresting. The roughness of the salty water mixed with sand tears a layer off my daughter's skin and sucks out her sense of normal as each reoccurring wave backwashes. She feels the sting but can't put her finger on *why* it hurts. One by one the energy of the *N* waves steal a piece of her. Precious parts of her are transported to the Carnies non-reality sea without her even being aware of it. *N* waves are unpredictable and strike with tremendous force. They can relentlessly stack up, crash and reset presenting a ceaseless cycle, which is what has been so detrimental for my daughter. She has

> She has lost so many pieces of herself in her father's Narcissist ocean, it will require a search and rescue team and a miracle to put her back together.

lost so many pieces of herself in her father's Narcissist ocean, it will require a search and rescue team *and* a miracle to put her back together.

Experts on PA agree that alienating parents become marooned in the first stage of child development. This is where survival skills are learned. To them, having total control over their child is a life and death matter. Dr. Richard Gardner, a forensic psychiatrist and expert in PA, agrees the alienating parent may be diagnosed as a Narcissist as well as a Sociopath, which is a person who has no moral conscience. Sociopaths don't distinguish between telling the truth and lying the way others do. Much like orders of protection can't fully protect a woman from her batterer, the clause in our legal separation agreement held no weight either. Page 16, section 2, of our separation and divorce agreement reads:

"Neither party shall do anything which may estrange the children from the other party, or injure the opinion of the children as to the other party, or hamper the free and natural development of the love and respect of the children of the other party."

I find myself wishing the same thing for my daughter that I needed, to get free from the man who is destroying her; she does not know her father's mental control and convoluted thought patterns jumble her mind. I believe one of the dynamics of abusing my daughter so intensely is that she shares my first name and he cannot disassociate that connection whether consciously or subconsciously. Destroying both of us is needed. I liken his efforts to someone who places a silencer on his gun and as inconspicuously as possible pulls the trigger. You stand bleeding while he stands smiling. The blood is dripping on his shoes, he notices and is surprised. "Oh, you are bleeding. Let me help you with that. I'll get a cloth and call an ambulance." When you point out that he is the one who caused the bleeding, he responds, "What are you taking about? I did not! You are crazy and when the ambulance gets here, I will tell them you are nuts."

Over the years my ex-husband has sent out some *deflectors*. They came as emails to divert our attention or explain or excuse his actions. The emails and notes he sent will enable you to share a seat on the roller coaster the Carnie commanded. The subject line for this email read,

"No more denials or blame shifting," 12:11 p.m. Thursday, February 25, 2010:

Dear [author]

[Married oldest son] and I spent several hours on the telephone last night. Something that should have happened years ago finally happened. I came to my senses and realized what an idiot I have been, how foolish, blind, and insensitive I've been once again. The shame of my past overt physical abuse and explosive anger has caused me to cover up and deny when I fall back into the old patterns. Instead of humbly accepting your admonishment the times that I have been loud or unkind, I thought you critical and unforgiving. I have been horribly wrong in twisting your intervention to mean I was right and you were wrong. The denial and excuses are going to stop because I want our children to be free from my unhealthy thinking as they grow to be adults.

I never grasped the intensity of the hurt that I've caused you and our children in recent days and months by my verbal manipulations. I've been blame shifting and dishonoring you in their eyes by painting you as unforgiving when you have been incredibly gracious, in the freedom of my visitations, and including me when the family gets together, and serving me as a welcome guest, and praying for me to repent and to do better as a dad.

You have been an excellent and godly mother and have made every effort to shield the children from mental and emotional trauma during the course of our separation by keeping your words about me respectful and appropriate. I will make every effort from this day forward to honor you in the eyes of our children as I should have been doing these past years. Very specifically, I plan to honor you by saying good and not bad things about you and your parenting. And also, I encourage everyone to be unafraid to correct me if I slip up. I've been avoiding accountability in this area and need to communicate on new levels with everyone.

I have copied this email to my pastor and his wife so that I will be held accountable by them on an ongoing basis in this area, as well as receive their godly counsel. It's normal to have a moment of weakness, resentment, or anger. It's normal to feel alone at times. It is not normal or helpful to play the blame game or to delude myself. I also want to be specific. I did pinch [our daughter] as you saw that time and I did downplay it then and blame shift. I did also say and do some hurtful things to the kids the past several months. I need you to know I am not writing this to cover my tracks or to alter your mind or recent decisions about my relationships with you or with visitations with the family. I'm also not saying all this to build up my image in your eyes or force you to think I've changed. I have to stop talking the talk but walk the walk.

Signed, [my ex-husband]

Did his letter provide you with a hear tug moment? Did you think it was sincere? If you did, you now know the cunning charm of a Narcissist. Not even a tiny twinkling of hope was provided to me by the portrayed inner reflection and heart-tugging script. Those with NPD have no capacity for that; this was simply another attempt at manipulating the cast. I believe my son, the pastor, and his wife perceived this letter to bear sincerity, but these fake confessions had visited my ears many, many times before, manifesting no changes. This letter is dated 2010 and yet in late 2012 he instituted a crusade that I was bipolar, crazy, and on psychiatric medicine, with a myriad of high-level crazy statements in between. His church discipline for dating while still legally married and smudging my character followed this letter as well. He is incapable of remorse or change.

Journal, April 2010

My youngest daughter told me, "Dad was making out with [a woman] and he told me he is going to marry her. He said, "Your mom controls me and when I marry [woman] I can do whatever I want. I can even take you to see my family."

My daughter told me she responded, "Dad, you need to stop kissing [woman] in front of me."

Later that week, my daughter-in-law informed me, "He wants to bring [woman] to my daughter's high school play." She expressed what my daughter expressed. Disgust. "You two are still married; there should be no dating until after the divorce."

The Christian teaching is if you date while you are married, you are committing adultery. While the ink was still wet on the legal separation papers, I told my husband if he wanted to date he could file the divorce at any time.

With contempt he yelled, "If you want to file the divorce, then YOU can, because then it's 'ON YOU' before GOD!"

I called his pastor. "Do you know my estranged husband is dating someone?" The pastor excused his action and my error: "No, you misunderstand. He has someone he is friends with, but that's it. He sees her in group settings."

I said, "He was making out with her in front of my daughter and he spends all his time at her house. He is over there right now." My daughter had just talked to her father and he told her he was over there. The pastor called him while he was at [woman's] house. So it's a come-to-Jesus moment. He is caught; he confesses.

This relationship has been going on for quite a while, but my estranged husband had made concerted efforts to hide that fact from his church friends and leadership. While I had the pastor's ear, I asked if he would also address my estranged husband's lies about my character and about why we are separated that he spreads around in church. My children innocently share with me the scenarios they hear their dad rotate through at church.

They don't mean to betray their dad. I think they believe when they overhear him telling some unsuspecting victim one of his stories, they can use this information to "help me get better" and are thereby helping their parents get back together. They include "She just won't forgive me," "She is very controlling," and "She had a bad childhood and it affected our marriage."

I did get to hear from one unsuspecting victim of this diatribe ear to ear. I went to hear my daughter sing at his church. An older woman with a sweet face walked up to me and gave me a hug. I did not know her personally. During the long hug, she whispered in my ear, "You have to forgive, honey; you have to forgive." How sad. She bought his fabrications and felt it was so real that she needed to share her advice.

To the pastor's credit, in this instance, and sadly the only time, he asked my ex-husband to stand at the front of the congregation and confess his adultery and lies about me. This confessing is a Biblical precept and in this case I think it was used properly. The pastor took away his privilege of teaching, leading, or worship team participation for a couple of months. My ex-husband often waved the flag, "I can't have done anything wrong or the pastor would not let me teach and preach." The pastor was lowering his flag for just a little while.

When my youngest daughter was in high school, she had a lightbulb moment about her father's manipulations and decided to take a break (one of many) from visiting him. Her father called me a few times and asked when he could see her. I said, "That is her decision. She is processing your ongoing intentional manipulations and she is tired of being pinched and slapped."

"I would never hurt my daughter. I am lonely," he sobbed.

My daughter was not interested. Frustrated that he did not make headway, he called more than one of her siblings to complain that their sister had not called him.

During this period, my ex-husband's father had passed away, so he took that opportunity to institute the exact action that got him in the position he was in: manipulation. Pretending he was troubled about **her** character, he reported to our other children, "I am concerned your sister is lacking compassion. She has not called me even though my father died, and you should talk to her about that." His father's death was not sudden or unexpected. This was an emotional ploy and tactical decision to "force" her to talk to him so he could regain control. His efforts produced results.

As each child called me, I told them, "If your father is going to call and complain to you that your sister has not called him, then he should be honest about the circumstance." Refusing to own fault, he accuses his daughter, the victim, of being uncaring.

Eventually she called him and I was present. "Can I talk to you? Do you have a minute?" Her father said, "Well, I have a radio interview on ___ station for __ that will air on __, but yes, I have a minute to talk to you."

It's all about him. This time my daughter caught it too. She was very mature in her conversation with him. She explained, "You should not be calling my siblings to say bad things about me; it's one of the reasons I do not want to see you. You are manipulating." He responded with great drama, "I have been going through a rough month too. Didn't we have fun times? I even called you for the annual Easter party so you could go have fun."

She answered, "Dad, you should go for counseling."

In a great blast of emotion, he lambasted her : "What more do you want me to do! I said I was sorry! I gave up my girlfriend for you!"

The Narcissist needed her to accept *he* did something for her and *he* gave up something for her, discounting the fact that he should not have engaged in that behavior to begin with. Narcissists are masters of language. Her dad uses words to deceive, coerce, and mislead. It is too much for a teenager to have to figure out and process. I tried to help her understand the nuances of the conversation and how much control and self-centeredness was in them so she did not absorb any of his accusations and traumatizing verbiage.

After about six weeks, my daughter began to see her father again and he quickly resumed his subtle and not-so-subtle abuse. First to reach my ears was his assertion, "Mom doesn't love you." She returned to acting out in anger and confusion at home. She was saying crazy things about me, so we had an intervention meeting with a friend. During this intervention, my daughter was on a roll, listing the charges against me with great conviction. Suddenly she put on the brakes. Her countenance changed and it appeared a lightbulb came on.

> I saw her recognize she was not saying things she experienced with me, but rather she was repeating the lies her father had indoctrinated her with.

She took a quiet moment. It was a visual moment of clarity. I saw her recognize she was not saying things she experienced with me, but rather she was repeating the lies her father had indoctrinated her with. She got hold of the fact that she was being brainwashed.

She went on to tell me that every time she visits her dad he tells her, "Your mom is crazy." When she complained to him that I made her do the dishes and clean her room, he replied, "See, I told you she was bad. If you think that was bad, imagine how it was for me."

He braided in absurd and crazy comments that he knew she would repeat to me. "Dad says you two could get back together if you would just forgive him." "Dad says since you're not going to church anymore, you're not a Christian, that's why you don't forgive him." So, was I crazy or loveable? Was he saying, "I will stop all my lies and let you have your daughter back if you come back to me?" Of course none of his lies are true, but like a sly lawyer who wants to sway the jury, you throw out a false statement to cause doubt. It's heard. The Judge disallows it. The crafty lawyer says, "Okay, strike that from the record." But he has accomplished his goal. The jury has indeed heard it. The doubt has been planted.

One time when the three of us were standing together, he bubbled up with this thought: "You know, we could reconcile." He wanted to give my daughter false hope and make me look like the villain if I did not surrender to his suggestion.

He got the response he wanted from our daughter: "Oh, you are going to reconcile!" His comment empowered her to say, "Mom, you should be open to it; Dad went to see the movie *Fireproof*." My young daughter did not understand that watching the hit Christian movie themed on marriage does not change a Sociopath Narcissist abuser. He played with her emotions. In her innocence, my daughter perceived the increase in fun activities after the banishment she had previously imposed equated to him being a better dad and therefore he transformed into a better husband. That's easy for a teenager to think.

She came home after a weekend with him and informed me, "You have a controlling spirit." This is sometimes a secular and definitely a Christian concept. She had just come home from church.

I questioned her source: "Who told you that?"

She said, "Oh, I can't tell you." Her father had indoctrinated the leadership of that church into believing I had a laundry list of problems but left himself off the list.

Dear Younger Me,

Sociopath Narcissists have a flexible reality that changes shape like Play-Doh. That shape shifting makes you feel confused, even unstable. You look at the same thing, yet he tells you something different that you see. Do not allow his wrong reality to influence or confuse you. Remember he is shaping power and control. Don't join him at the play table where he will be like a bully at the playground, demanding his rules and his game. Play-Doh comes in lots of colors with lots of messy possibilities and so does the Narcissist.

The downward spiral for my daughter began when she was about fifteen. I searched for a counselor who saw teens. Not all counselors do. My ex-husband decided he **had** to be part of the research since it was his money that would be paying for it. His Narcissism required he be part of the heroic rescue from the upheaval he had created. My panic blinded me from rejecting his suggestion that we use someone he and my daughter had met during a ministry event. I was not comfortable when she showed some resistance and even arrogance to my natural interview questions. I should have listened to my gut. My internal fear and distress over my daughter's fragile position prevented me from extending the search. My ex-husband applied pressure to choose "this one" because it was easy on his wallet, fifty dollars cash per session.

> I felt like someone had full throttle punched me in the gut.

One family session launched our time; then my daughter began sessions alone. One day my daughter announced, "My counselor says I could do well, but the biggest fear is you will pull me from counseling because you are the problem." I felt like someone had full throttle punched me in the gut and I was out of breath. What just happened? Unbeknownst to me, her father secretly began to see his daughter's counselor, as a client. He showed no empathy for his daughter's fragile condition and mental health, all he could focus on was that his fragile ego was surely going to take a tumble when facts came out and he simply could not allow that. He had to get in there and spin some false reality.

When I found out he was the source of information that formed the counselor's bold proclamation to my daughter, he defended his actions as honorable and gallant, "I care about our daughter too; I thought it would help if I saw the [same] counselor." My daughter told me her counselor said, "Your father is a good Christian, godly and righteous." My daughter informed me her father's report to the counselor regarding me was, "She is delusional. I don't remember ever hurting her or ever making her black and blue." He took his compulsive lying to the counselor's doorstep and used it to confuse, control and bolster his image.

Later I learned from experts that an abuser's denial can be so deep, he can minimize the physical damage inflicted on the victim to almost nothing. It became apparent to me that my ex-husband had premeditated this intentional evil. His selfish Narcissistic needs were paramount to his daughter's sanity.

Not a word from their mouth can be trusted; their heart is filled with destruction. Their throat is an open grave; with their tongue they speak deceit. Psalm 5:9

That counselor received a cancer diagnosis within weeks of her accusation toward me and died within months. The Carnie told me, "The best way I can help in her death is by stepping up to take over her Bible study." My failure to foresee what was being perpetrated in this scenario brings tears, embarrassment, even nausea.

Dear Younger Me,

You simply cannot trust someone with this level of disease. NOTHING he says or does can be trusted. Trust your instincts and know when something's not right. Do not for one minute think you are parenting with someone who wants the best for your child. He only wants what's best for him. He is constantly scheming how to maintain his image. Do not consult with him or take advice from him. Even if he is paying for something, ignore him. He is not truly emotionally connected to his child, so he can't care for the child's well-being. He only has room to be connected to himself. Narcissists use their children for selfish needs.

Journal, April 2010

My daughter and I have been having some conversations. She said, "You know, what Dad says and does do not match. He is a hypocrite. There are more things he said I should tell you."

I had to listen without showing any feeling or emotion, but I was devastated. Inside I was dying at the depth, intensity, and intended manipulation of the lies. It helped me understand why she would treat me so poorly after visiting him.

Things tumbled out of her mouth. Her face had a look of confusion as she thought through the list. I knew she was struggling. I could see she was reaching in her mind for all the things he had said over recent time. Clearly her fifteen-year-old brain didn't know what to think. She was offering them as facts but also maybe as confession that she believed them or was sorry she didn't tell me sooner.

1. You are a mental cripple.
2. You have never known how to love because you don't know how to forgive.
3. His family is okay; you're crazy.
4. You are not really saved or a real Christian.
5. You don't really love me; you only love my brother who looks like you.
6. You are mentally retarded.
7. You are not a good mother.

8. Only he understands me, not you.
9. He goes to church and Bible study; you don't.
10. He is a true Christian and a good person.
11. You have no friends and are not as social as he is.
12. He takes me out to eat and to see theatrical plays so I will know that is what guys who date me someday should do, you don't.

And lastly, she added, "If I don't act in a good manner or don't behave when I am with him, then he will look bad to you, so I have to act right."

When my daughter and I had normal teenage conflicts because I set appropriate boundaries, he latched onto that to insist, he was the lone parent to be trusted with her thoughts and feelings. For years, my teenage daughter heard this inventory of accusations regurgitated and revamped, so it simmered in her brain and produced antagonism. She did not know what to believe. The next time I saw him, I asked, "Why are you disparaging me to our daughter?"

He began his words with a change in his stance. Then came the tick in his face and then the stutter. Lies or pride always bring these three visible habits. "I don't know what you are talking about. I tell her good things about you."

My daughter reported to me his reaction on being busted for his words and actions. He interrogated her harshly, "Why did you tell Mom what I said?" Then the physical punishment came: he slapped her and pinched her on her arm. He was training humiliation into her with harsh questioning, pinching, and slapping as the penalty for disclosing his actions to her mom. The itemized log she shared made it clear that his empire of tall stories was expanding. Her father wanted our daughter to see me as worthless so that his worth increased by default. He gave her sympathy. It's tough to have only one parent with any value.

Journal, October 2011

My daughter made a 1 PM appointment with her dad to talk to him about his pushes, pinches, and manipulative behavior. Not long after the conversation, she came to me very upset. It took some time but she finally got this out:

1. He said you are a liar.
2. You don't love me.
3. You only homeschool me to look good.
4. You only care about appearances.
5. You are not saved.
6. You are mentally unstable.
7. You are just trying to make me like you because you are insecure.
8. Even if you don't love him, I should listen to you.

After she unloaded this burden, she ran off in a severe emotional state, wearing no shoes. Her father came to me and pretended to be bewildered as to why she was so upset. He said, "She is just emotional. I didn't do anything. I did the right thing. I told her she has to love and respect you – even if you didn't marry me for the right reasons. You are her mother." His continued conversation confirmed she had indeed repeated his words truthfully. He didn't even hear himself. He was convinced he was acting honorably.

I waited a few days and asked my daughter, "How did the talk become about me, when you went to talk about *his* behavior?"

All of a sudden her face lit up like a neon sign. "You are right. I went there to talk about HIS behavior and he turned it to you!" She was noticeably frustrated with herself for not realizing it till I pointed it out. This has been an ongoing problem. In his counseling up north, the therapist had said, "He has a hard time staying focused on himself." It was never that HE hit me and it was wrong. It was why *I* deserved it or caused it. He invents reasons why I do anything.

His behavior reminds me of pedophiles who kidnap kids and tell them their parents don't really love them. The pedophile lures information from the kids about their relationship with their parents and then twists it as ammunition. "They don't act like someone who loves you, but I will love you." Then he plies them with a much-desired toy or mouthwatering snack. "See, I love you." The pedophile breaks the barriers to make the kids subservient to abuse. My daughter's father was doing the same thing.

Emotional outbursts from my daughter rolled in with regularity. Reasoning became elusive and in exasperation she began to run away. Sometimes these emotional flare-ups happened when the boys were home from college, so they joined in the search party. They did not know what to make of their sister's behavior, so they wrote it off as teenage hormones. It was so much more than that.

When the two younger boys were older, in college, I tried to explain some of the dynamics but was met with resistance. "You always say bad things about Dad and Dad says bad things about you." They didn't understand the things I said were true and were meant to help them. Even though they were the victims of his abuse, both verbal and physical, they were not able to grasp that what I was sharing matched their personal experiences with their father. Their father's Sociopath verbiage made their thoughts clear as mud, so it was easy for them to feel accepting of his minimized version of things. They could not correctly label it, just like their sister, and me, for so many years.

Journal, October 5, 2011

My daughter met her dad for yet another conversation. She told him once again, "I don't want to see you for a while."

He replied, "Well, I'm sorry," then went on to blame others for his behavior and grandly offered her an opportunity to help him act better. "The thing I respond to best is if you are nice to me." He put the liability for his bad behavior on her instead of himself. I am familiar with this tactic; he has transferred that concept and responsibility from me to my daughter. My skin crawled.

My daughter saw though it, however, and told me her response was, "I was nice to you for the three years you lied about my mother, abused me, and pinched me." She told me that everything is jumbled in her mind but she has a tiny understanding of some things.

Assured his actions have not hurt his child, he magnanimously offered his daughter a way to help *him* because his Narcissistic needs are paramount. Empathy is nonexistent. This was the framework of my daughter's emotional see-saw. She loved her dad; sometimes she had fun, but sometimes she knew he kept her weirdly unbalanced. I tried to re-direct her schedule from spending too much time with him but sometimes she cried, "I know he does bad things, but I miss him." I am sure it was at her father's instigation that she yelled at me, "You cannot keep me from seeing him."

With our other children absent from the home, he fixated on her to fill his loneliness. Isolating her allowed his misleading babble to stand unchallenged. Whenever my daughter's expression read, "I don't even know how to explain what he did to me," I recognized that her dad intentionally put into play his crazy-making antics that left her utterly confused. As I had done many times, it was her turn to wonder, *What just happened?*

I had a bold revelation that sprung forth like a Jack-in-the-Box while I was driving in my car. When our daughter had windows of time she did not want to see her dad, the Carnie translated them as a rollback in his indoctrination and alienation operation. Absence would not simply be felt as standing still, but lost ground. When she buckled from her self-decided absence, his mounting anxiety generated intensified efforts to play catch-up. This revelation compared to my experience of his double-up efforts when I had clarity because of a supportive counselor and the bravery to be honest with friends. Mounting anxiety he could lose his daughter the way he lost me fed his fear.

At one point in this overwhelming chaos and emotion I investigated going *underground* with my daughter. Disappear. When my daughter began to be more and more unstable and distant from me, I wish I had. If she were an only child, that would have been a serious option.

Journal, October 18, 2011

I fear the damage my estranged husband has done has permanently broken my relationship with the children I have given birth to. They have believed his lies and manipulated every good intention, good word, and good deed to read as bad. My position as mother is destroyed. My son told me, "You have a victim mentality. Everyone can't stand you and no one is comfortable around you." Any interaction I have with them is colored by whatever lies he planted. They see no good in me. I hear it in their voices and the way they speak to me. The pain is too much.

Even though I don't live with this horrible man, I can't get rid of his damage. He walks around like a Super-Christian and deceives everyone. He asks for prayer, and shares his fake prayer information as a way to spread his lies. It's evil. I am so grieved I did not leave him sooner. I was ready to leave when we got saved, but thought this would change things. Instead he just started to misuse Christianity for his purpose.

I was dropping my daughter off at her friend's house; they go to the same church as her dad. Her friend's dad said to my daughter, "How are you and your dad doing?" My daughter said, "Fine." The man said, "I care about your dad. He's such a good guy and a godly man, so I want to make sure everything is Okay."

Translation: He goes to church with the Narcissist. The Narcissist went up for prayer and announced, "I need prayer. My daughter doesn't want to see me right now; she is upset and running away." He manipulates those who are intent on honoring his prayer requests.

My daughter smiled at me. She caught the game and did not offer her dad's friend any information he was fishing for. Later she told me she found out her dad was telling everyone to pray for him and making himself look like the victim and the hero.

This man, with deep compassion, offered to me, "He says he really is trying to be a better dad. He listens when she talks. He *is* trying." This unsuspecting man had bought into the opportunist abuser's deception and then delivered the verbal package, accomplishing his friend's goal of making his daughter feel strangely uncomfortable about her decision to temporarily vacate visitation. This was the poison circle created and honed in his church and other churches he ministered in.

A similar scenario occurred in that same time frame, which led me to believe the Narcissist was in a season of planting bad crops. A friend of my estranged husband crossed my path in 2011. "Your husband really loves you and considers you his wife. He really wants to have his marriage restored. I am praying for you guys." How could I explain a Sociopath Narcissist in a passing conversation? This friend was obviously ignorant of the nearly thirty years of various abuses and beatings my estranged husband had dealt to me or that he had recently pronounced his upcoming marriage to another woman while he and I were still legally married. Blissfully unaware of the church discipline my husband had received for slandering me, his friend accepted the carefully crafted words my husband had presented. He pleaded his case just as the Carnie planned because Sociopaths use people.

The Carnie changed his story as it suited him. To some I was crazy and bipolar and when he needed to look holy and godly, he was a saint waiting for his wife to realize he was magnificent and should return to him. He sang a different tune depending on the audience. I found it comical that he claimed to want to be married to someone crazy and bipolar. I wondered if he had a hard time remembering which people he told I was crazy and which ones he told he was still in love with me and wanted to get back together.

Dear Younger Me,

Narcissists are opportunists. He will exploit his friends by passing his false reality and cherry-picking details to maintain his image. Listening to his own propaganda produces a chemical high, so he does it as often as possible to maintain it. He hopes the newly inducted messengers will bear his good news because he is positive his minimized version is correct. There is nothing barring:

    A. *Return to marital bliss. (His false reality)*

B. Your being physically present to accept his abuse and lies (True reality) Recognize when the Narcissist in your life is manipulating friends and don't engage or defend.

Journal, October 20, 2011

My daughter was picked up at college to go to a luncheon with her dad. It was his birthday. She began a discussion about his behavior. She told me he would not own his behavior. She told me he threw out this honest confession: "I guess I want things to change without me having to change." Yes indeed, he wants everyone to adapt to his sickness, but not identify it properly.

Dear Younger Me,

You can spend your entire life trying to get a person with NPD to change but change will never come. They would sooner die or see you crush under its weight than change. You have to make the change; you have to leave.

Journal May 19, 2012

Catching up on all the events!

May 5: Dressed in extra fancy regalia at 10 AM, one son graduated with a doctorate. We emptied his dorm room and drove hours to make it to the same-day 7 PM college graduation for the next son. Draped in honor cords he received a business degree with a minor in entrepreneurship. We also packed up his dorm.

May 12: My daughter's grand homeschool high school graduation ceremony included a personalized Power Point presentation scrolling behind us while I had the honor of standing on stage, admiring her myriad of honor cords, bestowing her graduation diploma, and moving her tassel.

May 15: With her AA degree completed during high school, my daughter was admitted to the College of Education to continue her Bachelor's degree.

I believe it was in my daughter's senior year of high school that I located a counselor who saw teens. Weekly sessions were noted on the big wall calendar. When her eighteenth birthday arrived four months after graduation, her counselor said, "Legally I can't speak to you anymore." That was hard to hear. I had not heard her express any recognition that her client's dad was a Sociopath Narcissist, which would have given their sessions a solid direction and me some comfort.

My counselor and I, after years of sharing, had landed there. I remember incorrectly calling him a Psychopath Narcissist and she corrected me, "Sociopath Narcissist." Much like I went to my ex-husband's sessions up North to give truth every few weeks, I think this could have helped my daughter immensely.

My daughter was presenting the Narcissist false reality narrative; she did not know her father profited by her ignorance. Though she did not know the depth of the roots and all the fruits of her father's tree, my daughter's counselor did aid her in understanding that I had not done an adequate job of protecting her from her father. This revelation escaped her mouth as a startling burst of accusation but I was okay with that. I understood it was part of her healing and I wanted that for her. During one of our many conversations I enlightened my daughter-in-law about this concept.

"Ha!" she exclaimed. "You couldn't even protect yourself!"

Sadly, that was true and it hurt. This same concept was introduced to me in counseling years earlier. My mother failed to protect her children, and I failed mine. Many of my siblings have not entertained that thought; they protect our mom as only a victim along with us. Safe and protected is something we all like to feel and I grieve that I did not accomplish that for my children.

A friend went to county social services to seek help when she realized her husband was dealing drugs through his medical practice. He was using his children to aid in the sales; the children participated, sometimes knowingly and sometimes unknowingly. Social services, upon interviewing the husband, determined the mom was *just* having a hard time letting go now that they were teenagers. The final judgment was, "Their father is an upstanding medical professional!" This father used his children for his image and profit line. Her Narcissist won.

Eventually he was arrested, along with other staff. The authorities closed all his clinics. It was splashed all over the newspapers and regurgitated on every TV news outlet. He was one of the many prescription pill mills busted that year. He lost his medical license and went to jail for nearly a decade. The kids' perception of life and how to make money was distorted by their father, and they all went down long dark roads that still break my friend's heart.

I desperately wanted the county employees to see his name in the media blitz, recognize my friend's plea was valid, and apologize, but that didn't happen. Her Narcissist didn't apologize either. He said, "It is all a misunderstanding, I'm a good guy!" After my friend's experience, distaste for the social services system sat in my mouth, as well as a fear that if I engaged county services to help me, they would accuse me of failing to protect my children and take them from me.

Dear Younger Me,

If abuse has been going on in your home for some time, Social Services could indeed consider taking your children from you. That is a scary thought. Your abuser will say he is a good guy. You have to be forthcoming about his abuse tactics and slay his good-guy image. Prepare. Defend. You do not need to label your abuser, rather show his pattern. Provide specific examples, dates and details of any forms of abuse dealt. Let your documentation lead the ears and eyes receiving the information to naturally land the label. The goal would be for you and your children to be placed in housing together, not for you to be removed from your children. I think contacting Domestic Violence Services is a better option than Child Protective Services (CPS).

Journal, February 8, 2013

My daughter is hell-bent on finding an apartment. She allowed me to view a few complexes with her. What she can afford is in scary, unsafe areas. She blames me for not being able to afford something better. Everything I say is poison; when someone else offers the same thing, it's gold.

Journal, February 15, 2013

My daughter found an apartment. She can afford it for two months, and then she thinks money will magically fall from the sky. I gave her many things for her new place: her bed, brand-new, high-end culinary tools, pots and pans, an expensive vacuum, silverware, and lots of other items, but nothing I gave seemed to have value. Her boyfriend's mother usurped any value I added.

Within six months of her graduation, I did not recognize my little girl. Her last kindness toward me was probably graduation day, after that she began to verbally abuse me. It felt as if my heart would burst when her horrible words struck me. "I am going to kill that F****** B****. Her messages and texts to me were vile, very, very vile.

Her barrage of ongoing cursing and an extended period of disrespect caused me to ask, "Would you be happy somewhere else?"

Rather than softening to humility or tenderness at her cruelty toward me, she jumped at the possibly of *somewhere else*. Her version of, "She threw me out" was privately applauded as a successful piece to her father's alienation plan. In the first weeks of her move she talked to me, and then no more. In three short years, she lived with three different men; was placed on psychotropic medication, with all its possible undesirable side effects exhibiting themselves, was arrested by the police, and was involuntarily committed to a psychiatric facility.

Once my daughter moved out of our home, she resisted any help from me. I amassed a collection of self-help books I thought would enlighten her. I designed some notepaper with her initials in calligraphy and penned, "I wish someone had given me books like this when I was twenty years old."

Her response to my doorstep delivery was a text: "Stop giving me self-help books." My husband dished out a similar thought to my friend when she gave me the book *The Verbally Abusive Relationship*. The Carnie would never want our daughter to get informed and make a break from him, like I did.

Journal, April 21, 2013

My daughter did not call me on Easter; she spent it with her dad and her boyfriend's family. I had a visit from close friends who wanted to see my daughter, even if it was brief, so there was a short visit, during which time she announced in front of my friends, "You know you are certifiably insane, right?"

Narcissists will never admit their behavior; that is built into their dysfunction. They will deflect, divert, project, and minimize. They portray themselves as people who would never purposely hurt anyone. They will not acknowledge Parental Alienation tactics. "I can't help it if my daughter will not see her mom" is one of my ex-husband's popular catch-phrases. He delivers that counterfeit report quite regularly.

Journal, May 20, 2013

I got a call from the pediatrician's office, asking about the emergency room visit over the weekend for my youngest daughter. I didn't know about any emergency room visit. But I acted as if I did.

I called my estranged husband because I knew he had been with her. He admitted he took her to the ER, without telling me. She had stomach cramps. Not informing me violates our separation agreement, but I didn't make a big deal out of it. I had previously told him these cramps or pains were normal when our daughter is menstruating and she sometimes gets bowel issues from the normal swelling all women

get at that time of the month. Some worse than others. It does not require a trip (or expense) to the ER.

My daughter has been very dramatic about any illness lately and she's looking to label herself with different ailments. It's getting a bit concerning. Attention? He said he felt obligated to take her and didn't want to tell me because the examination, including x-rays, proved my assessment was true. It was her period combined with mild constipation. He said he didn't want me to know because, "I was right."

I called my daughter to ask how she was feeling and offered to visit her. She told me she was going to stay with her voice coach until she felt better and I was not welcomed. Somewhere between her May 2012 graduation and February 2013 the Carnie had broken my daughter's connection to reality. Unbeknownst to me she now embraced every convoluted morsel that fell from her father's lips. She no longer battled or tried to untangle his lies but succumbed and embraced them.

He also managed to successfully transfer the false narrative to our daughter's unsuspecting voice coach. Let's call her Pam. I am not so sure the ease of deception says something about the voice coach's weakness, character, or naivety, though her actions did cut me to the core. The credit for the ability to deceive a second person doesn't lie with the first, but rather displays the powerful deceptive acumen of the third person who excels in a Narcissist Personality Disorder.

The card on Pam's boxed-up belief read "inattentive, mentally ill, and horrible mom." I found Pam's susceptibility to the indoctrination incomprehensible. She had been in my home dozens of times. At her invitation, I was a guest speaker for a women's retreat at her church. When her son needed stitches for an injury, I was the one she asked to provide transportation to the emergency room. She bonded with me over the fact that I was there for her son's first major childhood boo-boo. She trusted me to hold her only child on my lap and comfort him while he got stitched up.

Yet suddenly she believed the false narrative of a Narcissist and his accomplice daughter. Pam was not able to discard the nonsense *word salad,* tossed with evil elixir dressing, served by her student. Her brain left no room for questioning. Mine did, so I sent her a text. Her responses confirmed she had been propagandized.

Victoria: Do you have time for a conversation?
Pam: About?
Victoria: My daughter, a few things, too much to text.
Pam: More specific, I am not exactly sure what you want to talk about. I don't have time for a game, U have not been there for your daughter.

My heart broke. I cried. I ended the conversation right there.

Later, I attended one of my daughter's singing venues that Pam had arranged. Pam gave me uncomfortable glances and gossiped about me with her table companion. When I went to sit with Pam, she let me know I was not welcomed. When I went to thank the owner of the venue for having great entertainment, she asked me why I went in to talk to the owner. Suddenly, in her eyes, everything I did had an evil intent. She treated me with distain or indifference, sometimes even at her church where she led the worship team.

How could Pam so easily adopt as her own verbiage, "U have not been there for your daughter" when she watched me homeschool my daughter, invest in her interests, taxi her all over town, make costumes, take her to counseling, and support her many gifts? I even played with her toddler son on the floor while she gave my daughter singing lessons in my home. At Pam's holiday and end-of-the-year recitals, I helped set up, tear down, and baked homemade cakes with creamy icing that read, "Pam's singing stars."

Later down the road, Pam became the object of my daughter's wrath over a convoluted issue, which made her question her behavior toward me. I would have welcomed a humble visit to my door or even a phone call, but I had to settle for an apology on Facebook. I share this sad and frustrating snippet to show you how much carnage can be done when Narcissists must, at all costs, maintain control and power to the point that they enjoin others to their malignant cause. I am sad that many, including myself, have adapted so easily to Narcissistic deceptive behavior.

While I was doing my best as a mom to try to make sweet memories and teach the precepts I wanted my children to have built into their characters, I was unknowingly parenting with a person who was not capable of doing that, though he presented himself to the outside world as if he was a capable and godly parent. This kept our circle of friends either confused or conned. One of the whopper misrepresentations he twisted together to create a rope from which to hang me was, "Mom only homeschools you to look good."

My daughter-in-law, who also homeschooled, laughed heartily, "No one homeschools to look good. It's too hard and too time consuming! There are much easier ways to look good!" Her comment made me laugh too.

Instead of immediately recognizing that the Carnie's perversion was his disorder functioning, I was offended. My youngest daughter couldn't recognize it either and he knew it. She was just a kid who had words of doubt steadily dropped on her like a nagging drip from a faucet that creates an indent in the porcelain after years of wear. Rather than quickly discounting the value of any of his negative statements or mixed messages, they settled in my teenager's heart. Then, like tiny strokes of a razor blade, they slowly wore away the love and confidence she once felt for me.

Sometimes my ex-husband's negative comments were perfectly obvious, though sometimes they were the kind I didn't catch at first, but returned to haunt me and marinate in my brain for hours. He often presented reminders of his gestures for my daughter to fawn over. "I took you out to eat, I took you to a play, and I took you to the Father-Daughter Dance." It wasn't enough to bestow something; it needed to be *used*. Much like her father escorting me to a Broadway play was used as ammunition, so were the things he did *with her*, even though he would not own or be blamed for the things he did *to her*. To our daughter and outsiders, he would present his grand scorecard as part of his smoothing-over process to lay down any frizzy hairs of doubt. To him, keeping score proves he's a *mensch*.

Presenting our positive homeschooling experience as something I did to attain a good image made me stand up and take notice. His words were another piece tossed onto the mountain of evidence that his Narcissist personality disorder took no rest. I believe he saw homeschooling as a competition he could not win and that I stole something from him by providing something so important. He needed to create a jagged road for me to tread in my new position as teacher, guidance counselor, and principal. I homeschooled because our daughter expressed a desire to be homeschooled on many occasions and this seemed a perfect juncture to do so. Saving tens of thousands in Christian school fees he would have been required to pay did not relieve him of his insane jealously that I had control over this important area of our daughter's life. She graduated high school with seeds of hate in her heart, planted by her dad. I missed that those seedlings were about to break ground and that he was going to yank her from me. I was getting glimpses of her rebellion, the result of the Carnie's declaration, "You graduated so you don't have to listen or answer to your mother anymore." She boldly let his words vomit out of her mouth one day and it crushed me.

When my daughter graduated high school at seventeen, she was feeling very adult about her accomplishments. Her father thought so too. Now that she had graduated he felt he did not have to answer to me, and kept affirming to her that she didn't either. Although we have a section in our legal separation paper forbidding contact with his family, as soon as our youngest daughter turned eighteen, her father took her to his sister's house in another state, without asking me or telling me. "She is eighteen. I don't have to answer to you anymore, besides she is so pretty and talented, I want to show her off." His need to look good superseded the wellbeing of our daughter. This visit was to the sister who knocked me unconscious, and that same anger

> His words were another piece tossed onto the mountain of evidence that his Narcissist personality disorder took no rest.

would allow her to transfer her and her mother's false narratives to my unsuspecting child.

Journal, May 28, 2013

My son is displaying classic abusive techniques. He told me I have subjective value. I bought him food I know he likes and my kindness was wasted. "Unless you also cook it for me, I am not eating it. I have better things to do with my time. Cooking has subjective value too."

I gave him (and another son) a contract to live by if he wanted to live at home. His response was, "How dare you do this? I am going to post this on Facebook and let everyone see what kind of person you are, and I'll show your business client what you are doing too. If you take back the computer you bought for me, I will call the police and have you arrested. I have the receipt, so even though it's in your name and on your credit card, it's mine." The recent college graduate defended his character: "I can't be so bad. Look at all I have accomplished. No one will believe you!"

I thought a hundred and fifty dollars a month for room and board was a bargain. The contract included taking out the garbage on a rotating basis, cleaning the shower he used, and making sure he paid his car payment, which was in my name, or I would have to take over the car and its payments so my credit wouldn't be ruined. My generosity was rewarded with put downs and threats.

Journal, December 17, 2013

Today someone very important in my life told me my daughter told them I starved her. I only fed her ramen noodle soup and stole her money. I am really worried about her, is she as mentally ill as her father?

Journal, December 2013

My estranged husband sent me a note:

"My daughter [name] made it very clear to me that she does not want me to tell you anything about her life. I will abide by her wishes and keep what she tells me in confidence. She is emancipated and you are no longer her custodial parent. I pray each day according to Colossians 3:12-14 for you and her to have your relationship restored."

Colossians 3:12-14: "Therefore as God's chosen people, holy and dearly loved, clothe yourselves with compassion, kindness, humility, gentleness, and patience. Bear with each other and forgive what even grievances you may have against one another. Forgive as the Lord forgave you, and over all these virtues, put on love which binds them together in perfect unity."

[Signed, the abuser]

In October 2013, seven weeks prior to this communication, final dissolution of our marriage was pronounced. The above note arose out of a need to strike back, and our daughter was the perfect contrivance. He was the guillotine that separated mother and daughter, but he offered scripture to soften the blow of the surgical wound. On paper, his poison pen offers sacrificial prayers for restoration as the smoke screen, but secretly he is ecstatic at the silver platter opportunity to fill his need of *Power Over* us.

His Narcissism pushes back any doubt that by presenting these wonderful concepts, those reading might realize he has epically failed to apply any of them to himself. Using the word *my* as ownership and stating her first name (also my first name) are covert control messages, when stating *our daughter* would have sufficed. He throws her emancipation in to stress he is no longer allowing me control in our daughter's life but then underhandedly presents his control veiled as a gesture of *favor* to his daughter. This *ipso facto* makes him maintain her favor, which builds her trust in him. No one should have to analyze this so much or so deeply, but not doing so kept me in the NPD web.

I am sure this is why I tested vigilant or hypervigilant in a one-hundred-question test my counselor gave me years ago. To be vigilant means you are wary and keenly watchful to detect danger. Nearly one year to the day, the Sociopath would compose a confession note that blows apart his Colossians 3 pretense and makes it sparkling clear that restoration was never on his docket. As you read this book further, make sure you don't miss the note dated December 2014.

When asked why he was separated from me, in the beginning, it was enough to offer the smaller lie, "She won't forgive me," and to the Christian audience, a broken-hearted alm, "I am not even sure she's a Christian anymore," to help them pray better. Once I filed for final divorce, he went from DEFCON 3 to DEFCON 1. He pondered ways to hurt me for taking a sledge hammer to his fraudulent world.

The Carnie consistently gathered up his imaginative tales like a veteran sand sculptor carefully chooses only prime grades of fine sand to create an awe inspiring sculpture. Like any good artist, the liar has marinated the concept in his mind before he commences. Both artists instinctively know placement of their revered Magnus Opus is key. The sand sculptor is keenly aware a rising tide can take his artistic expression out to sea before it can finish taking shape and the Narcissist uses the same thought process. The artist closely studies the base he has complied, and then backs up a few yards, bites his lip as he ponders if its elevation is majestic enough to start the fine tuning. No. He must heap on a million more grains, but it does not exhaust him. Years of practice provide the untiring methodical skill and stamina. In real life, sand sculptures are only as good as their foundation. The Narcissist doesn't care about a strong base; the outer image is all that matters. Every experienced sand sculptor knows the key to making the exterior of his creation stay intact longer. Spray it down. The Carnie carefully wets down his pyramid of lies with a solution of 10 % truth. He carefully controls the application because truth is scant in his creations. The thin coating of truth must stand under the occasional chisel of casual questioning that he welcomes to prove his point, but not reveal the lack of substance underneath. It is of utmost importance that the smidgens of fact help maintain the facade of his story under cursory examination. The Narcissist artist puffs with pride when he marshals a coterie of the naïve and easily deceived and they are conned and engaged by his sculpture of well-placed lies. The gravitational pull of the earth and moon will eventually cause the glory of the sand sculptured masterpiece to erode. The same cannot be said for the Narcissists masterpiece, it will take more than the rising tide to wash them away. Some say sand sculpting is the ultimate performance art but I beg to differ. Sociopath Narcissists are a strong competitor for that title.

My daughter was forced to attend all of her father's art shows and because he already had years of experience conning the women in his life, his work was not entry level. Narcissist artists make art from lies for selfish reasons, and try to share their ideas and visions with others as part of their dysfunction. The Carnie had a carefully curated following. There were those he already conned and those who were choosing to stay blissfully ignorant, which I believe my daughter saw as affirmation of her father's view. Since I left his fan club he desperately needed a replacement. Tragically he chose our teenage daughter and began the indoctrination to seal her allegiance to him and carefully lead her to believe I was a traitor and deserved alienation. His master level lies heaped on a still in development teenage mind that was already reeling from adolescent hormones and self-doubt was fertile ground to make her a dedicated fan of his counterfeit concoctions. He carried a plethora of material around in his mental portfolio and his elevator pitch was perfected and ready on demand for her, his church groups and general followers.

Lie after lie lead to confusion and frenzy for my daughter so I brought her back to counseling once again- yes, our attempts to get help began and stopped a few times, sometimes because of our life schedule and sometimes because of the counselors schedule. I did not grasp the size of the wrecking ball her dad was swinging back then and I think her counselor missed it too. I, too, returned to sessions with the counselor I gleaned from when first arriving in the South. I wanted a checkup to make sure I was staying in balance during this trying time. I needed assurance that my anger over the Carnies multiple Magnus Opus 10% truth creations were not causing me to lose focus and drown in his sociopath watered down fabrications while flailing to defend myself. I was in distress because my daughter had run away barefoot in pajamas more than once. I feared that in her emotional confusion she would get in a car with someone who would abduct or rape her. Sometimes she ran a mile or two; once she ran more than ten miles and called for a ride home. Pride could be seen on her father's face for being part of the search and rescue team, especially if he found her first. Her sprints were the result of her emotional upheaval caused by his black voodoo, but he took zero responsibility. Instead he pitched himself as a demigod.

When I was in counseling and my daughter was about 16 my counselor told me, "Your daughter is old enough to hear the truth." Up to that point I had never really fully conveyed to my daughter the severity of her father's actions or told her about what I had endured. Telling her truthful facts did not clarify as I had hoped, however. It just confused her more. In angst my daughter screamed at me, "I don't know who to believe. I feel crazy!" At that time my counselor and I had not fully weighed the major indoctrination my ex-husband had seated that left zero room for truth. After she graduated high school her dad sequestered her from me leaving himself uninterrupted time for his statements to go unchallenged and fill her brain with his alienating narcissistic lies. By the time she was 18 and 19 years old it seemed he had performed surgery. He had opened her skull, played with its contents and installed aftermarket parts. I had very rare occasions to talk to her or have any input but on one occasion she did have something to say to me and she delivered it as if it were gospel: "Now I know the truth about you! Dad told me the truth: you are Bipolar and you are crazy! You have been unstable for a long time and you take medicine. You try to control me."

He just employed *projection*, one of those nasty dangling symptoms from that big black Narcissist umbrella. I had heard general whisperings of what he was trying to convince her of, but she laid it out in one big crystalline soundbite. The fictitious bipolar statement was one he then began to spread like strawberry jam for everyone to taste, using his daughter to keep the jar full now that she had embraced his fantasy as fact. Creating a picture of instability would make most people afraid to ask me whether her statements were true.

Just before she divulged her poorly sourced proclamation, my counselor was teaching me the concept of "Not adapting to sickness," something the Carnie had trained me to do. I was sharing this with my youngest daughter, hoping both of us could apply it to achieve better boundaries with her dad, but instead she raised her voice to just below a scream and blasted me, "I am so glad I am getting away from you, so I don't adapt to YOUR sickness!" His venom was running rampant through her veins. I collapsed in grief.

James 3:6 says, "The tongue also is a fire, a world of evil among the parts of the body. It corrupts the whole body, sets the whole course of one's life on fire, and is itself set on fire by hell."

Sometimes God gives us living proof that His scripture is true. Narcissist tongues are a world of evil.

My daughter continued to send me disgusting texts, cursings, accusations, threats, and hateful remarks. Then she disowned me.

One night I got a phone call. I was still awake, plugging along on a work project. Automatically I answered, "Hello?" Then I glanced at the clock on the computer. It was just after midnight. Phone calls after midnight can't be good, they usually mean tragedy or a problem.

I was met with an obviously disguised voice, deep and threatening. My heart raced. "We know what you did, how do you live with yourself? You stole her money. Are you scared? You better watch out, we know where you live." I did not say anything. I listened carefully for background noises and voices. Definitely two people. They finished and hung up. I called the police. I told them I had the phone number because it showed up on my phone screen.

Before they even arrived at my front door, they had traced the number. It originated out of the same town where my daughter lived. That and the phone carrier name they easily traced. They took my case very seriously. While I thought it was my daughter and a friend she had riled up by feeding her friend the same lies she was being force fed, the police left room for a stalker or other crazy threating person. They gave me a case number and told me that one more phone call would be grounds for pursuit and arrest.

What would make a previously normal and loving young girl act this way? Brain Shear. That is a medical term for when brain matter slides within the skull because of rapid acceleration or deceleration. Her father, a Sociopath Narcissist has bombarded her brain with mega meteors of slander and the impact has made her brain shift in her skull. The Carnie then nonchalantly throws in a touch of plausible deniability by sprinkling a pinch of truth to his fiery phenomenon. Truth and lies rock her brain causing whiplash; her brain has been brutally bruised. The breaking and tearing has put unnatural stress on her gray matter. Without all parts working together in normal capacity something falls short and the brain and body can't function or can have deficiencies in function. It results in judgment issues and memory issues. The Carnie has used our daughter like a test dummy, tossing her around in his Narcissistic vehicle. Data for test dummies are used to determine the probability of injury. Her probability of serious injury is 100%. I believe brain shear is a twin to what is happening to my daughter's brain. The intense Sociopath Narcissist lies and selfish actions of her father have caused our daughter's brain to shear. His overwhelming need to control and fabricate to maintain *power over* her has caused her to have not just memory and judgment issues but many other visible issues. She is not the only one who lacks awareness of what is truly happening; there are others, even family members, who simply do not understand the magnitude of the pathology of the true blue Sociopath Narcissist drive and cover tactics. My heart races when I recall the times his tactics made me use poor judgment and when I disregarded truth for *his* version.

Narcissists will often launch an offensive, using information you offered in sacred marital trust or even childlike innocence, to open old wounds, or to make you feel shame or trauma to punish you. They'll use anything they feel will advance their cause, so I should have expected her dad to use personal husband/wife confidences with our daughter to cement his case against me. "She is not as good as she thinks she is," I can almost hear him tell her in a way that would make her believe he was *forced* to share this very personal thing to defend his honor. "I would never tell you this except I just *have to*; you understand, right? Your mom had an abortion!"

I get another phone call. The number that appears on my cell phone screen is my ex-husband's, but it's my youngest daughter's voice I hear. She had not really talked to me for more than two years at that point, so the call surprises me. No small talk; she gets right to it. In a challenging tone, she says, "It's me. Did you have an abortion?"

Intense grief and sadness come over me. "No," I offer strongly, and then softly, if not weakly, "I am not talking to you about that."

She hung up. It would be typical for him to twist our word exchange. "Mom is a liar. She murdered her baby." Why do I use such strong but truthful words? "You murdered your baby" was his defense as to why I should forgive him for his sexual romp with the teenage babysitter. Years before, he had pleaded in a condemning manner, "You have to forgive me; you murdered your baby!" While I was taken back and hurt he would use *that* as a weapon in his warfare tactics to get me to step back under his umbrella of control, I did not let it sway me. It did portray his shear desperation. Desperate for control and power *over me,* he will use any weapon necessary.

> Desperate for control and power over me, he will use any weapon necessary.

When I took my child's life (commonly called abortion) I was young, scared, and at least on some level bought the lie that my baby was just a bunch of cells in the early stages. My more mature, knowledgeable stance on snuffing out a child's life as an answer to an unwanted pregnancy is quite different. Today's technology and sonograms prove it's a baby, not an indiscriminate group of cells. I am compassionate to women who are as fearful as I was when facing an unexpected pregnancy. I am thankful we have a much greater understanding and far more help available than we did forty years ago. By sharing this event in my life that fewer than a handful of people have ever known, I am taking the air out of the Narcissist's balloon. It's not useful as a weapon against me. It is said. I made a choice, one I would not choose today. It does not define who I am or my character like the abuser tries to convince my children and others of.

More than a year after graduation, my daughter made a solo trip to visit some friends we homeschooled with during her high school years. The mom called me and said, "Your daughter was just here. I am so sorry, something is very wrong. I know you so I know these things are not true, but your daughter just said you are mentally ill, bipolar and are on medicine. She told so many stories that sounded *not normal*. I gave her love the best I could."

I explained to my friend a bit about what her father was doing. From the bottom of my heart I thank her and acknowledge her for being healthy enough, brave enough, and mature enough to call me directly. I thank her for knowing nothing my daughter said was true. In reference to my ex-husband she said, "I met him once and all I can say is he is *interesting*." That was her being polite! She asked, "What can I do to help?"

I said, "Let me think about it."

By the time I got back to her, I had no chance to offer any suggestions. She said, "My husband said I can't get involved." I said, "I understand." I do understand. This does not have a quick fix, because Sociopath Narcissist are not fixable.

Sometimes people leave wiggle room for the abuse. They are influenced by the abusers soft-pedal of actual events. I do not think the Bible does and I do not believe GOD does.

Colossians 3:19 (ESV)
"Husbands, love your wives, and do not be harsh with them."

Psalm 11:5 (ESV)
"The Lord tests the righteous, but his soul hates the wicked and the one who loves violence."

1 Peter 3:7 (ESV)
"Likewise, husbands, live with your wives in an understanding way, showing honor to the woman as the weaker vessel, since they are heirs with you of the grace of life, so that your prayers may not be hindered."

Galatians 5:19-21 (ESV)
"Now the works of the flesh are evident: sexual immorality, impurity, sensuality, idolatry, sorcery, enmity, strife, jealousy, fits of anger, rivalries, dissensions, divisions, envy, drunkenness, orgies, and things like these. I warn you, as I warned you before, that those who do such things will not inherit the kingdom of God."

2 Timothy 3:1-8 (ESV)
"But understand this, that in the last days there will come times of difficulty. For people will be lovers of self, lovers of money, proud, arrogant, abusive, disobedient to their parents, ungrateful, unholy, heartless, unappeasable, slanderous, without self-control, brutal, not loving good, treacherous, reckless, swollen with conceit, lovers of pleasure rather than lovers of God, having the appearance of godliness, but denying its power. Avoid such people. ..."

Dr. Richard A. Gardner wrote something I experienced firsthand: "The child's campaign against the parent is without merit, but the child absorbs all the untruths the alienating parent plants." My daughter's visit to our homeschool friend's home where she confidently informed her friend's family that I was bipolar, crazy, and on medicine, is a prime example of a child absorbing the alienating parent's fabrications. Another drop I can add to that pool of examples is a time my daughter talked to two pastors serving in the same local church and she laid out her accusation against me. They told me they realized the accusations were outrageous, some not even believable, especially since they know me. My daughters indoctrination is so deep that she thinks it's infallible and sympathy worthy. Sadly, she spreads it like wildfire, which fills her growing need for attention by accepting sympathy for her supposedly sick mother.

One of my other children decided to have a conversation with their indoctrinated sister. It did not go well. "Mom, it was frightening how incited she got. As soon as I mentioned you, her countenance changed, her voice raised, and she got demonstratively mean and angry. It was scary. I stopped because it was so weird." To entertain positive thoughts about me, my daughter would have to perform mental gymnastics to wind her way through the insurmountable mountain of misinformation. Instead she shut down the voice of truth to quell her inner tempest.

Dr. Gardner goes on to say that Parental Alienation Syndrome is more than brainwashing or programming because the child has to participate in the denigrating of the alienated parent. This is done primarily in the following eight ways:

- The child denigrates the alienated parent with foul language and severe oppositional behavior.
- The child offers weak, absurd, or frivolous reasons for his or her anger.
- The child is sure of himself or herself and doesn't demonstrate ambivalence (i.e., love and hate for the alienated parent), only hate.
- The child exhorts that he or she alone came up with ideas of denigration. The independent-thinker phenomenon is where the child asserts that no one told him or her to do this.
- The child supports and feels a need to protect the alienating parent.
- The child does not demonstrate guilt over cruelty toward the alienated parent.
- The child uses borrowed scenarios, or vividly described situations that he or she could not have experienced.
- Animosity is spread to the alienated parent's friends or extended family.

It distresses me that I can check each of these as well-worn. Some of you may recognize I have shared examples of these in prior pages, but I have more. My daughter once told me she was not going to see me anymore because she was afraid of me. I asked, "Have I ever hit you, pinched you, or abused you in any way?"

She got quiet. She tipped her head, appearing to think deeply. Then she offered with a whisper of the assertion she had just used to accuse me, in almost a question rather than a statement, "Once, when I was eight you pulled my hair?" That is the second bullet point in action. "Don't blame dad for me not seeing you. You are the reason I am not seeing you; you are to blame" is bullet point four in action via a text message. Texts were always particularly foul: "I don't need your love as I hate you and could care less about you. I am reporting you to the police. You are not my mother anymore. Why don't you go F*** yourself? It'll relive some stress." Bullet point one in action.

The more I research, the more concrete evidence and understanding there is for the evil my ex-husband holds so dear. It is comforting in some realm that all his actions have names. How can a Narcissist-obsessed parent be effective in erasing a child's love for a parent who showed the child only love and not abuse? MajorFamilyServices.com quotes these five things:

(1) Relentlessly bad-mouthing the target parent's character, in order to reduce his or her importance and value

(2) Creating the impression that the target parent is dangerous and plans to hurt the child, in order to instill fear and rejection of that parent

(3) Deceiving children about the target parent's feelings for them, in order to create hurt, resentment, and psychological distance

(4) Withdrawing love if the child indicated affection or positive regard for the target parent, in order to heighten the need to please the alienating parent

(5) Erasing the other parent from the life and mind of the child through minimizing actual and symbolic contact (Baker 2007)

These points are an amazingly accurate description of my circumstances and what my ex-husband has achieved. The Carnie is a stellar student, achieving an A plus. A Narcissist with OCD would never accept a B.

Dr. Frank Williams, a child psychiatrist, describes the goal of cutting a parent out of a child's life as a *parentectomy*. In these cases, a child will succumb to the alienator's programming or brainwashing and experience fear, anger, and hatred toward the target parent. When parental alienation is severe enough, children have no choice but to align with the disturbed parent against the target parent, thus destroying their relationship with the target parent.

In 2017 social media posts proved my daughter was having a banner year in the company of her Narcissistic father. She posted "Happy Father's Day to the man who helped me become the woman I am today." The truth of that statement makes my knees buckle and tears flow. Truly, she does not understand the horrific scope of that statement. One of my children reached out to me after reading that, "Wow, if she only understood what she was saying. She is a mess because of him!" Today she is mentally unstable, has trouble defining fact from fiction, seeks attention from the wrong places, claims a multitude of unsubstantiated illnesses and makes medically impossible claims.

While my ex-husband was busy mangling our daughter's psyche, which I was helpless to prevent, I was busy working and checking a few things off my bucket list. My life adventures rubbed against the Narcissist's grain and had an unbearable sting. I was supposed to be incapacitated, financially devastated and already back in his arms. His ire was palatable and I was not even in his presence. I knew it well. So in last quarter of 2017 when the news headlines proclaimed a slew of sexual molestation charges it provided the Narcissist timely fodder for his next bamboozle. He persuaded our daughter I sexually molested her. It was an easy slide; he had already laid the groundwork. She quickly took to social media to claim her dramatic Harvey Weinstein-esq # Me Too story. This fabrication was carefully crafted in the Carnies workshop, and then sold at the high price of our daughter's sanity. If using our daughter causes my destruction, it is a price he has already rationalized as justified. The Carnie is her script writer and puppeteer but he knows his student will garnish the story on her own and then he can claim no blame. His social media response to being called a great father by the victim of his Sociopath Narcissistic whirlwind was this, "The obstacles and challenges that you faced and successfully overcame were not stumbling blocks but stepping stones for you. I am proud of the woman you have become." He affirmed, took credit and even pride that his Sociopathic indoctrination took root and flourished abundantly. One of the dead giveaways that her Carnie was the source of her script in her *#Me Too* social media rant was, "My mother had to con my dad into having sex to conceive me." This of course made the Narcissist a victim, an all too common ploy. The Carnie's script had her claiming I demanded half dozen sonograms during one of my pregnancies and I threw a tantrum in the doctor's office. A few sensible friends offered, "That was stupid, what insurance company pays for 6 sonograms just because you want them?" In my daughters immaturity she could not process that I used the same doctor for all my kids and no physician would keep you in his practice if you threw a screaming tantrum in their office. She willing takes every Narcissist morsel as truth and regurgitates them without regard for her own reputation.

> If using our daughter causes my destruction, it is a price he has already rationalized as justified.

Dear Younger Me

The Sociopath breathes deep and exhales a Narcissistic breeze. Take cover. Don't expose yourself or throw your arms open wide to breathe in or receive his blowing wind. It will contaminate your whole body, inside and out. Don't let youth or immaturity keep you from bundling up and shielding yourself.

Chapter 18

Unsuspecting Participants

My daughter's melodic voice blessed her with the opportunity to participate in many local and well-known national singing competitions. After that whirlwind settled, she lent her voice to local venues needing entertainment. A young man at one of these venues took a fancy to my daughter while she was still living home. This young man's mom enjoyed the new girlfriend's companionship a bit too much; I had some unease about conversations she shared. My daughter, too young at seventeen, and enjoying the attention too much, could not grasp the inappropriateness of being used as a confidant by a nearly sixty-year-old woman. Let's call her Andrea.

Hearing intimate and personal details about Andrea's marriage and family dynamics made my daughter feel special. When I explained that healthy adults don't share these kinds of details, my daughter offered, "I told her she should be your friend."

According to my daughter, Andrea started the sharing of intimate details with, "Don't tell anyone, not even your mom." About a year later, when the Carnie laid the beautifully wrapped mental illness package at his daughter's feet as if it were a classified hushed secret he had been honorably keeping since she was born, she ran to Andrea. Now they were bonding over mutual dysfunctions.

It wasn't long, as I predicted my daughter could not afford her apartment, that Andrea invited my eighteen-year-old virginal daughter to live in her house, along with her husband and son, an only child. My questioning was met with, "Well, she has nowhere to go and she told me you threw her out." Then she added these exact words: "My son is a good boy; nothing will happen."

I offered the obvious: "But you are not home with them all the time; you work."

In an uppity defensive tone I heard, "Oh, you're telling me I won't know what's going on in my own home."

My daughter eventually confessed to the sexual activity that went on right under Andrea's nose. Down the road my daughter and Andrea's son broke up but Andrea let my daughter stay in her home and dismissed her son's fury. Andrea liked having a pretend daughter too much to let her go; she bought her clothes, took her for manicures, bought her more than one car, paid her car insurance, and even put her cell phone on her plan. Her husband was on board with most of this. He was there for the purchase of the first car, which was posted on a popular social media site.

During one of the times I ran into Andrea she told me, "I *had* to buy her a car since you didn't step up to buy her one."

At another unexpected meeting she told me, "You should give me money toward everything I have spent on her."

My last conversation was two years ago and lasted three hours while standing in front of a local food store. She made it clear to me she had created a rationalization and false narrative she could live with. She was my daughter's codependent rescuer and liked it. I pondered whether my daughter would be angry with her someday when she realized Andrea was not protecting her.

A few days later I saw her son and said in a peaceful and nice tone since we were in a public place, "Please look me up and call me when you are thirty-five. That's about when you will be ready to understand and apologize for what you did to my daughter."

Soon after these two events, which happened back to back, Andrea texted me, "I thought we had come to some kind of understanding; good to know I just wasted three hours." I think her understanding is I am out and she is in. She was angry because I held her adult son accountable for his behavior. I thought I had done it in a nice way. I could think of a few other scenarios that would not have ended in kind words.

"Do not rescue her; she needs to have these life lessons before coming back to the top" was the counselor's advice to me. Andrea was not on board with this advice. Instead she allowed my daughter to live rent free, chore free, and carefree. During our three-hour chance meeting I queried Andrea, "Do you give my daughter any domestic tasks to do?"

"I don't feel that is my job to make her do chores; she should have learned that at home." It was stated as a put down, but I did not allow it to land.

My daughter began to date another guy while still living at Andrea's house. Let's call him James. She left Andrea's house to attend college. She lived on campus and dated James. Andrea did not let the relationship naturally dissipate; she chose to stay emotionally entrenched. I got a small glimpse into one of the tools of emotional entrenchment when I received several emails from her directed to my daughter but sent to me whether she intended to do so or not. One shared Andrea's medical diagnosis, including a video from her doctor. "Honey, just in case you want to and have time to listen to what *Dr. Smith* said to us individually at our 11/10 appt. xoxo." She said *us* because her sibling received the same potentially terminal diagnosis and they were both being treated at the same well-known hospital.

My daughter shared with me that she went to the hospital to see Andrea and ran into her son. "She is my mother; what are you doing here?" was his greeting. Oddly, I read a tinge of enjoyment in my daughter at creating havoc and that bothered me. He was ignorant that his mother had adopted my daughter as his sister and that blinded him to see that his mom had extended her the same visitation rights.

Andrea traveled to visit my daughter at college, brought her food, and continued to pay her bills. Andrea started to be secretive about her visits with my daughter to quell her son's dissatisfaction and still does. She told me, "My son does not get to choose my friends."

My daughter married James. They went to the local city hall with no parent's knowledge, permission, consent, or blessing. My daughter quit college and they moved forty minutes in another direction, but Andrea still wanted her mother status. So she visited, attended my daughter's singing events, brought her and her new husband food, and purchased furniture for them. My daughter often flaunted these things on social media and her four siblings were as bewildered as I was.

I provided Andrea with my ex-husband's multiple letters of confession. She heard my cries, saw my tears and grief, but refused to give up her mantle. Interestingly, Andrea shares my birthday and marks the day with my daughter. Andrea emailed after one of our talks, "I will tell you that it always dumbfounded me how your ex-husband was your biggest supporter, correcting [daughter] anytime she had something disparaging to say about you. He always sang your praises and repeated to [daughter] what a good mother you have been and gave specific examples."

> He is juggling his image, moving the curtain as needed to veil his true actions.

Dumbfounded is a good word. Andrea is watching his carnival show. He is juggling his image, moving the curtain as needed to veil his true actions. My daughter faithfully parrots the script her father has given her, but if anyone gets too close to his con, he is forced to quickly move both of them off script. That juggle caused Andrea's confusion.

The same happens to my daughter as she tries to decipher which position her ringmaster is working from so she can know which version of her mom she is supposed to present and when. "Does my mom love me? Is she mentally ill? Evil? Or wonderful and praiseworthy?" It will depend on which club the juggler has in the air and how fast he throws it. His cascade can be forward or backward. He just wants it to be smooth; a misstep can tarnish his image. Sometimes he just tosses the club a bit higher until the observant eye moves on, then catches it and continues his show.

All four parents were heartbroken when social media reported our children married on Friday December 12, 2014. The four of us had started meeting in November of 2014 to brain storm how to help our wayward kids. They were both worked for a Christian institution, so we committed to get together and pray for our children once a month. I really did not want to include my ex-husband in the meetings but suffered through the discomfort. Our first meeting was at my home at my large cherry dining room table. The seven-hour meeting was fueled by a nice assortment of snacks, fruits, and beverages. A few hours into the meeting, James's mom joyfully announced, "Wow, you are really nice and very normal."

"What were you expecting?" I asked.

"Well, your daughter warned us you are bipolar, crazy, unstable, and on medicine."

I said, "That is not true, but thank you for letting me know what she is saying. I am sorry you had to hear that."

Astonishment overtook both of their faces. James's father tilted his head, leaned toward me for emphasis. Making sure to have total eye contact with me, he asked me very directly, "So, you have never been diagnosed with mental illness or are on medicine for mental illness?"

I said, "No, I never have."

Turning my head to the right, looking to my ex-husband but addressing everyone, I said, "But he has. He tells her these lies." My ex-husband did not flinch; he was very comfortable with his lie. The Bible teacher and preacher disregarded Exodus 20:16 that says, "You shall not give false testimony against your neighbor" and Ephesians 4:29, which says, "Let no corrupt communication proceed out of your mouth, but that which is good to the use of edifying, that it may minister grace to the hearers."

I suggested it would be helpful for my daughter to work with truthful information. "My ex-husband needs to come clean about his never-ending stream of lies." A hornet's nest had just revealed itself and I could see James's parents desperately wanted to sidestep it.

I could read their question: "I thought this guy was a Christian."

I requested the letter be run by the three of us before presenting it. The Narcissist skipped fault or embarrassment and went straight to hero. With pride he offered, "I can do this; I'll be as honest as possible to help my daughter. I'll get to it right away; this will really help her." Taking this stance, he perceived his image would be unscathed.

Future meetings did not reflect being taken down a notch. Denial of spreading lies was firm until these outsiders held his feet to the fire. Had it been just me, I would have gotten tossed by blame and diversion.

> The Narcissist skipped fault or embarrassment and went straight to hero.

The goal was for the new in-laws to hand deliver the letter of confession to the newlyweds, who lived with them for a short time. Anxiously waiting for just the right moment for her to be mentally prepared for its contents, I never did hear if it happened or if the Carnie's pastor got a copy. I forwarded his email containing the letter to key people so it could not be discounted and I am sharing the December 2014 letter here.

Dear Younger Me,

Narcissists have no moral compass and no shame. They are self-deceived. Absorb these facts; they are critical in maintaining boundaries. Never put yourself in the presence of the Narcissist and think you have an ally. Because they are Sociopaths, they will create a problem and then swoop in to rescue. It makes a good story for them to tell. Be on high alert. The self-centered Narcissist is a roaring lion looking for whom he can devour. Don't be on the menu. Be vigilant.

In January 2015 my daughter discovered I had visited with her new in-laws. She began to send me a barrage of questions and some threatening texts. In her mixed-up mental state she convinced herself I should know nothing about her life circumstances in spite of the fact she posted every nuance of her life on many forms of social media. Her questionable scenarios and outlandish stories regularly blurted with no filter would spur a half dozen people to contact me for clarification, the rest were able to figure out fact from fiction without my input. Because she believed her behavior was *normal* she could not grasp that her siblings would not be communicating their concerns to me as well. My cell phone displayed 11 consecutive incoming calls and dozens of texts from my youngest daughter, yet she was convinced *I* was harassing her. The following separate texts are all from my daughter.

> My cell phone displayed 11 consecutive incoming calls and dozens of texts from my youngest daughter, yet she was convinced I was harassing her.

You are a stalker
Did you hire a personal investigator to spy on me?
Who did you hire?
So, did you pay someone?
Stop ignoring my calls!!! I have the right to talk to you
If you have nothing to hide then face me
You love control so much don't you?
Get away from me and my family
I am reporting you to the police for stalking unless you talk to me.
You are not my mother and will not be ever again. You are a creepy stalker.
I will be filing as soon as possible.
I don't need your love as I hate you and could care less about you.
Enjoy your miserable life.

To help you understand the roller coaster of confusion the Carnie commanded, let me first share an email sent to me in March 2014 before I share the Carnie's December 2014 response. This note expresses his heartfelt apologies for previous less-than-honorable conduct, but while confessing to one ignoble act, he actively juggled a myriad of others in his attempt at personal and parental character assignation.

(I have omitted some words to permit anonymity.)

Dear [Author],

The landlord at church failed to renew the lease. Everything needed to be moved to a new location in only a week's time. The reason I am sharing this is that through this arduous experience, I came to realize and appreciate how organized you were for our move from the North to the South, and the enormous amount of work that you accomplished for the move. I am saddened and deeply grieved that because of my OCD at that time that instead of treating you with the dignity, respect, and appreciation that you rightfully deserve, I was stressed out, overwhelmed, and mean spirited. Although it is ten years too late, I offer my humble, heartfelt apologies.

Signed, [Ex-husband]

In this 2011 note he professes he did not treat me with the dignity, respect, or the appreciation I deserve. His thought disorder totally disconnects that while he is asking for forgiveness for treating me poorly, this behavior is currently unceasing and prolific. This is part of his dissociative disorder. The contents of this note and supposed heartfelt feelings are conceived in his Sociopath Narcissist art studio and rise out of the creative juices of a lunatic artist. It's here that he paints canvases that portray me as retarded, unforgiving, a mental cripple, unloving, a heathen (2010), crazed, a liar, unsaved, mentally unstable, insecure, unable to love, an inadequate mother (2011), and a medicated bipolar crazy person to be feared (2013-2014). His canvases are usually strategically showcased, so he was not counting on being unveiled in front of his new Christian in-laws.

Faking repentance and pretending this was a slip of a brush stroke rather than the stamp on all his artistry let him calmly offer to be part of the solution for the problem he created. His only retribution was to confess to his lousy work when a mental facility or jail would have been more fitting. One last point that cries out to be revealed in his note:

by adding *at that time* to his admission of OCD, he is minimizing his lifelong dysfunction.

The following is his less-than-full disclosure account of his slander.

December 2014

Dear [Daughter],

I am writing to you because you need to know the truth, which I was either too mentally imbalanced or self-serving to reveal to you before now. I have no other agenda than taking the first painful step to reveal to you the awful, warped, and harmful things that I have said to you that have destroyed your relationship with your mother and harmed you mentally and emotionally.

Before I begin with specific examples of the lies and exaggerations, which I, being self-deceived, even believed to be true and were not, I know there is no reason for you to trust or believe me now. That is why I have put this information in writing and I am sharing this letter with [James's] parents and your mother. The purpose is that you know that I am being held accountable and cannot deny or rationalize away the truth, which I am about to share with you.

In hindsight, I realize the evil that I committed by not supporting your mother, who attempted to raise you with healthy boundaries, which were in your best interests. I painted her as controlling, when she was actually being caring and protective of her little girl. If you complained about one of her rules, I agreed with you to win your favor. How foolish and selfish of me to cause a wedge between the two of you. What kind of a father would provoke his daughter to rebel and belittle her own mother? Sadly, the answer is a loathsome and self-centered one.

I portrayed your mother to you as having mental issues and being emotionally incapable of loving you. In actuality, it was I who had severe emotional and mental issues. In my corrupt mental processes, I assumed that since your mother didn't love me that she could not love anyone.

The truth is that your mother did love me until my pattern of physical and emotional abuse destroyed that love she had for me.

I was also wrong concerning your Social Security Benefits payments. Your mother kept a detailed account of your Social Security income expenditures. Half of the money paid for your trips, vocal lessons, gifts you purchased, personal items, and so forth, while the other half went toward your support. She was a very good steward of the funds entrusted to her. Your mother has always worked and had an income. Any money that she has given to your brothers was her money.

Your mother always loved you. You were the baby girl that she always wanted. She nurtured you from birth and demonstrated her love by breastfeeding you. Your mother always made an effort to make "special memories." Whether it was simply a day at a park, a family vacation, Thanksgiving, or an event where you were singing, every occasion was sure to be photographed and scrapbooked. When it came to your birthday, she took hours to make special hand-made cards, posters, signs, decorate the dining room table, make you a special breakfast, and bake you a cake. Your mother homeschooled you, enrolled you in voice lessons, took you to church, and numerous other activities while working part-time and doing all the many chores required to keep your home clean and comfortable. She always gave you hugs and kisses and told you how much she loved you. Your mother still, and always will, love you.

Therefore, as God's chosen people, holy and dearly loved, clothe yourselves with compassion, kindness, humility, gentleness, and patience. Bear with each other and forgive one another if any of you has a grievance against someone. Forgive as the Lord forgave you. And over all these virtues put on love, which binds them all together in perfect unity. Colossians 3:12-14

With deepest regret and sincerest apology,

Daddy

My daughter-in-law read her husband's father's words and said, "He has not gone far enough. This is only a good start." She is very smart. Upon rereading his letter, I was taken by the fact that by his own words he has defined himself as having NPD. Of course it is the rest of his actions he does not note in this particular letter that clarifies and rounds out the diagnosis. He describes his behavior using the same terms that are seen in medical definitions of Narcissism and NPD, including projection. Here he also confesses to physically abusing me, something he has tried at different times to discount. His confessions cause absolutely no change in his behavior, but the acts he committed and confesses to are all true.

Soon after he wrote this December 2014 letter, he called to challenge me about the use of the Social Security money addressed in the letter. He negated his typed words of trust and proper stewardship during his ear-to-ear questioning. He wanted an excuse to loop me into his Narcissistic wrong thinking and weave blame and doubt. Although I did not realize it then, these are the exact tactics noted in books about abusive men.

> ...he is confessing to operating a 24/7 slander café, percolating and serving lies to anyone who graced his presence.

In this letter, he is confessing to operating a 24/7 slander café, percolating and serving lies to anyone who graced his presence. This café has been open for years, serving naive and unaware patrons. While his forked tongue disparaged me at every turn, he thought the following words and accompanying passionate plea would pull at my heart strings: "You know, I always thought we would get back together and have that miracle story to tell. I pictured us giving our testimony and telling our story in front to the church of the marriage that God saved."

Perhaps, like me, his actions can allow you visualize this word picture. A man stands before you; one hand is lovingly caressing your arm while delivering words that warm you, while the other arm is nonchalantly tucked behind. You feel safe; you allow yourself to enjoy the comfort of the gentle expressions flowing from his mouth. Then at that exact instant his concealed arm swings forward, yielding a freshly sharpened switchblade that filets your solar plexus, leaving you to hemorrhage on the floor while he strolls away claiming innocence.

Titus 3:1-2 (NIV)
"…be ready to do whatever is good, to slander no one, to be peaceable and considerate, and always to be gentle toward everyone."

In April 2015, just a few months after his December 2014 confession, the Carnie tried to take me on a wide fan turn. He tried to wiggle out of a binding email agreement by telling me it was not witnessed. His fear tactics don't work on me anymore, so when I responded with proof, strength, and logic, he backed down. Laughably, he told me, "I will no longer be offering you Christian charity" when informing me he was not going to honor what he promised even though he was legally required to provide part of that.

Dear Younger Me,

Abusers try to engage you in conversation – any topic will do. As you are trying to disengage, step away, and get healthy, they will throw out "bait" to see how they can catch you and reel you in. They feel that any talk, whether positive or negative, is a connection, and therefore, success.

Do not take their bait. They want you to step into their fantasy world again. They persist in trying to find a crack in the door – any door.

It's a big concept to grasp, but you have to learn it. You can resist, say no, and still be Christian in your refusal. The book Boundaries by Townsend and Cloud will help you learn about healthy boundaries.

My ex-husband ended his December 2014 letter with a scripture. He uses scripture to subliminally demand what he wants shown to him, then scripture to abuse, and then scripture to ask forgiveness for the abuse. This is his spiritual abuse cycle. In Henrietta Mears' timeless book *What The Bible Is All About,* she states, "If anyone thinks he is a Christian but does not control his tongue this man's religion is worthless. The religion that does not influence the tongue is not a vital or true one." My ex-husband put forward this scripture to tell us we should show him kindness, yet these mentioned attributes, typical of my subversive ex-husband, are the exact adjective actions he has failed to exhibit toward his children and me. He lacked compassion, lacked kindness, lacked gentleness, lacked patience. He most definitely did not show love. Those who have NPD and yet claim to be Christians easily disregard scriptural precepts; they lie and bear false testimony to maintain position. Their personal elevated position is more important than a scriptural position.

Proverbs 12:22
"Lying lips are an abomination to the LORD: but they that deal truthfully are his delight."

Luke 17:2, Matthew 18:6, and Mark 9:42 deliver this precept: there should be a millstone tied around the neck of someone who causes His child to stumble, and that person should be drowned in the depths of the sea.

A millstone is huge, much like the weight of the Carnie's lies that have caused all our children, but especially our youngest daughter, to stumble and fall.

The book of James covers the concept of being in control of our tongues, and leaders and teachers are even more accountable to God for their words and actions. My ex-husband self-claims both these titles. James explains a small bridle can turn a huge animal. The rudder can turn a huge ship.

James 3:3-6
"When we put bits into the mouths of horses to make them obey us, we can turn the whole animal. Or take ships as an example. Although they are so large and are driven by strong winds, they are steered by a

very small rudder wherever the pilot wants to go. Likewise, the tongue is a small part of the body, but it makes great boasts. Consider what a great forest is set on fire by a small spark. The tongue also is a fire, a world of evil among the parts of the body. It corrupts the whole body, sets the whole course of one's life on fire, and is itself set on fire by hell."

James 3:9-11
"With the tongue we praise our Lord and Father, and with it we curse human beings, who have been made in God's likeness. Out of the same mouth come praise and cursing. My brothers and sisters, this should not be. Can both fresh water and salt water flow from the same spring?"

These verses admonish us for being double-minded with our mouths and words. In real-life vernacular it is saying, "Hey, Carnie, you just preached a sermon at your church in the morning and taught a Bible study in the evening but then told some big lies about your ex-wife to a bunch of people. That's evil, don't you think? You know the scripture says your ex-wife is made in the image of God and you are letting lying and praising come out of your mouth at the same time? This should not be." Another version of this would be "Hey, Carnie, you have been telling everyone the reason for your divorce is 'She is not forgiving.' You know that is not true. What's up with that?"

The goal of learning God's precepts is to help align our thoughts and words to God's expectations. Sometimes it takes years to model ourselves after these new concepts. Bridles for Narcissists won't stay in place; they throw them off. My ex-husband's bridle is nonexistent. His Narcissism will not allow the scripture to take hold and change his character. It's why you cannot trust Sociopath Narcissists; they will say one thing and do another.

The book of James in the Bible even covers the subject of favoritism. He says, "Don't do it!" I am going to apply this thought a bit differently. This will take some mental acuity on your part as you follow the way an abuser would misuse this concept. My ex-husband has claimed I am guilty of showing favoritism toward one of my sons to help give substance to his often-repeated declaration that I don't love the child he is currently showing favoritism to. Informing my daughter, "Your mother doesn't love you; she only loves your brother who looks like her," he invites her to be comfortable in repeating it to others. He selfishly fills his loneliness as they bond over this *truth*. They feel emotionally close because she is his favorite. While showing this favoritism to my daughter, he effortlessly slides in his parental alienation statement, "I am the only one who loves and understands you." He insists everything he says is true and presents his credentials of Bible teacher and author as his evidence. Any reservation is quelled by his reassurance, "I am in leadership at church and they would not let me teach and preach if I was not telling the truth."

His favorited child assumes every morsel is gospel because she has heard church leaders and members disparage her mother too. An alienated child believes, "If my mom doesn't love me, I have to choose someone else to love me." This false concept secretly planted in her subconscious has caused her to bounce from guy to guy, looking for love and letting Andrea usurp my position.

This has all been particularly heartbreaking. As a teen she and I attended many mother-daughter conferences on dating and purity. Her weekly girls' group called Bright Lights placed emphasis on valuing yourself, character building, and growing your gifts. Sweet memories were made at Strong in the LORD and the Radiant Purity Conferences. She and I adored the sand drawings they created that were projected onto a big screen. During the Revolve Tour for teens, she heard author Chad Eastham speak and reveled at his on point spiel, which led her to read many of his books. My daughter's laughter and engagement in the activities were such a joy to take in at that conference!

> It was so important to him that he destroy me that if he destroyed our daughter in the process it was of no consequence.

I did not realize during these teenage years I was swimming upstream. I was building, but behind my back the Carnie father was tearing down. It was so important to him that he destroy me that if he destroyed our daughter in the process it was of no consequence. It is why one of my counselors introduced me to the book *People of the Lie* by Scott Peck. In my opinion my ex-husband, based on my documented personal experience, is an example of *People of the Lie*.

Before my daughter was indoctrinated, she was kind, sweet, loving, happy, and she loved and respected me. She and I went to Bible study and we attended church together. Here are some examples of the love she expressed to me prior to my ex-husband's Parental Alienation:

To my darling and dear mother, I love you!

Thank you is so much less than you deserve today, dear Mom; I love you! You always ground me when my brain is nowhere to be found.

Happy 50th birthday, Mom! May God Bless you and keep you and make His face to shine upon you and give you a long, joyous life. Momma, thank you so much for being there for me and for putting up with me. I know it must be hard to be a mom and I want to let you know how much I appreciate it. Besides, it's pretty dang awesome that I have the coolest momma around. You are great, grand, and awesome and are doing a GREAT, FANTASTIC job raising me. I love you so very much and hold you dear to my heart. If I ever said anything different than that throughout the years, forgive me 'cuz I must have been pms'ing to not think what I do now! I am so glad that we have grown closer over the years and that I am getting to know you better. I love you! Have a great birthday. I hope you put the gift to good use! I love you!

My daughter has been in a fierce storm for many years now. You can see her manic ride when she posts on social media. It causes many to ask, "What is wrong with her that she posts crazy stuff?" She also posts things that are clearly not true, highly exaggerated and dramatic. I offer these small tidbits without oversharing because my ultimate goal for my daughter is to heal, not to push her away. But these subtleties are important to note. I can't help others, including my family, to learn without saying some things that might sting at first, but can ultimately bring understanding and healing.

In an effort to use some discretion I am leaving out certain details that can stay in my journal and probably forever in this momma's crushed heart. During my time in counseling, it was requested I read John Oldham and Lois Morris's book *New Personality Self-Portrait: Why You Think, Work, Love, and Act The Way You Do*. When arriving at the section about the personality disorder continuum charting, when a *style* becomes a *disorder,* we spent some time there. She had a few things she wanted me to discover on my own regarding my youngest daughter.

With this new information, I was led to question whether my daughter had chosen *this* as a coping mechanism because of the Narcissist's excessive efforts. Had she crossed from a style to a disorder? Dramatic to Histrionic? Had the abuser's unending lies, misinformation, covert and overt abuse crumbled her in places we can't see? The body has to pick something to cope. My body chose migraines and then teeth grinding. Much like my two responses resolved, I am hoping my daughter can have resolution too. She has spent at least *eight intense* years under the Narcissist's plethora of maladaptive behaviors; many of those were teen growth years where he isolated her.

In 2014 a psychiatrist who was not aware or recognized she was being abused by her Sociopath Narcissist-disordered father, placed my daughter on medications. The treatment should have been to remove her father and get her intense counseling. Instead the psychiatrist put her on excessive doses of psychotropic drugs and every single negative side effect you hear quickly whispered at the end of the pharmaceutical TV commercials happened. It took her body a year to recover from the severe effects, and I believe some of those effects still linger though she has relabeled them to something else.

This is the slushy mess, along with a divorce from James that an unsuspecting new character stepped into. Let's call him Sam. Sam wanted to help save our daughter from this storm. There is a system of tornado watches and warnings used to alert the public to danger. This system gives people in the storm's path time to get to safety. I wish there was a system to alert someone like Sam that he was about to be spun into the eye of a Narcissistic storm. At the very least he should be able to read the safety pamphlet so he knows what he is dealing with. This man was about to enter the outer bands of the storm with limited information provided by a faulty system: the voice of a Sociopath Narcissist.

From what I know, Sam is a nice guy, married, has time on his hands, and is friends with the Narcissist. Sam takes great compassion on our daughter; after all, his friend said and his daughter agrees that her mother is mentally ill and does not love her. Sam is all in. He will help however he can. His Bible-believing friend said it and his daughter, the victim of successful Parental Alienation, backs it up. Sam is comfortable with the facts. He is going to help rescue her from her bad decisions; it's the least he can do to help.

He reflects back, perhaps with a tear in his eye, about the sweet little girl who used to play in the pet shop he managed, who now stood before him lost and in shambles. She has been through an EF5 tornado, and he wants to help with the restoration. What Sam does not know is that the EF5 tornado was created and hand spun like a cotton candy roll at the county fair by his good friend. The Carnie is allowing his altruistic friend to step in and try to fix his unconfessed destruction. Sam will build by the day, book her at venues to sing, drive her to national contests, and treat her to special things.

The Narcissist, however, will tear it all down by night. Our daughter will sing nice and smile big, but where it counts in her inner health, her mish-moshed mind, there will be no healing. Unless the man who is spinning the storm is made to stop, the tornado will never be called, "All clear."

Chapter 19

A Sociopath as a Husband and a Father

Being a husband or a father has never stopped the Carnie's from his need to rob people of reality. He is a special kind of thief, slick, cunning and tricky. He does not steal glittery things from a jeweler's case but he lifts truth right out situations and circumstances. He creates fantasy fakes, replicated without license or conscience. His knockoffs are good. They are not recognizable right off the bat. Not to the naked eye, or to the innocent victims or the blissfully unaware friends in the circle or on the fringe. Genuine articles of truth have been watered down, rebranded, remolded, rephrased and replicated and he is prepared to swear on a Bible his lies are real.

Sociopath behavior does not consist of a single trait. Sociopathy is a syndrome, a whole cluster of symptoms related to each other, many of which I have cited as examples through my ex-husband's actions. They demonstrate a pattern of disregard that is pervasive, particularly in terms of the feelings and rights of others. Sociopaths can be

> Sociopaths can be charming and intelligent, but they lack remorse, guilt, or shame because their brains don't contain the proper wiring.

charming and intelligent, but they lack remorse, guilt, or shame because their brains don't contain the proper wiring. The Carnie occasionally let remorse show through, but it wasn't there to stay. The show evaporated quickly. Like my ex-husband, all Sociopaths hate to lose, which can lead to them defending their lies at all costs. They simply want to control and dominate. They may exaggerate wildly in their lies, but somehow make their absurd tales seem believable. Sociopaths are delusional to the extent they think things they say become truth just because they say them and the more they say them the truer they must be. I believe my accounts have given you some factual examples.

In 2010 one of my adult children's friends placed a complimentary remark about me on social media. There ensued some silly banter between the grad school college friends. Even my son chimed in with a funny observation. Suddenly a bucket of ice was thrown on the warm banter. The Narcissist entered and wrangled in the conversation. While I had been legally separated from him for nine years at that point and had zero relationship and limited conversation, he weirdly demanded, "You have offended my wife and you owe her a public apology." His Narcissistic ego created that story and hoped everyone would bandwagon to it. Then he threw in some scripture for good measure: "Do not covet another man's wife – even if you have lusted in your heart you have sinned." He picked projection and control as his symptoms of the day. Observers surely joined me in my oft-repeated statement, "What just happened?" Demonstrating his acumen in his sociopath Narcissist flip of facts to fit his fancy, while claiming on social media that I was his wife, in that same window of time he told our daughter he was going to marry another woman whom he had been dating. (I described this in *Destruction of my daughter*.) His lack of conscious did not allow him to register that hypocrisy.

Projection is a subconscious defense mechanism where someone takes their own negative feelings they have about themselves and imagines that they belong to someone else. In December 2017, I was with my son and his friend when I had a rare encounter with the Narcissist. He accused me, "Our daughter is having seizures because you poked her arm during your homeschooling and now no one can touch her arm or she has a seizure." He accused me of something *he* actually did, quite regularly. My youngest son, who is becoming more astute about Narcissistic behavior, was immediately able to recognize what happened. He told me, "Mom. you don't do that, Dad does". When in the trenches with a Narcissist a good defense is knowledge of his patterns until you can get out and cut of all ties. I am glad my son is learning to recognize the patterns.

Dear Younger Me,

Always expect the Sociopath to lie; it's what he does. Don't be shocked, or let him draw you in to feeling his lie is truth. Stand firm. Don't waiver. Are you shocked when a dog barks? Or a cat meows? Do not be shocked when the Sociopath Narcissist lies, or stacks them high. The content may change, get bigger, or more offensive, but the words are still a lie.

In mid- 2017 one of my children shared a conversation he had with his dad years before. It was about his dad dating a woman I mention in a prior chapter. I clearly heard and identified each Narcissistic statement and tricky word play the Carnie served up then that was now being brought to my ears. Dad said to me, "I liked dating her because she took interest in the things I was doing and liked everything I did. I like the affection, being hugged and kissed. I like how it makes me feel. You know, I have been separated along time, so it's ok." My chest grew tight and my insides swirled as I listened to my son relay the con to me. Frankly, it scared me how easily my son embraced his dads words as truth. "Dad is right; anyone would like these things, its normal. Mom you had been separated for about 9 years at that point and nobody cares if you date if are divorced or not." My adult child fully missed the shady ploy and wanted me to agree with the assessment his father delivered as if his father was the wronged one and deserved unreserved affirmation. To my son, his father seemed sincere. He saw the way his father sort of hesitated in-between words, as if he was being gut-wrenchingly honest, the accompanying pleading expression, and the occasional crack in his voice convincing him his words can be trusted. I have seen it all before.

My son heartily joined his father in his false reality excuses. He does not understand the mind of a Narcissist. His father wanted him see him as a victim of circumstance and swell with compassion. Just as he swayed people to believe he was the victim while he abused me. Should I be astonished at his tactics to get our child to see his actions in a Narcissist view? I had to breathe deep, keep my tears at bay and try to maintain my outward composure. I wanted to work from facts, not emotion so I offered nothing substantial at the time, but working from facts here is what I know to be true about his father.

1. He is in leadership at a church but was caught lying to his pastor about dating this woman
2. He committed adultery by dating when he is legally married
3. He was haughty in his display of adultery in front of our young daughter
4. He bragged to our children that he is marrying someone else while still married
5. He could have simply filed for divorce and then freely dated but refused to do so
6. He would not file because he had already stated to me he wanted me to do the filing so I would feel condemnation for doing it. But he felt no condemnation committing adultery and causing confusion to our children
7. He felt no embarrassment telling his son of his escapades
8. He tried to create a scenario where he was deserving of compassion
9. He purposely used our son's world view on dating and sex to gain his favor.
10. He would condemn the same behavior by someone else

My son does not grasp that his father needed me to be the one to file for the divorce so he could successfully alleviate any blame in his Narcissistic world. "I didn't file, my wife did so it was not my fault. She is bad, I am good."

In speaking with my son, his father instituted a tactic he does often. He reinvents and re-writes history. Using this tactic he makes sure I never have closure. All the things my ex-husband did to me that my son was too young to know about, or things I chose not to disclose or was too embarrassed to tell, the Carnie is now telling our children and his friends. He often uses the *first to market advantage* which works excellently for a Narcissist, he sells the story he convinced his victim to hide, but he rewrites it swapping details and denying any liability.

I would like to revisit the December 2014 letter I showed you in a previous chapter. In it my ex-husband made some big confessions. His confessions don't hold as truths in his mind for long, but the letter contains some great content for analyzing.

> One of the most toxic things Narcissists do is distort reality.

One of the most toxic things Narcissists do is distort reality. In that letter, we see him admit to what mental health professionals call projection. "I portrayed your mother to you as having mental issues and being emotionally incapable of loving you. In actuality, it was I who had severe emotional and mental issues. In my corrupted mental processes, I assumed that since your mother didn't love me that she could not love anyone."

These words are a double whammy. First he projects, nailing his mental illness to me, then the Narcissist says, "If she can't love me [the great and awesome me], then she can't possibly love anyone else; therefore, my daughter, she can't love you." He sees himself as too great to pass up; anyone who does not love him must be crazy! He then uses the wrong context. It is not, "He **had** severe emotional issues." It is he **has** severe emotional issues. My ex-husband spins some fantastic lies and yet people believe them. My friend recently queried to me as we discussed the Narcissist, "The bigger the lie the easier to believe. Why is that?" I do wonder why people believe my ex-husband's lies. Why do they repeat them? Why do people, especially in the church, not call the accused and ask for clarification? The Bible tells us to do that.

The quote, "Any money that she has given to your brothers was her money" bears more discussion. Why would any money I give my other children be a topic for discussion with her? The answer is twofold. The Narcissist has a need to see me fail, so he projects that I have no or limited money to give anyone; therefore, I must be providing money that is hers to my sons. Similar to him inventing other reasons for the marital problems other than his abuse and dysfunctional behavior, he keeps reaching for other places the money went because he cannot accept the documentation and explanation. He simply *must* invent some kind of treachery he can tell our daughter to create chaos. My ex-husband does not care that his imaginary tales damage the sibling relationships. It is too important to keep up the lies to build up his protective father image.

Journal, January 2014

My counselor explained to me my ex-husband has a thought disorder. Even if he hears anything, it won't matter. It won't last. He can't hold the concept. She was really trying to impress upon me to grasp what my problem is and what my problem is not.

This is the way this Sociopath father acts:

1. He creates a problem, intentionally.
2. He denies he created the problem/unable to recognize he created the problem.
3. He makes himself the hero/volunteers to rescue/help with the problem/or pray for the problem he created.

Repeat again and again and again.

This thought disorder was clearly seen at a recent wedding where he gave the father-of-the-bride speech for his oldest daughter's special day. The bride asked him to keep the speech short and simple, and she asked that it not be religious. The fact that she felt the need to express this is telling. This is usually a warm-fuzzy moment used to express the passing of the baton from father to the new son-in-law and perhaps share a personal memory with the bride. The Narcissist with a thought disorder ignored this concept that was clearly told to him and recited ALL of 1 Corinthians 13 from memory. To say the bride was not happy is an understatement. But that is not what was important. It was only important that the Narcissist had the attention and did what HE wanted and HE was happy. When the bride confronted him about his actions, with no repentance, he gave his rationalization for why he thought it was just fine.

In another example, my son relayed this to me: "I was visiting with Dad and he started to tell me that something that happened yesterday didn't really happen. But I was there; I know it happened. I said to Dad, "Dad, STOP IT! That did happen!" I was so proud of my son. He stayed in reality and did not let his father's denial and discounting deceive him. I am grateful that my son was so astute and *willing* to call his father out on his lie. I wish it could happen more. My kids are so confused by their dad's behavior that this kind of correcting does not happen often, if at all. This is the first time I was hearing that one of the kids was willing to stand up to his twisted lies. The bride was willing to stand up to her father too, so maybe the tide is turning. My son became contrite at the realization of his father's dysfunction: "Mom, I am so sorry. For years I believed his lies; I didn't know. I didn't understand. I see it now." The veil is lifting; his vision is clearing.

My ex-husband has so deeply indoctrinated my children into the lie that I am deficient and crazy that some of them believed him; some treat me like they have undergirding doubt of my quality as a mom and as a person. He makes them question what their own eyes have seen and ears have heard. As a young adult, my youngest daughter has sometimes adopted these techniques. She tells her version. People are drawn in. She is copying learned behavior dyed and set by her abusive father. I am praying the truth presented here will lead her learn to walk in real truth.

Dear Younger Me,

A childhood controlled by a maniac makes it easier to accept control from a husband who uses brainwashing as a tool. I want you to know control is not love; it's fake protection. He is not protecting you; he is protecting himself from letting anyone else have control in his life. Stand up for yourself right away and let any abuser know control is not acceptable. You can set boundaries and reject their fraudulent control that is not based in love or health. Escape the marriage before you have children; do not have children with a Sociopath Narcissist. Staying with a Narcissist is an ungrateful, full-time, draining job. Hand in a letter of resignation.

I must point out my ex-husband will use the words of the above *Dear Younger Me* to accuse: "Look, Mom wishes you were never born." Please, don't take in his calumny!

Recently my ex-husband took our daughter to be on a local Christian talk show. In his magical world, he thinks speaking on a Christian talk show makes him a Christian. The invitation came as a promotion offer for our daughter's singing abilities and her dramatic interpretation of her life's circumstances. The programing was creatively danced around so no talk of God came from the young guest during the segment. My ex-husband's charade presented the illusion of a supportive father, not a demonic abuser. For the Narcissist, this event met his selfish needs perfectly. His image was validated and he got to snap up a few minutes of air time to talk about his books and promote his special End Times theology. Score one for the Narcissist. It was another successful day of holding the harsh realities at bay; no one knew it was all a dysfunctional, absurd pretense intended to create a pleasant or respectable appearance.

The dysfunction of magical thinking enables my ex-husband to engage in sometimes subtle and unsettling behavior such as psychological warfare. It is all meant to keep me teeter-tottering on the emotional roller coaster. Every month as required, since the divorce was finalized in October 2013, I receive a check. It comes in a white business-size envelope that is dropped in my personalized bronze street-side mailbox.

In the last quarter of 2016, while I was in the process of writing this book, an unusual thing happened: the amount of the check was twenty-five dollars more than usual. I pondered why as I sat at my kitchen table, strumming my fingers. My intuition told me there was something else wrong and not just in the number on the check.

I was not going to call and question him. I have learned my lesson about engaging a Sociopath Narcissist. He can be untiringly creative to see what it takes for that to happen. Create something positive; use something negative. It does not matter. As long as he can engage, he has won. Five minutes was enough time to consider the tactic, the same amount of time it would take me to drive to the bank and deposit that check.

December 1st, the next check arrived. It was back to the regular promised and legal amount due. Suddenly, I yelled "Bingo!" My birthday is in November; he had sent me a birthday present. The man who poured the mother lode of abuse for decades and purposely alienated my child from me had sent me a birthday present.

When we are being attacked with fists, knives, guns, or a bat, we can easily identify the threat. We know those things will hurt when they make contact with our body's fragile outer covering. Mental and emotional games are more difficult to identify and harder to explain to others. I am quite sure he told key people in his world about his twenty-five dollar birthday gift. This action could be seen as proof he has always been a thoughtful, nice guy even after the divorce. Creating this false reality is less painful than admitting, "I am a Sociopath Narcissist who destroyed my family, and using this birthday gift is part of my sickness."

While food shopping, I ran into my ex-husband and my daughter. She would not even acknowledge me. In some ways, she is an innocent by-stander to the harm that was done to her and her response to it. The lies she believes and the acts she is participating in are extensions of the sickness that has claimed her. Her decisions and choices are not conscious ones but are influenced by the indoctrination she has lived under.

Dear Younger Me

Narcissists use language like a pro. It is used for hiding, deflecting, avoiding, masking and manipulating. Work to develop real eyes that will help you realize when you are being served real lies. It takes practice, wisdom and knowledge. A Sociopath Narcissist does not want you to have real eyes. They want you to have a veiled vision to easily accept their version.

She lives under the indoctrination of a Narcissist magician. When a magician asks, "Pick a card, any card", they are lying. The trick to guessing a person's card is that there never any guessing. The Cardician is a master manipulator so he sets the deck assuring the trick will work, for him the card is already chosen. Then it's about getting the unsuspecting victim to pick the right card- then abracadabra! It's Magic! Narcissism is the same. There is a lot of Hocus Pocus. The Narcissist leads you to the card. The card is the perception the Narcissist wants you to take on. He is a conjurer. It's a big show and only the Narcissist himself knows the legerdemain he will have you believing. He gets his unknowing but willing participant to pick his version and the audience is witness to the fact that it seemed random. Buts it's all magic and only the Narcissist and other dysfunctional Narcissists understand the prestidigitation.

The circumstances I lived under were difficult and so hard to explain to others. I felt so alone. Sometimes I cried so hard my eyes were bloodshot, some days I screamed and shook my fists at God, and some days I put on my happy smile and faced the world head on as if I didn't have a care in the world. As I reflect, I appreciate something my counselor in the North told me: "I want you to start taking care of yourself; do some things for you. Go to the health club, exercise; nourish yourself, whatever that might be." At the time, I did not know why she was saying that, but I certainly do now. She could see I was losing my vitality. I was being verbally put down and physically threatened on a daily basis, so taking care of myself was one of the things I neglected. I did not feel strong, my energy was zapped, and my only activity was trying to survive. I was not being nourished at home; I was being diminished and my spirit was most definitely being crushed.

Proverbs 18 is a key chapter about the human spirit and the way people can deliver crushing death or life-giving joy with their words.

Proverbs 18:21
"Death and life are in the power of the tongue."

Proverbs 18:14
"The human spirit can endure in sickness, but a crushed spirit who can bear?"

The Bible talks about the Spirit bringing life, but a person working in power over another crushes the personal spirit; there is no grace or love the Bible speaks of. I think this is why verbal abusers are so offensive; they crush and diminish the personal spirit of the victim, with no remorse. I certainly related to the voice of David in Psalm 143:4, "Therefore my spirit is overwhelmed within me; my heart within me is desolate."

CHAPTER 20

CAN A NARCISSIST THRIVE IN THE CHURCH?

Feel free to skip this chapter if you feel the subject matter does not apply, but I would be remiss not to share how my ex-husband, the Narcissist, thrived in his church, while abusing me and the children, and how leadership mostly ignored it, definitely minimized it, and believed the abusive Narcissist rather than the victims of the abuse. I leave room for naivety, ignorance, and even deception delivered by the abuser.

At least one in four women will experience abuse from her partner at some point in her adult life; tragically, that rate is no different in Christian homes. Research shows what I already know, that Christian women stay longer and sometimes suffer more severe abuse than their non-Christian counterparts. Many Christian women caught in the cycle of abuse believe "I can't leave this abusive marriage because the Bible says divorce is wrong." Abusive men promote and twist Biblical text to suit their need to control with no pang of conscience.

There may be women in the body of the church who, like me, feel an incredible sense of injustice when the abuser in their lives is not held accountable and the abuse is disregarded or minimized by those in leadership positions. It is an inconceivable violation and leaves the abused feeling violated again when they ask for help and provide proof.

Fear, isolation, finances, love, and cultural, social, and spiritual values were all factors that influenced my decision when to leave my abuser, and it is the same for all women. Stories told by victims help others perceive differently; there are subtleties to Sociopath Narcissist behavior that need to be taught and recognized so leadership can help and not hurt the victims. My hope is those in leadership can be more informed so they, like the astute counselor up north, will tweak their questions and modify their methods to unveil the Narcissistic behavior and deep-cover tactics. Friends, family, leadership and those who counsel must train their ears to draw out all the facts and not just the view the abusers promote.

Because of today's "selfie" culture, researchers say one in four men can be diagnosed with simple Narcissism or Narcissist Personality. The titles Sociopath, Narcissist, and Abuser can be separate attributes or all wrapped in one package, like my ex-husband. In all three, orientation is always toward control and dominance and includes covering those facts as best they can. Many people who hold even one of those titles don't operate in the same reality as others. You express something from reality A; they receive it and respond from reality B. If you don't grasp this, you will stay frustrated all the time, just as I was.

> Up until now he has been able to bar the gates maintaining his pretend kingdom.

It behooves the church and leadership in general to become informed about personality disorders as part of the sin spectrum because my ex-husband spent decades constructing his castle of conceit while standing in the church praising God. His moat of protection was the pools of people he charmed and perpetrated his strategized lies to. Up until now he has been able to bar the gates maintaining his pretend kingdom. Dismantling his castle will clear the way for his family members to rebuild their lives.

As a matter of fact, not conjecture, my counselor stated, "Abuse has been the experience of more people than not. "We are everywhere." Victims and perpetrators are even in places of worship. All the while he's sitting next to you, the abuser will rearrange the power and placement of life-giving scripture meant to reach your heart. He neutralizes its nourishment so he can wrangle for control over you in opposition to God. No place of worship, whether denominational or non-denominational, is unscathed by wounds or trauma of some nature. Narcissists show up as pastors, leaders, Bible study teachers, or congregants. Most church leaders are sincere in their faith, serve with love, are sacrificial in their work, and display humility. Some admit they are sinners just like everyone else. I am grateful when I see true servants in the church with humble hearts. I am proud to say I know some.

I have also come across some interesting studies on Narcissism in the church, done by particular denominations. There is an awakening. Maybe it's only my awakening. But it's there. The more we talk about it, the more women will not feel so alone. If my embarrassing, uncomfortable story, and honesty helps even one woman, I have done my duty. The first person I could help might even be in my own family circle. When the tumult settles, that person can use this knowledge when sitting with a qualified counselor to untangle misconception and live a happy, healthy life.

> If my embarrassing, uncomfortable story, and honesty helps even one woman, I have done my duty.

When my kids were little we learned Behemoth was God's word for dinosaurs. The word *dinosaur* is not in the Bible because it was first created and spoken much later. The concept of the Trinity is in the Bible but the word *Trinity* is not. We don't see the word *Narcissism* in the Bible, since like many other words, it was established and understood much later. But the Bible does address the precepts of being self-centered, having envy and arrogance, and wanting attention. God is not slack in describing the negative attributes of attention seeking, verbal abuse, and physical abuse.

Romans 2:8
"But for those who are self-seeking and who reject the truth and follow evil, there will be wrath and anger."

2 Timothy 3:1-2
"But realize this, that in the last days difficult times will come. For men will be lovers of self.…"

James 3:14-16
"But if you have bitter jealousy and selfish ambition in your heart, do not be arrogant and so lie against the truth. This wisdom is not that which comes down from above, but is earthly, natural, demonic. For where jealousy and selfish ambition exist, there is disorder and every evil thing."

Philippians 2:3
"Do nothing from selfishness or empty conceit, but with humility of mind regard one another as more important than yourselves."

Proverbs 25:28
"Like a city that is broken into and without walls, is a man who has no control over his spirit."

Romans 8:13
"For if you are living according to the flesh, you will die; but if by the Spirit you are putting to death the deeds of the body, you will live."

Psalms 141:3
"Set a guard, O LORD, over my mouth; Keep watch over the door of my lips."

1 Timothy 4:8
"For bodily discipline is only of little profit, but godliness is profitable for all things, since it holds promise for the present life and also for the life to come."

This is just a sampling of the precepts God has given to help us align our character to His expectations. None of them allow for verbal, mental, emotional, spiritual, or physical abuse to anyone, including a spouse.

At different times in my life I have been in charge of children's Sunday school, missions, and Vacation Bible School (VBS). I have led a morning women's Bible study in my home for nearly a decade. Along the way took a course at a local church and obtained a certificate in Biblical counseling, and trained to earn a lay pastor title. I have always explained to the women in my studies the church is a place where people come to learn about God, but they come with problems in all stages of sin. Sin is simply missing GOD's mark of perfection, with the Ten Commandments as a good measuring stick. The Ten Commandments are found in Exodus 20:1-17. In the church you will find people who have been on the path of growth for twenty years but act as if they started yesterday, and some who started yesterday act like they have been Christ followers for twenty years. Don't be surprised by sin, in both the saved and the unsaved. Saved is a scriptural precept, meaning once you accept Christ you are saved from the punishment of hell. Unsaved means you have not accepted the gift of Jesus' death on the cross for your sins; therefore, you are not saved from the punishment of hell. I recognize it is not just men who are Narcissists; women can be, but at a statistically much smaller percentage. I have encountered women Narcissists.

The church my ex-husband attends is a small congregation. On the average, about thirty attend. In its fifteen-plus years of existence it has stayed a small congregation. The pastor works a Monday-through-Friday day job, and his wife gives music lessons. On Friday nights the church celebrates God in a Messianic Shabbat service. For those who are unfamiliar with this concept, it is a worship service that is celebrated with all the traditions of a Jewish temple but includes recognition of Jesus (Yeshua) as Messiah. It resembles the way the first believers in Jesus in Bible times would have worshiped and mimics a traditional service order. It meets the needs of those who enjoy learning about Christian Jewish roots, lively Davidic dance, Hebrew prayers, and celebrating

Shabbat with candle lighting and Challah. For Jews who know Jesus is the Messiah, it allows them to have the traditional style of worship they perhaps grew up with.

This same congregation holds a contemporary Sunday church service in the same location. The two services go by different names under the same leadership. Some people attend both services and some just one. My ex-husband had visitation on the weekends so this is where he brought the three smaller children on a more continual basis and the older two when they visited. The leadership of this small church saw his proclivity to want to teach and read his published books. Small churches need all the help they can get. They need people who help teach, set up, tear down, and clean up. My ex-husband can fill in at the pulpit or take over for a Bible study and he will tithe (his OCD would not permit otherwise), and that money is needed in this small congregation. He will participate in grunt work because the more he does, the more he has laid the groundwork for proving how good he is. His position is validated and his good father image is affirmed.

Most pastors are not equipped to deal with Narcissist abusers; seminary does not teach such things. Part of my ex-husband's boldness came from the fact his pastor could be conned many times over. I am not sure the pastor grasped the abuser would soon forget promises he made to him just like he forgot the promises he made to me. Early on, I asked to meet with my ex-husband's pastor and his wife. We met at a local coffee shop. A mom and pop place where we could sit for a long time, refill our coffee, and not be disturbed. I explained why I was separated from my husband and recounted some of his actions. They said they saw some of the attributes I mentioned, but I saw no light of understanding pop on. Perhaps their vision was blurred by the fact that Narcissists are extremely skilled at managing their image and carefully put themselves above the rest.

At another meeting they said, "We feel he is doing better." I wondered by whose scale they were measuring results because the children and I were being abused every day.

In one of our meetings the pastor's wife read me a text message sent by a man who frequently visited their congregation. "You need to get rid of [my ex-husband]; he is the reason you are not growing." I think this stranger grasped what I was not successful in relaying to this small church leadership. They did not act on that man's suggestion either. I called the pastor and periodically shared truth, but he got tired. After accepting a few phone calls he said, "I cannot fix what God doesn't fix." Still, they promote his teaching, endorse him on social media, support his ministry in glowing terms, and allow him to preach. They believed the Carnie's fabrications, and the content of subsequent phone calls let me know they were shading me with the same crayon as him. I was once again swimming against the tide. I was delivering truth but the abuser had an audience with them more and often, giving them plenty of time to discount or rationalize anything I had to say. Finally my counselor told me to stop talking to them. My counselor was right; the more I tried to tell them, the more they resisted. She told me, "God will be the keeper of your reputation." This was hard, really hard. He was getting away with it, at least here on this earth.

> "I cannot fix what God doesn't fix."

One day I got a small glimpse into the distaste that sat in their mouths for me and the atmosphere my daughter was exposed to at church when I arrived for my daughter's weekly singing lesson with the pastor's wife. When the lesson was over, I privately and calmly addressed the pastor's wife about her outburst at me upon arrival. As I was exiting, she yelled across the large room that boomed her words for all her other students and parents to hear: "Oh, now I see where [my child] gets her rebellion!" Properly correcting her was rebellion. That gave me a small peek into the unkind or confusing behavior she probably displayed in front of my daughter and even in front of my other children.

A few days later she called my home and left a voice mail apologizing for her behavior. After that I talked my daughter into going to church with me on Sundays. I had asked her prior to this, but she always resisted a change, probably because her father was trying to dissuade her. He did not want to miss that window of control. Now she was ready and I was happy to have time with her. I especially treasured this period. My child's father didn't stop his behavior; he just got his days of subterfuge switched.

Dear Younger Me,

Places of worship are not spaces to let down your guard. Any house of worship gathers sinners in all different stages of growth and repentance. It can also be a hiding place for those with serious illnesses, including pedophiles. Worship and learn but don't believe it is a one hundred percent safe place. Know how to recognize unhealthy leaders and unhealthy followers. Always feel free to leave. Don't think more highly of anyone just because they are in a church. Everyone is on a path of healing; some leave the path and become predators. Some just lack awareness. Make a difference by making sure you develop and maintain Biblical precepts that display love, caring, honesty, character, and integrity. Be a Christ follower in body, mind, and spirit.

The pastor and his wife were recipients of the February 2010 letter previously shared where my ex-husband admitted to verbal manipulation, physical violence to my daughter, being deluded, and using *old patterns*. If only they understood what *old patterns* was code for. Code was used for a reason. He would only answer for what he *got caught* doing, not for what he was doing and didn't get caught for *yet*. As grave as the letter was, it was gravely minimized. It was a partial confession, much like the 2014 letter.

> In the church, apologies, repentance, and forgiveness can get you pretty far.

The pastor let my ex-husband off the hook on one point by saying to me, "Well I pinched my son, and it's not really a big deal." That would be one point the abuser would not have to spend time minimizing; he got someone else to do it for him. Rather than perceive his letter as the tip of the iceberg, they processed, "He has confessed these things and it is all better." The Narcissist in the church assumes everyone will be kind and forgiving. But the cycle will continue. In the church, apologies, repentance, and forgiveness can get you pretty far. The Carnie knew this so he included this as part of his repertoire. He would apologize sometimes dramatically at the church altar, sometimes directly to people, sometimes with great emotion. A good example is when he screamed, "What more do you want? I said I was sorry and I gave up my girlfriend for you!"

There were a series of three more emails from the pastor and his wife sent after that 2010 email. I am choosing to omit these because they are unbelievably sad to read from the Monday-morning quarterback position. They defend the abuser and use a verbally abusive tone and content directed toward me and my youngest daughter. They tag my daughter with Narcissistic labels. I could imagine she was trying on some things she saw her father do at church and blatantly get away with. When her father modeled it, it was accepted and affirmed; when our child modeled it, she was "bad, a know-it-all, and rebellious" according to their email. My daughter was being micromanaged through a myriad of control mechanisms by her father and the pastors observations were the result.

The Narcissist tried to mold his daughter into his box of perfection. As a result, she felt pressure to be pretty, perfect, and appear to know it all because that is how her Narcissistic father groomed her to be, a reflection of him. He transferred the need to control from me to her. Sadly, the pastor and his wife were not able to see that. In the subsequent seven years since the 2010 letter, they did not budge from their position. At one time they offered this statement in an email: "If your daughter hasn't been safe for these past seven-plus years, then we've all been blind!" *Blind* is a good word; *conned*, *manipulated*, and *duped* would be others. Like me, when the gravity of what they allowed hits, I am sure they will have some sleepless nights.

> Like me, when the gravity of what they allowed hits, I am sure they will have some sleepless nights.

Isaiah 5:20

"Woe unto them that call evil good, and good evil; that put darkness for light, and light for darkness; that put bitter for sweet, and sweet for bitter!"

Dear Younger Me,

Narcissists see a child as a stream of Narcissistic supply for affirmation used to regulate their sense of self-worth. If your child has a Narcissistic father, introduce as many male figures who are not, so that the child has someone else to emulate and he or she can see that a Narcissistic personality is not the only choice. Abuse, Sociopath, and Narcissistic traits can be generational, but with knowledge, you have a window to hinder or reverse those traits in your little ones.

Word came to me there was a man in his mid-to late-thirties dating a sixteen-year-old in my ex-husband's church. Let's call him Peter. I questioned my ex-husband about this. As if it were normal, he told me it was not his first time dating a minor. Later I found out he also got reprimanded for slapping a few of the teens on the buttocks, and was caught in engaging in *grooming* emails to a teen at the church. I ran into this man and he told me he was a tailor and wanted to make my daughter an outfit; I just needed to let him measure her.

What was equally disturbing was my ex-husband's rhetoric. With great compassion toward Peter he announced, "He didn't do anything wrong! The parents gave him permission to date their sixteen-year-old, but now they have reneged on it and called the police." My ex-husband was so indignant that Peter was going to have a police record he went to jail to visit him and offer help. He told me he lent Peter a large amount of money for his business.

Most frightening, I recognized the same excitement in my ex-husband's face, the nervous tick and stutter I had seen when he was having sex with the babysitter. It was undeniable to me; he was fantasizing he was the one having sex with that sixteen-year-old. His words strongly suggested I join him in compassion for the pedophile because he told me, "It just wasn't his fault."

How do we get the primarily male leadership to believe and not dismiss the primarily female victims? How do we get leadership to acknowledge the severity of an abusive Sociopath Narcissist hiding in a church and other places of worship? There is a difference between plain old self-absorbed Narcissism where someone thinks he is all that and a bag of chips, and the Narcissistic Personality Disorder, but both need to be addressed. The Sociopath Narcissist abuser is unable to follow God-given directives, especially in the areas of the Narcissistic symptoms and character traits I listed earlier in the book. I know it sounds strange, as if Narcissism is stronger than the creator of the heavens and the earth. This is my experience and it is backed up by people with great education, research statistics, and initials behind their names.

Sociopath Narcissists have no real conscience or permanent remorse. They can exhibit these IF and only IF it helps them attain the goals of power and control and presents them as good people, rescuers, and helpers. They hold onto seemingly good attributes for only as long as it benefits the show; then they let those attributes slip away without a trace.

The temporary appearance of these attributes can give the victim and others he is hurting a false hope. They believe he has real remorse and maybe it's real change. Victims, family, or church friends can have a real excitement rise. They talk about it and let the dream of healing go to huge heights. Then all the air is let out and hopes are dashed when he goes back to the exact same behavior, lies, and mental games. Sometimes it is the next day, sometimes a few weeks or a month. The longer it disappears the harder the fall when it all comes back and brings bigger demons with it. If it takes a month to come back, or more likely, if it takes a month for the abuser to get caught, the abuser uses this time to keep the church fellowship deceived. He will tell those in church, if he is forced to talk about it at all, "I am doing well," even if he is not. He believes it and that is all that matters. He will talk about the miracle God is doing. Those whose ears are privy to the con then innocently repeat the glory story to others. It's part of the plan.

The revelation he is back at the same old antics a month later does not travel like the wildfire of the glowing report that was fabricated earlier. The abuser never tells the pastor of his evil tricks and tactics because he doesn't think his actions are evil; his disorder tells him he needs the evil to survive. He will smile and brag about the good God is doing. The Carnie often offered, "God provided this study and that speaking engagement" as the cover-up phrase. He entices others to agree with his assessment and then lets the praise run over him like warm honey. His fragile self-esteem is safe in the warmness of praise.

Some may ride his roller coaster of hope for a few miles before realizing they were conned. When this plays out in the church the few miles becomes hundreds of miles because the abuser works the precepts of apology and forgiveness to the hilt, allowing the deception to be drawn out as long as possible and then hopefully forgotten. The cycle of hope, no hope, hope, no hope creates an exhausting up-and-down confusion mostly to the victim and sometimes to others he is conning. Narcissists try never to take blame for anything, so they allow themselves the privilege of falsely pointing at their victims. His selective perception makes lying a necessary tool and an acceptable evil. The fact that it breaks God's precepts and commands has little bearing on his decision. He resists the Holy Spirit. I can relay this with such sharp detail because it is my personal experience.

Some may feel perplexed because the Narcissist in their midst is an esteemed leader; they find it hard to believe *he* could be the problem. Some sincerely believe the abuser's defense. They have seen him give to the poor, buy a meal for someone in need, and pray a long sanctimonious prayer, which leads them to believe he can't be the problem. Remember, they have concocted personalities and rotating masks that are presented as needed.

When an abuse victim in a place of worship shares truth and presents proof about what she has endured and the church body does nothing, the victim is left with the following thoughts to ponder:

The pastor/leadership:

- Believes the abuser's lies and sins of commission and omission.
- Discounts or minimizes the truths of abuse brought by the victim.

- Refuses to acknowledge there is a Sociopath Narcissist in their church.
- May also be a Narcissist and therefore is unable to help.
- Incorrectly believes the abuser is the victim.

Sometimes there is a pastor/leadership Narcissist and a congregant Narcissist. One Narcissist in the position of pastor/leadership may not hold the other Narcissist accountable. Instead he makes excuses for the Narcissist congregant or else he may have to face those same traits residing in him. Some believe God would not allow *that* person to do such a thing or that God would not allow bad things to happen in the church. Of course history tells us otherwise. We can't overlook the evil that has happened in the mainline churches or any other place of worship where men have taken advantage of those weaker than themselves. God does not approve but he allows our fallen world to exist and with that fallen world comes the ability to choose sin.

Many ask me, "How can you have faith in God after all this?"

My answer is still the same. God is good, and mankind is the problem. Sinful nature is clearly on display. I am grateful for my strong faith. I know there is a God because I have seen Satan. My ex-husband's illness is deeply seated in his marrow, imprinted in his being. Like a magician, he escapes public awareness by ensuring everyone is watching the right hand while the left commits the prestidigitation. His illusion is to keep everyone admiring his list of accomplishments while he tumbles lives and crushes bodies, minds, and spirits. The rug should be pulled on all his ministry busy-ness and he should be made uncomfortable in using the church to hide his disgrace.

> I know there is a God because I have seen Satan.

Page 84 of the book *A God Who Hears* by W. Bingham Hunter has a very honestly written section titled, "The Silence Of God," and he quotes Arthur C. Custance (*The Silences of God*, 1971):

It is His seeming indifference, at times, to the needs of human beings when appalling suffering over takes them. Countless millions of people have suffered because of famine, or war, or drought, or disaster in circumstances in which it hardly seems appropriate to say they deserved it. At such times thoughtful men do not become atheists because they find it irrational to believe in a spiritual world which is above and beyond demonstration by ordinary means, but because of emotional insult, the feeling that if God is really such a being as we as His children claim Him to be, He could not possibly remain silent. He would have to act manifestly, mercifully, savingly, and publicly.

Hunter also says, "Confidence in God's love, presence, and providence does not require that we deny the objective reality of evil or say that pain really does not hurt." I know it does hurt, very much. I join in some small part in Jesus' word in Mark 14:34: "My soul is overwhelmed with sorrow to the point of death." W. Bingham Hunter ends with his owns words, "The silence of a wise and good God is shattering." My good and wise God was silent. God wanted me to walk out the pain of the abuse dealt by the hands of a man who claimed to know Christ and could quote God's Word from memory but could not and did not apply it. If I don't know why in this lifetime, I am confident I will in the next, standing in front of my wise God.

CHAPTER 21

ZEBRAS DON'T CHANGE THEIR STRIPES: THE NARCISSIST WILL NEVER CHANGE

As I come to the end, I want you to know I do not think my ex-husband will change. My youngest daughter needs to be protected from her father. All the children need to heighten their awareness so they don't adapt to his sickness and the false reality he tries to have them believe. Speaking truth when presented with lies will prevent them from being drawn further into their father's deception and alleviate the muddled mindset.

It has been said that withholding forgiveness from those who have hurt us will keep our spirits locked into its wounding. That is why I forgive but do not forget and I urge you to do the same. Forgetting is not part of forgiving. You are God's precious child; you are allowed to use wisdom and knowledge to protect yourself. Unfortunately it is possible after being separated from the abuse to forget how bad it actually was, as my helpful counselor pointed out to me. For this reason it is important to maintain the knowledge. I like to refer to it as keeping it on the back burner. After escaping, the information can be held in your recess and not in the forefront of your mind as constant

> Forgetting is not part of forgiving.

angst, but rather information gathered, boxed, and in storage. You may need to refresh when the abuser comes back around to say, "We should get back together; I love you." Your boxed-up information can provide a wealth of knowledge and helpful information for other victims.

Narcissistic Personality Disorder is not like other mental health disorders that respond to medication; there is no medicine specifically for this disorder. God has not chosen to perform a miraculous healing and my ex-husband has chosen not to treat or tame his symptoms. I agree with Shannon Thomas, LCSW-S, when she asks, "Will he change?" (southlakecounseling.org/when-a-Christian-meets-a-sociopath)

> No, he won't. Sorry to be so short and blunt about it, but God will not change a Narcissist, Sociopath, or Psychopath. How do I know this to be true? Because I have never, not once, ever, never seen someone changed by God who didn't want to be changed. Think about it for a minute. Has anyone ever gone to bed a complete high-grade jerk and woken up radically transformed into the loving image of Jesus? Nope. I have witnessed individuals do a whole lot of praying and soul searching and surrendering and such, and then become completely new people. It's actually one of my favorite things about the blessings of God. Narcissists, Sociopaths, and Psychopaths don't think there is anything wrong with them. Their disorder convinces them everyone else is wrong. They are incapable of change. Speaking of change, go ahead and take a look at my blog about the Four Levels of Change. Don't believe me? Think about a clinically Narcissistic person and the truly positive lasting change that occurred within them. Can't think of any? Neither can I and I am a therapist.

The Biblical use and Merriam Webster dictionary definition of the word *repent* means to turn away from sin. Forgiveness and repentance are a pair, but are separate and on opposite sides of the coin. A person can be forgiven, but without repentance, there cannot be reconciliation because there is no safety. Victims like myself know we live in a world where the victim is often blamed, so we enter the process of sharing with some trepidation. Abusers need to discount and I expect the Carnie will do that. Interestingly, when he does that he will be displaying part of his illness. Now that you are informed, I hope you will recognize that too. My ex-husband has walked this destructive behavior so long that most of our children have at least some understanding that something is very wrong. Their comprehension will be multiplied by reading this book. They will discover the depth of his disorder.

I have opened Pandora's Box but I have given the tools to manage the storm, and my children can take control of the outcome. When Pandora opened the box, she let out the seven deadly sins but closed it before the last attribute could escape. One was left in the bottom. It was not able to escape before the lid came down. Elpis was still in the box. *Elpis* in Greek translates to "hope" or "expectation." I reopen that box and release hope. I want my children to have the expectation of understanding, the hope for healing, and a healthy future.

My ex-husband's Bible knowledge assures me he has encountered Numbers 32:23 and its well-used precept, albeit usually stated apart from its original context: "… take note, you have sinned against the Lord; and **be sure your sin will find you out.**" His sin is against the LORD but also his children, me, his friends, his church, and his followers. God handles all wickedness. I rest in that, not in angst, vindictiveness, or lack of forgiveness, but just because God said so.

I too will be held accountable to God for not protecting our children. Praying more, giving chances, rationalizing, or my own real fear, did not help. God was waiting for me to do my part, align my health to His Word. I could not do that without help; my bathtub was too dirty. Perhaps late, I am traveling the right road now nonetheless.

The abuse is what happened to me; it is not who I am. I have been through a refining fire and made it through to the other side. Diamonds start off ugly, brass, dull, gems without luster and gold and silver impure. There is a process that brings out the purity, the shine, and the best of what is hidden. God has allowed the process. I am obligated to shine, for Him. I am His creation. This story has been difficult to write but also therapeutic on many levels. I have pulled together the big and little threads of streaming thought and woven them into a permanent tapestry of life. I know once I have finished this book, I never have to tell this story again; I can let the book do it for me. The book will let truth live on, not the false narrative of the abuser. There is a war between guilt and grace, but most days I choose grace while creating my sacred space of safety and healing. I hope my children will join me.

CHAPTER 22

HELP IS AVAILABLE

Can you relate to some of these stories? Do the facts ring a bell? Do you need help? Please seek outside help, secretly if needed. Call your local city or county Domestic Violence Hotline for help with recommending free or reduced-fee services to get you started. Many counselors will work on a sliding scale if you share your need. 211 on your phone or 211.org online is a national free and confidential service that helps people across North America find local resources. It operates 24/7.

Be sure to ask your counselor for references, and inquire if he or she has any past experience helping women escape abuse. Probe a bit about the counselor's training in the area of Sociopath Narcissistic behavior; ask which books he or she has read and which books he or she recommends for women to read. Ask the counselor whether he or she has attended any teaching seminars on this particular dysfunction.

A stumbling block for many women when vetting a counselor is they themselves have not settled in their minds that it is the abuse making them so miserable. That can be an obstacle to immediately acknowledging you need a specialized counselor. Abused women can enter counseling convinced they can do something differently that will make everything better. The abuser reinforces this. Where possible I advise against couples counseling with a Sociopath Narcissist abuser unless the counselor is highly trained. It is best to visit his sessions only occasionally to be a voice of truth. The counselor needs to hear a voice of truth. The Narcissist will abuse you in counseling and an inexperienced or unskilled counselor will allow it, even believing the abuser is the victim.

The National Domestic Violence Hotline's trained and caring staff can offer sound advice, help making escape plans, and provide emergency housing when necessary. Because of public interest and a bonafide need, these hotlines have grown and are now available at the county and even city level in all the United States. Popular talk shows; a plethora of books; and journalistic outlets in print, on TV, and online cover this subject as a way to help the victims of physical, mental, emotional, and spiritual abuse heal and recover. Victims are not quite as timid about sharing their painful stories because they know they can help other women be strong, speak truth, and protect themselves and their children. I applaud that effort and you should too.

How do you recognize when a friend might be being abused? The National Domestic Violence Hotline lists these things:

- Their partner puts them down in front of other people.
- They are constantly worried about making their partner angry.
- They make excuses for their partner's behavior.
- Their partner is extremely jealous or possessive.
- They have unexplained marks or injuries.
- They've stopped spending time with friends and family.
- They are depressed or anxious, or you notice changes in their personality.

Other signs you may see are:

- Your friend's husband feels he has the right to dictate your friend's behavior, privileges, responses, or opinions.
- You may see him blame her for his behavior.
- You may see him insist on controlling all of their money.
- He may criticize her appearance, weight, or clothes.

- You see him become angry when she has a different opinion than his or she doesn't take his advice. He may humiliate her in public.

How do you help a friend you think may be being abused? Your support can make a great difference to someone who is abused. Remember, she probably feels very afraid, so she may reject your support or seem defensive. Also remember abuse is not a "private" matter; you can talk about it. Be sensitive; express your concerns using a tone of concern and compassion. If she feels encouraged, she may gain some inner strength and be more able to make decisions. If she feels judged or criticized by you, she may be afraid to tell you or anyone else about the abuse again.

Acknowledge that they are in a difficult situation. It may take more than one conversation to be able to have them share their world and fears. Don't give up after one conversation. To be able to seek outside help they may need assistance with babysitting or transportation. If you can, do that for them.

Help her see that what she's going through is not right; she may need to be brought back to a true reality after the barrage of manipulative information from her abuser.

Advice From: *To Be an Anchor in the Storm: A Guide for Families and Friends of Abused Women* by Susan Brewster:

- Believe her. Most battered women don't lie or exaggerate their abuse.
- Recognize that emotional abuse is truly abuse.
- Open ears; shut mouth. You can't be listening when you are talking.
- Respect her decisions; don't judge her. Don't give advice; giving advice tends to take away her power.
- Ask open-ended questions. Ask her to clarify what you don't understand. Try to understand not just the words she speaks,

but what she is attempting to convey to you – the meaning between the lines.
- Be a mirror. Reflect her statements back to her. This lets her know you are really listening and trying to understand her.
- Speak only for yourself, not for her. Express only your feelings and observations, not your beliefs.
- Support without over-controlling. Control yourself, not her.
- Be patient. The establishment of trust can't be forced.

What you can do if you are experiencing any form of abuse:

- Contact a crisis center or shelter for information and support.
- Attend a domestic violence survivor support group.
- Seek counseling.
- Go to a shelter or stay with family or friends.
- Take legal action.

ACKNOWLEDGMENTS

I feel the necessity to say I have no plans to kill myself; I am now enjoying a wonderful life. My ex-husband has not been able to destroy me with his vast array of abuse techniques, but this message may create a need to shoot the messenger and or increase attempts to destroy my character and reputation. I don't think my battles have ceased. Experience has taught me to expect further. Yes, I am independent and free of living with a monster but as to the future behavior of the Carnie? That is anyone's guess. Through this writing process I have attained a measure of peace and tranquility. Those things are invaluable, and many times I didn't know they existed.

I thank the LORD for sustaining me, and for being my firm foundation. Thank you, Jesus, for your supreme sacrifice; I am eternally grateful.

Psalm 119:50, "My comfort in my suffering is this: Your promise preserves my life." Proverbs 14:10, "Each heart knows its own bitterness, and no one else can share its joy."

To a friend who is a true jewel in my life, thank you for painfully reading my early revisions. You held my hand, never complained, and loved me through it.

To my cheerleader son, you are my son of encouragement. Although this was a difficult and painful process for you, you never wavered from telling me to keep speaking truth, even when that truth made you cry. You walked this writing process with me and helped me stay focused. You are very brave. Thank you for understanding. I take great comfort in knowing you will never follow your father's abuse pattern. Speak life; walk in truth. 143 xo

To my youngest daughter, I apologize for not being able to protect you or effectively help you. Though this story will have been hard to read, it is necessary. I hope the knowledge I have imparted helps you get well, though I recognize it's a lot to process. I pray for you to be set free from the mind control and unhealthy behavior of those who surround you and are not walking in truth. Much like I laid Patricia Evans' book on my counselor's table and said, "This is my life" and received help and direction for the first time, I hope you might be able to take this book and lay it on the table of a highly trained and qualified counselor, say the same, and receive guidance.

To all five of my children, as I say on many Mother's Day celebrations, "Thank you for making me a mommy." I know I failed you all on many levels; my efforts fell short. One of my counselors reminded me sometimes all we can manage is *good enough,* but it is all we could do. It is all I could do. Forgive me for my failures. I hope speaking this painful truth will help you understand and heal. I recognize it will be painful at first. Wait for the healing to follow; it will come.

I love you. 143 a million xo

PTediting. Patient Pauline, you made me be brave and stretched me further than I knew possible. Thank you.

EPILOGUE

In September 2017 I had completed what I felt was a publishable draft of my book so I called for a meeting with 4 of my 5 children. I wanted them to know what it said before I published it. I gave no reason for the gathering, leaving it to their imaginations as to why I would have made such a request. I was nervous. My imagination ran as wild as theirs. They wondered why and I wondered how. How would they respond? Within weeks they arrived in my home and we spent a long weekend together. A miracle happened. No one was upset, no one was offended, even when they recognized themselves. They were compassionate, engaged and interested. They did not dispute any of its contents. They even felt it would help others who were struggling in abusive relationships. At one point the kids gathered in the backyard, standing around the unlit fire pit. I wondered what they were saying but didn't want to interfere with their private discussion. When we regathered in the dining room they said, "We think you should seek a publisher, you did a really good job writing this, we are impressed." Our time together was better than I could have ever dreamed. I had their blessing and support. We talked, cried, laughed and started some honest conversation and baby steps in the healing process. They all agreed their youngest sister might not be receptive to the facts I presented because of her mental and emotional space right now, but they felt it should be published.

LEGAL DISCLAIMER

I would like to thank those family members and friends who lovingly supported me in this endeavor, including confirming my facts and memories and sharing their own. This is my truthful recollection of events. I have related them to the best of my knowledge, and identities have been hidden or generalized for protection. This book is not intended to hurt anyone but to share my actual experiences to help my children gain understanding and heal, and to help women recognize domestic violence, narcissistic personalities and physical, mental, verbal, emotional, and spiritual abuse. I recognize that others may choose to remember the events described in this book differently than I do. I regret any unintentional harm resulting from the publishing and marketing of *Dear Younger Me: Victim to Victor*.

The information and advice or strategies may not be suitable for your situation; you should consult with a professional where appropriate. Information quoted, cited, or offered, including websites, may change or disappear between the time of writing and publishing.

Resources to Help

National Domestic Abuse Hotline
1-800-799-7233
1-800-787-3224 (TTY for the Deaf or Hard of Hearing)

Sonya Perkins, Clinical Social Work/Therapist LCSW

RECOMMENDED WEB SITES

cryingoutforjustice.com
Verbalabuse.com
BPDcentral.com
Breakthroughparenting.com/PAS.htm
kathyescobar.com
carolineabbott.com
saferelationshipsmagazine.com

RECOMMENDED BOOKS

Caroline Abbott with Debbie Stafford, *A Journey Through Emotional Abuse: from Bondage to Freedom* (Franklin, TN: Carpenter's Sons Publishing, 2013).

Lundy Bancroft, *Why Does He Do That? Inside The Minds Of Angry And Controlling Men* (New York, NY: Berkley Books, 2002).

Susan Brewster, *Be an Anchor in the Storm: A Guide for Families and Friends of Abused Women*, Seal Press; second edition, May 17, 2000.

Dr. Henry Cloud, Dr. John Townsend, *Boundaries*, Zondervan, 1992.

Jeff Crippen and Anna Wood, *A Cry For Justice: How The Evil Of Domestic Abuse Hides In Your Church* (Calvary Press November 1, 2012).

Bill Eddy, LCSW,JD and Randi Kreger, Splitting: Protecting Yourself While Divorcing Someone With Borderline or Narcissistic Personality Disorder (New Harbinger Publications 2011)

Patricia Evans, *The Verbally Abusive Relationship: How To Recognize It And How To Respond,* (Holbrook, MA: Adams Media Corporation, 1996).

Marie M. Fortune, *Keeping The Faith: Guidance For Christian Women Facing Abuse*
(HarperOne, first edition, June 23, 1995).

Sandy Hotchkiss, PsyD, LCSW, *Why Is It Always About You? The Seven Deadly Sins Of Narcissism*, (Free Press, a division of Simon and Schuster 2002).

Joe S. McIlhaney, Jr., M.D., Freda McKissic Bush M.D., *Hooked: New Science on How Casual Sex Is Affecting Our Children,* Moody Publishers, 2008.

Donald Stewart, *Refuge: A Pathway Out Of Domestic Violence and Abuse* (New Hope Publishers (AL) (March 2004).

Susan Weitzman, PhD, *Not To People Like Us: Hidden Abuse In Upscale Marriages,* (New York, NY: Basic Books, 2000).

WORKS CITED/ATTRIBUTE/PERMISSIONS

George R. Bach and Ronald Deutsch. *Stop! You Are Driving Me Crazy.* (New York: GP Putnam's Sons, 1980, p. 16).

Susan Brewster, *Be an Anchor in the Storm: A Guide for Families and Friends of Abused Women*, Seal Press; second edition. May 17, 2000.

Arthur C. Custance, *Hidden Things of God's Revelation*, Vol. VII: The Doorway Papers, second edition. 2015. E.M. White and R.G. Chiang, editors, Doorway Publications, Ancaster, Canada. p. 4. Used with permission

Patricia Evans, *The Verbally Abusive Relationship, How to Recognize It and How to Respond* Adams Media, (an F&W Publications Company© 1992, 1996).
Used with permission

30 Days to Taming Your Tongue
Copyright © 2005 by Deborah Smith Pegues
Published by Harvest House Publishers
Eugene, Oregon 97402
www.harvesthousepublishers.com
Used with permission.

Dr. Richard A Gardner, expert in Parental Alienation Syndrome
April 28, 1931 - May 25, 2003

Susan Hall, *The Theology of Domestic Violence: Views from the Edge* (Seattle: Mars Hill Graduate School, January 2006).

Sandy Hotchkiss, PsyD, LCSW, *Why Is It Always About You? The Seven Deadly Sins of Narcissism,* (Free Press, a division of Simon and Schuster 2002).
Used with permission

Robert Lewis, *How to Raise Modern Day Night Focus on the Family*; revised & enlarged edition (February 1, 2007)

Max Lucado, *You'll Get Through This: Hope and Help for Your Turbulent Times*
Thomas Nelson Publishers, 2015.

Henrietta Mears, *What the Bible is All About, Living Bible Edition,* 1987, Tyndale House Publishers.

John Oldham and Lois Morris, *New Personality Self Portrait: Why You Think, Work, Love, and Act the Way You Do.* Bantam; revised edition (November 7, 2012).

Scott Peck, *People of the Lie*, Touchstone, second edition, January 2, 1998.

Shannon Thomas LCSW www.southlakecounseling.org/four-levels-of-change/
Used with permission